KNOWING BODIES, MOVING MINDS

Towards Embodied Teaching and Learning

Edited by

Liora Bresler
University of Illinois, Urbana-Champaign, U.S.A.

KLUWER ACADEMIC PUBLISHERS
DORDRECHT / BOSTON / LONDON

A C.I.P. Catalogue record for this book is available from the Library of Congress.

ISBN 1-4020-2022-8 (PB)
ISBN 1-4020-2021-X (HB)
ISBN 1-4020-2023-6 (e-book)

Published by Kluwer Academic Publishers,
P.O. Box 17, 3300 AA Dordrecht, The Netherlands.

Sold and distributed in North, Central and South America
by Kluwer Academic Publishers,
101 Philip Drive, Norwell, MA 02061, U.S.A.

In all other countries, sold and distributed
by Kluwer Academic Publishers,
P.O. Box 322, 3300 AH Dordrecht, The Netherlands.

Printed on acid-free paper

Printed in the Netherlands.

TABLE OF CONTENTS

ACKNOWLEDGEMENTS

The impetus for this book originated in conversations with Judy Davidson who had an important role in writing the prospectus. Many shaped my personal experience of body/mind connections. In particular, I am deeply and warmly indebted to Rose Bronec, Patricia Knowles, Jean Korder, Marcia Stevens, and Lisa Sullivan. My children, Guy and Ma'ayan, and husband, Yoram, provided wholehearted and enthusiastic support for my body/mind explorations.

I am grateful to Teri Frerichs, Technology Resources Office, for her indispensable help with typesetting, Yu-Ting Chen from the University of Illinois, André Tournois and Marianna Pascale from Kluwer for their excellent, dedicated and careful editorial help. I would like to acknowledge Michel Lokhorst, my Kluwer editor, who manifested keen interest beyond the call of duty, extraordinary skills and involvement in this project.

ENDORSEMENTS

"The development of language and the invention of the alphabet and other writing systems have made us, uniquely on this planet, a "symbolic species"--to use Geoffrey Deacon's term. That preternatural symbolic ability, which we see re-enacted in children in their first few years, is so astonishing, and has been so momentous for human experience, that we are occasionally forgetful that our odd brain is a part of an odd body. Our brain works with what this body, with its peculiar senses, delivers to it. The basis of all our forms of understanding is that given to us by our body's interactions with the world. Somatic understanding precedes all others, and persists while our symbolic forms of understanding develop, and it shapes those symbolic forms of understanding in profound and subtle ways. Understanding human cognition, then, requires our careful attentiveness to the body that is their foundation. We have attended to the body's role in our cultural lives and especially in education far too little. It is a pleasure to welcome this splendid book that shows many of the ways in which attention to our body, to its senses and understanding, can greatly enrich our ability to educate our embodied students."

Kieran Egan, Faculty of Education, Simon Fraser University, Burnaby, Canada

A visionary scholar assembles a multidisciplinary team of experts in the arts and human sciences, to generate a "new theoretical cluster" that addresses the global concern about reviving the cognitive body in classroom education sites. The contributions in this volume are written with insights from cultural body studies, reflective personal body experiencing and researched educational challenges. The book is a timely guide on cherishing embodied knowledge as well as perceiving body communications, and should be of interest to all who own a sensitive body or educate in mind-body correlation.

Meki Nzewi, President of the Pan-African Society of Music Education

Everyone who has been observing the Arts from the back of a classroom and felt a bit of frustration about one's inablility to write and talk about the *essence* of it all, can now rejoice. The book you are feeling in your hand or reading about or looking at with your eyes contains what we all have been waiting for; a rich, updated and immensly interesting collection of aticles about the connections of bodies to knowledge, to minds, to Arts Education and Scooling and to our very selves.

By focussing on embodied knowledge in education the editor and the writers have given an important contribution to our understanding of the shortcomings of the many dualisms that dominate our world and to what wholeness really means. This book should not only be on every curriculum for educators. It should be read by everyone, who believes in the uniqueness of the human body and human culture.

Stord Norway, November 2003

Associate Professor
Magne Espeland

As someone whose research concerns the lived and told stories of teachers and children, Bresler and her colleagues offer me much to consider. Attending to children's and teachers' lives using a lens of embodiment opens new possibilities for reimagining the school landscapes which shape those lives.

D. Jean Clandinin
Centre for Research for Teacher Education and Development, University of Alberta

BIOGRAPHY

Wayne Bowman is Professor and Chair of Music Education at Brandon University in Brandon, Manitoba, Canada, where he teaches graduate courses in the philosophical and social foundations of music education and in music education research. A trombonist, his university instructional experience also includes extensive work with jazz ensembles and applied low brasses. Bowman is Associate Editor of *Action, Criticism, and Theory (ACT) for Music Education*, and has published widely on matters germane to the philosophy of music and of music education. His book *Philosophical Perspectives on Music* was published in 1998 by Oxford University Press.

Liora Bresler is a Professor at the College of Education at the University of Illinois at Urbana Champaign and a faculty in the Campus Honors Program, where she teaches courses on arts and aesthetic education, and qualitative research methodology. Bresler was involved in a number of National research projects. She is the author of sixty some articles, and has contributed chapters in books including the two Handbooks of Music Teaching and Learning. Most recently, she has co-edited a book on context and culture in arts education (Bresler and Thompson, 2002 by Kluwer), and a book on International Research in Education (Bresler and Ardichvili, 2002 by Peter Lang). She is an editor for the book series: *Landscapes: Aesthetics, Arts and Education*, for Kluwer; is a co-editor (with Tom Barone), of the *International Journal for Arts and Education;* and a guest editor for international issues in *Arts Education Policy Review*.

Judith Davidson is an Assistant Professor in the Leadership Program at UMass-Lowell's Graduate School of Education, where she teaches courses on qualitative research, action research, and school planning. Her research interests focus on organizational cultures and change. Her most recent book is Living Reading: Exploring the Lives of Reading Teachers (Peter Lang, 2000). Her publications have appeared in Teacher's College Record, International Journal of Educational Leadership, and Educational Researcher. She lives in Lowell, Massachusetts near the banks of the Merrimack River with her cat companions-Scooby and Oreo, and is a passionate, and unconventional, gardener.

Charles Garoian is Director of the School of Visual Arts and Professor of Art Education at Penn State University. His scholarly articles are featured in theoretical journals on art and education and his book *Performing Pedagogy: Toward an Art of Politics* is a State University of New York Press publication. Garoian has performed, lectured, and presented workshops nationally and internationally.

Alma Gottlieb is professor of anthropology, African studies and women's studies at the University of Illinois at Urbana-Champaign, and is currently president of the Society for Humanistic Anthropology. Gottlieb has held fellowships from the John Simon Guggenheim Memorial Foundation, the National Endowment for the Humanities, the Social Science Research Council, and many other agencies. She is the author, co-author or co-editor of six books, most recently, *The Afterlife Is Where We Come from: The Culture of Infancy in West Africa* (2004).

Minette Mans is an Associate Professor in ethnomusicology and music education at the University of Namibia, and has focused her research on indigenous musics and dance in Namibia for the past decade. She publishes widely and sits on several international editorial advisory boards. As 2002 ˆ 2004 Chair of the ISME Music in Schools and Teacher Education Commission, and Vice President of the Pan African Society for Musical Arts Education, she plays and active role in music education internationally, while also serving nationally as Chief National Examiner for Integrated Performing Arts. Mans also provides outreach service in education through the Swedish South African Research Network. In 2002 she won a stipendium as Guest African Researcher 2002 at the Nordic African Institute, Sweden. Her new book with CD *"Discover the Living Musics & Dance in Northern Kunene Region"* will appear in 2003.

Pirkko Markula, originally from Finland, is currently a senior lecturer in sport sociology and a member of the Qualitative Research Unit in the School of Sport and Health Sciences at the University of Exeter, United Kingdom. She is an ethnographer with special interest in poststructuralist feminist analysis of dance, fitness and health. Her most recent research project focuses on the meaning of mindful fitness forms for the fitness industry.

Michael Peters is Professor of Education at the University of Glasgow (UK) and the University of Auckland (NZ), and he holds a post as Adjunct Professor of Communications Studies at the Auckland University of Technology, New Zealand. He has research interests in educational theory and policy, and in contemporary philosophy. He has published over 100 articles and some twenty books in these fields, including: *Critical Theory and the Human Condition* (2003) (Eds.); *Heidegger, Education and Modernity* (2002) (Ed.); *Poststructuralism, Marxism and Neoliberalism* (2001); *Nietzsche's Legacy for Education: Past and Present Values*, (2001) (Eds.); *Wittgenstein: Philosophy, Postmodernism, Pedagogy* (1999) with James Marshall; *Poststructuralism, Politics and Education* (1996); *Curriculum in the Postmodern Condition* (2000) (Eds.); *Education and the Postmodern Condition*

Kimberly Powell received her masters degree from Harvard Graduate School of Education and her Ph.D from Stanford University in art education. Her research focuses on aesthetic development, civic engagement, and sociocultural contexts of learning. She is currently a senior research associate at The Pennsylvania State University, has taught courses in qualitative methods and art education, and works with the American Journal of Education.

Janice Ross is a dance historian, dance educator and critic who teaches in the Department of Drama at Stanford University. From 1990–2003 she directed the program in dance education for the School of Education. For 10 years, she was the staff dance critic for *The Oakland Tribune* and her articles on dance have appeared in *The New York Times* and *The Los Angeles Times* among other publications. She is the author of, *Moving Lessons: Margaret H'Doubler and the Beginning of Dance in American Education.* She is the recipient of a 2001 Guggenheim Fellowship for a book on the dance/theatre works of Anna Halprin.

Sue Stinson is Professor of Dance at University of North Carolina at Greensboro, where she teaches undergraduate courses in teacher preparation and graduate courses in research and curriculum. She served as Department Head in

Dance 1993–2002. As a dance educator, Stinson has taught in settings that include public and private schools, day care centers, and community agencies. She is active in national and international professional organizations in dance education. She has presented her scholarly work nationally and internationally, has contributed chapters to a number of books on dance and artseducation, and published in these journals: *Ballett International; Bulletin of the Council for Research in Music Education; Choreography and Dance; Dance Research Journal; Design for Arts in Education; Drama/Dance; Educational Theory; Impulse: The International Journal of Dance Science, Medicine, and Education; Journal of Curriculum and Supervision; Journal of Curriculum Theorizing; Journal of Physical Education, Recreation and Dance; Musical America; Pro-Posicoes*(Brazil); *Visual Arts Research; Women in Performance;* and *Young Children*. Since the mid–1980's, her research has focused on how young people interpret their experiences in dance education.

Richard Shusterman is Chair of Philosophy at Temple University, Philadelphia. Educated at Jerusalem and Oxford, he has been awarded senior NEH and Fulbright Research Fellowships and has held academic appointments in Israel, France, Germany, Canada, Finland, and Japan. Author of *The Object of Literary Criticism* (1984), *T.S. Eliot and the Philosophy of Criticism* (1988), *Pragmatist Aesthetics* (1992, now in its second edition, 2000, and translated into twelve languages), *Practicing Philosophy: Pragmatism and the Philosophical Life*(1997), *Performing Live* (2000), and *Surface and Depth* (2002), Shusterman is also editor of *Analytic Aesthetics* (1989), *Bourdieu: A Critical Reader* (1999), and The Range of Pragmatism and the Limits of Philosophy (2004), and co-editor of *The Interpretive Turn* (1991) and *Interpretation, Relativism, and the Metaphysics of Culture* (1999). An expert in somatic philosophy, where he has developed a field called somaesthetics, Shusterman also works professionally on body-mind reeducation as a certified Feldenkrais practitioner.

Joseph Tobin is the Nadine Mathis Basha Professor of Early Childhood Education at Arizona State University. His publications include *Preschool in three cultures: Japan, China and the United States, Re-made in Japan: Everyday life and consumer taste in a changing society, Good guys don't wear hats: Children's talk about the media and most recently, Pikachu's Global Adventure.*

Daniel J. Walsh is associate professor of early childhood education at the University of Illinois at Urbana-Champaign. He is most interested in how cultural beliefs about young children and their learning and development form contexts for young children's learning and development. He is the author of *High Risk Children in Schools: Constructing Sustaining Relationships* (with Robert Pianta) and *Studying Children in Context: Theories, Methods, and Ethics* (with M. Elizabeth Graue).

ALMA GOTTLIEB

FOREWORD:

FALLING INTO TRUST

"The body is a mirror that limns the observer's gaze and the object of that gaze, reflecting one back upon the other."

(Roberts and Roberts 1996, p. 86)

In Beng villages in the rain forest of Côte d'Ivoire, children learn critical life lessons through the body. On any given day, one might notice children of varying ages—as young as three, as old as fourteen or fifteen—playing the falling dance/game of lolondalɛ. A small group of children, usually no more than a dozen or so, forms a circle. Everyone claps hands and gaily sings the nonsense words to a short ditty that accompanies the playful routine. Half the children sing one line, then the other half repeat those words in an echo that serves as a variation on the common call-and-response vocal style of many African musical traditions. Altogether, only five short lines comprise the entire song:

No no
No no
Nona nofi
Nona nofi
Siyagita
Siyagita
Bandarandara
Bandarandara
Hooptageti!
Hooptageti!

Right after the children start singing this lively tune, one of them volunteers to stand in the center of the ring, surrounded by her playmates in an enveloping circle. As the singing children reach the final line of the air, the child in the middle deliberately falls backwards. As she does so, all the other children of the circle extend their arms outwards to catch the girl so that she falls backwards not onto the hard ground, where she would hurt herself, but into the soft but strong, waiting arms of her young friends and relatives, who keep her safe. Then the children gently bounce her upright, leaving her to regain her balance and rejoin the circle. Right away, another child jumps into the middle and the children start singing again,

1

Liora Bresler (ed.), Knowing Bodies, Moving Minds, 1-5.
©*2004 Kluwer Academic Publishers. Printed in the Netherlands*

climaxed with the new girl in the center falling backwards to land, as her predecessor just did, in the protective arms of her companions.

Often the dancing circle consists entirely of girls, but sometimes boys join in. Children start observing this dance activity from birth, as the game is performed outside in public view, where babies spend much of their days from dawn to dusk (Gottlieb, 2003). As soon as they are old enough to walk unassisted without falling, toddlers may begin haltingly to join in the game; by three years of age, many are regularly participating. Thus *lolondalE* often attracts a multi-age group: children as old as pre-teens participate routinely, and teenagers may join in if they have time off from their work. In the right mood, if they find themselves unexpectedly free from the multiple demands of full-time farming plus full-time domestic work, even the odd young, married woman may join in a round of *lolondalE* on occasion.

The game of *lolondalE* is, most obviously, a quite enjoyable diversion; from an aesthetic perspective, it is, as well, a graceful performance that is actually more choreographed than its spontaneous nature might imply. At yet another level, I propose, the song-and-dance routine is also a serious educational project. For educators know that all children's games, no matter how apparently trivial, teach significant lessons and values.[1] What are the lessons and values taught by *lolondalE*?

> I suggest that the major aim of this body game is to teach the very serious lesson that life is in good part about trust. In Beng villages, this is an important lesson that begins at birth and is often taught through the body. Immediately after childbirth, for example, a long line of wellwishers forms outside the doorway of the house in which the newly delivered woman gave birth. Ideally, a member of each household in the village comes to congratulate the woman and engage with the baby. And the baby's mother or grandmother typically offers the visitor a chance to hold the baby—an offer that is often accepted.

> In the weeks following this postpartum ritual, the Beng infant continues to be introduced somatically to visitors: normally, someone who travels from another village to visit a new baby should immediately be handed the child to hold. In reality, the guest may decline the chance to hold the baby. However, it is generally considered imperative to make the offer, whether that person is a relative or a stranger.

For all such visits, it is optimal for the baby to be awake so that the two can be properly introduced, according to formal greeting routines (see Gottlieb, 2003, Chapter 6). Of course this exchange could be problematic if—as happens often in the lives of infants —the baby happens to be sleeping when a guest arrives. In such cases, it is common to awaken the little one to be handed over to the visitor, especially for high-status guests, relatives visiting from afar, or relatives from the other side of a large village who do not get to see the baby every day.[2] Right from the start, then, a baby becomes used to being passed around from person to person, trained to trust the strong arms holding him (and, later, the strong back that will carry him).

Indeed, after the first two to three months of life—once the mother returns to working in her fields—a typical Beng baby does not spend more than an hour or two at a time with any given person. In a quantitative study that I conducted,[3] the most common length of time that infants remained with a given caretaker was a mere five minutes. The next most common duration for remaining with a single caretaker was ten minutes; after that, the next three most common durations were fifteen, twenty and twenty-five minutes, respectively (the latter two times were tied for fourth place). During the 41 two-and-a-quarter-hour sessions that we observed, the babies were engaged with an average of 2.2 people, but in many cases they were engaged with three to four people, and in two cases they were engaged with five or six people.[4]

In Beng villages, the somatic teaching of trust extends from holding the baby to breastfeeding. For the Beng, breastfeeding is a social act, and a biological mother is only one of many potential breastfeeders who may nurse a young infant. A casual attitude toward wet nursing offered as an improvisatory feeding strategy produces the possibility that Beng babies experience the breast as a site not just of nourishment but also of sociability (cf. Kitzinger, 1995, p. 390).[5]

One result of such high levels of social stimulation is that few Beng babies develop the sort of "stranger anxiety" that is common among middle-class, Euro-American babies toward the end of the first year and stretching into the second year. Indeed, Beng mothers actively endeavor to prevent the development of "stranger anxiety" and disapprove actively of the few babies who show signs of it.[6] A baby should agreeably go to anyone, even a stranger; a baby who cries on being given to an unknown person is insultingly called "*gbãlɛ*," or clingy.

In emphasizing this set of early childcare practices and games of young childhood, I do not wish to imply that social life in Beng villages creates an idyllic setting in which communal child care and universal trust govern all daily interactions. Indeed, later, as children mature into adults, Beng youth learn different lessons beyond their early training to trust a wide variety of people. They will learn the more morally problematic lesson that not all people are in fact to be trusted—that there are, in particular, many who pose a threat to their wellbeing through their strong mystical powers of witchcraft.[7] But at the young age at which babies are routinely passed around and, in a few years, children begin participating in *lolondalɛ*, teaching trust is much more important than is teaching suspicion. Life in this face-to-face community demands it.

Several years after observing *lolondalɛ* in Beng villages, I found myself teaching an introductory class in anthropology to a group of some two hundred students. The course met in a large room of fixed seats and attached desks—just the sort of enormous and impersonal lecture hall I myself had managed to avoid while a student at a small, liberal arts college. Trying to deconstruct the institutional rigidities of the unforgiving space, with its implicit assumption that the teacher knows all and the students know nothing, I decided one day to enliven the unit on childhood cross-culturally by bringing Beng games into the lecture hall. Without offering much preview—surprise and drama are, after all, two of the few delights we can offer in such grim pedagogical settings—I simply asked for a few brave volunteers to join me on the stage and try out a West African game. Several courageous students climbed the stairs to meet the challenge, and I positioned them in a circle, recruiting one to stand in the center. They eyed me expectantly, awaiting instructions. First, I gave the small group a singing lesson, teaching them the Beng song that accompanies *lolondalɛ*. Then I told the students in the outer ring to hold out their arms, and I instructed the student in the center to fall backwards, into the waiting arms of her companions in this venture. A murmur went through the lecture hall: the rest of the students were clearly worried about the fate of their classmate. *What if they didn't catch her and she fell onto the hard wooden floor,* they seemed to be thinking, *wouldn't she risk a serious injury?* The student in the center of the circle—and the center of all this attention—hesitated. She giggled nervously, looked around cautiously at the outstretched arms surrounding her, raised her eyebrows, giggled nervously some more, . . . and remained firmly upright. I teased her gently: "Don't you trust your classmates? Can't you see they're waiting to catch you?" She still looked nervous, but perhaps she was now thinking, *Can I pass this course if I don't follow the teacher's instructions?* I feared I might be on the edge of abusing my pedagogical authority. Still, I tried one last mild tease, and the student allowed herself to fall backwards—slowly, barely. Her classmates caught her, and she jumped quickly into the edge of the circle, showing evident relief. *Narrow escape,* she seemed to be thinking.

I gently taunted the group some more.

"See, it was easy? She didn't fall, you all caught her beautifully. Who'll try next?" I expected an eager volunteer from among the outer circle. None came forth. *Sure, they'd managed to catch the first student without causing injury, but could we repeat this feat a second time?* They were perhaps worrying. I decided to end my pedagogical abuse and thanked the brave group, then returned to my impromptu lecture.

The students' reluctance had supported my point quite dramatically: seemingly innocuous children's games teach important lessons in values that a given society endorses. To put the contrast at its starkest, in our society, games teach, above all, the value of competition; in Beng villages, *lolondalE* teaches the value of cooperation. In both cases, they do so in good part by aesthetic lessons imparted through the body.

In the chapters that follow, you will be treated to a wide variety of case studies of such lessons. This book blazes new paths in exploring the myriad ways in which the body both encodes cultural values and creates personal meanings. From Japanese preschoolers roughhousing to the epistemological knowledge imparted by dance/drama education in American elementary schools, you will read of dramatic and subtle ways alike in which cultural values are etched through artistic-somatic techniques. From the repression of young children's sensuality in American day care centers to the overt celebration of sensuality in Namibian dances that also celebrate political resistance to (current or past) oppressive regimes, the authors of these chapters explore the multiple ways in which the body is artistically configured and refigured. A remarkable discussion of teen jazz dance classes in California youth detention centers reminds us poignantly of how bodily interventions reshape people's consciousness—in some cases charted in that chapter, reorienting people's lives to imagine new life plans beyond prison bars. Across the world, people learn critical life lessons—sometimes destructive, sometimes productive, but always palpable—through aesthetic engagements with the body. This is a bold book filled with a dazzling array of aesthetic-bodily engagements around the world; prepare to experience the cerebral version of yogic enlightenment.

ENDNOTES

[1] For one ethnographic example from West Africa, see Lancy (1996).

[2] The practice of waking a sleeping baby to introduce to visitors has been documented elsewhere in West Africa (e.g. among the Fulani—see Riesman 1992:113, Johnson 2000:185) and may be fairly common on the continent.

[3] I carried out this quantitative portion of my research with the assistance of Dieudonné Kwame Kouassi, whose assistance I acknowledge here with gratitude. In total, we observed 25 babies in 43 observational sessions over a total of 5,745 minutes, or 95.75 hours. Of the 43 sessions, 41 were 135 minutes in duration; 1 was 120 minutes in duration; and 1 was 90 minutes in duration. The babies ranged in age from three months to twenty-four months, with the average age being 11.4 months.

[4] For tables, see Gottlieb (2003: Chapter 6).

[5] For more on Beng breastfeeding practices, see Gottlieb (2003: Chapter 8).

[6] For more on "stranger anxiety" in Beng villages, see Gottlieb (2003: Chapter 6).

[7] For more on Beng witchcraft, see Gottlieb (1989), Gottlieb ad Graham (1994).

REFERENCES

Gottlieb, A. (1989). Witches, kings, and the sacrifice of identity; or, the power of paradox and the paradox of power among the Beng of Ivory Coast. In W. Arens & I. Karp (Eds.), *Creativity of power: Cosmology and action in African societies* (pp. 245–272). Washington, D.C.: Smithsonian Institution Press.

Gottlieb, A. (in press). *The afterlife is where we come from: Infants and the culture of infancy in West Africa.* Chicago: University of Chicago Press.

Graham, P. (1994/1993). *Parallel worlds: An anthropologist and a writer encounter Africa.* Chicago: University of Chicago Press.

Johnson, M. (2000). The view from the *Wuro*: A guide to child rearing for Fulani parents. In J. DeLoache & A. Gottlieb (Eds.), *A world of babies: Imagined childcare guides for seven societies* (pp. 171–198). New York: Cambridge University Press.

Kitzinger, S. (1995). Commentary: Breastfeeding: Biocultural perspectives. In P. Stuart–Macadam & K. A. Dettwyler (Eds.), *Breastfeeding: Biocultural perspectives* (pp. 385–394). Hawthorne, NY: Aldine de Gruyter.

Lancy, D. (1996). *Playing on the mother-ground: Cultural routines for children's development.* New York: Guilford.

Riesman, P. (1992). *First find your child a good mother: The construction of self in two African communities* (David L. Szanton, Lila Abu-Lughod, Sharon Hutchinson, Paul Stoller & Carol Trosset, Eds.). New Brunswick: Rutgers University Press.

Roberts, M. N., & Roberts, A. F. (1996). Body Memory: Part I: Defining the Person. In M. N. Roberts & A. F. Roberts (Eds.), *Memory: Luba art and the making of history* (pp. 84–115). New York: The Museum for African Art.

LIORA BRESLER

PRELUDE

In his discussion of the concept of culture, Clifford Geertz, the famous anthropologist, refers to Susanne Langer's "*Grande Idée*"—certain ideas that burst upon the intellectual landscape with a tremendous force, becoming the conceptual center-point around which a comprehensive system of analysis can be built, promising to resolve many fundamental problems at once (Geertz, 1973, p. 3). The concept of embodiment, I believe, is one such *Grande Idée*.

Embodiment can be defined as the "integration of the physical or biological body and the phenomenal or experiential body," suggesting "a seamless though often-elusive matrix of body/mind worlds, a web that integrates thinking, being, doing and interacting within worlds" (Varela, Thompson, & Rosch, in Hocking, Haskell, & Linds, 2001, p. xviii). Csordas (1999) points out that the distinction between body and embodiment is reminiscent of Barthes' distinction between text and textuality: The former is a material object that occupies space in a bookstore; the latter is a methodological field that is experienced as activity and production (Csordas, 1999, p. 145). To work in a "paradigm of embodiment," is not to study anything new or different, but to address familiar topics—healing, emotion, gender, power, from a different standpoint (ibid.). This book aims to do just that within the field of education, examining schooling, in general, and curriculum and arts education in particular, through these new lenses.

The attention to the body has entered the world of scholarship from several directions, including Philosophy, the Social sciences, and the Arts. The body is conceptualized through multiple lenses, including the Neuro-physiological, the cognitive unconscious, and the phenomenological (Johnson, 1999; Lakoff & Johnson, 1999), the cultural (cf. Csordas, 1994), and the sociological (cf. Turner, 1996).

The notion of *Somatic society,* coined by Bryan Turner, is related to the shift from "the laboring body" to "the desiring body"—a locale for pleasure and playfulness (Turner, 1996). I see this shift as closely connected to the widening gap between schools and the outside world (cf. Sarason, 1990). As *Grande Idée*, embodiment has profound implications for many areas of society, but particularly for education and the ways we think about how children learn, how teachers can teach, and how schools could be organized. There is a vital need to examine what somatic modes of attention, those "culturally elaborated ways of attending to and with one's body in surroundings that include the embodied presence of others" (Csordas, 1999, p. 151), mean for schooling and for curriculum.

The body played an important role in various ancient philosophies and cultures, including the Greek and the Celtic. In Hinduism the body has been regarded as a vehicle to free the mind. In particular, the philosophy of yoga claims that the

7

Liora Bresler (ed.), Knowing Bodies, Moving Minds, 7-11.
©2004 Kluwer Academic Publishers. Printed in the Netherlands

alignment of body and mind is essential for spiritual freedom (Eliade, 1973). The body has served as a grounding element in different Buddhist traditions and practices (cf. Hahn, 2000). In contrast, western philosophy and spirituality of the past 2000 years have largely ignored, if not condemned, the body. Spawned by the late 19th century philosopher Friedrich Nietzsche (1886/1960), the centrality of the body to mind and being was taken on in the 20th century by French philosophers, most notably by Merleau-Ponty (1962), Sartre (1956/1966), Foucault (1977) and Bourdieu (1979/1984, 1980/1990).[1] In North American philosophy, the body/mind has been addressed by John Dewey (1928, 1929) and more recently, by Lakoff and Johnson (1999) and Shusterman (2000), among others.

John Dewey, a philosopher, psychologist and educator, addressed the body as part of his notions of experience and growth—two key concepts in his thinking. In his introduction to F. M. Alexander's book,[2] Dewey wrote:

> Men are afraid, without even being aware of their fear, to recognize the most wonderful of all the structures of the vast universe—the human body. They have been led to think that a serious notice and regard would somehow involve disloyalty to man's higher life. The discussions of Mr. Alexander breathe reverence for this wonderful instrument of our life, life mental and moral as well as that life which somewhat meaninglessly we call bodily." (1918, p. xiv)

In a paper addressed to the medical profession in the New York Academy of Medicine, Dewey claims:

> The very problem of mind and body suggests division; I do not know of anything so disastrously affected by the habit of division as this particularly theme. In its discussion are reflected the splitting off from each other of religion, morals and science, the divorce of philosophy from science and of both from the arts of conduct. The evils, which we suffer in education, in religion, in the materialism of business and the aloofness of "intellectuals" from life, in the whole separation of knowledge and practice—all testify to the necessity of seeing mind-body as an integral whole.

> The division in question is so deep-seated that it has affected even our language. We have no word by which to name mind-body in a unified wholeness of operation . . . Consequently, when we endeavor to establish this unity in human conduct, we still speak of body *and* mind and thus unconsciously perpetuate the very division we are striving to deny. (1928/2002, p. 24)

In an essay titled "Nature, Life and Body-Mind" (Dewey, 1929) addressed to fellow philosophers, Dewey develops the notions of body/mind in the context of the relation of mind to nature. Surveying the history of body/mind since the Greeks, observing that "Greek thought, as well as Greek religion, Greek sculpture and recreation, is piously attentive to the human body" (ibid. p. 249), Dewey traces the dichotomy of body and soul in Pauline Christianity, where the body is portrayed as "earthy, fleshy, lustful and passionate" compared to a "Godlike, everlasting" spirit. He notes the distinction between the corruptible flesh and an incorruptible spirit. "Appetites and desires spring from the body, distract attention from spiritual things;

---

[1] See also Hoy (1999) and Dreyfus & Dreyfus (1999).

[2] We learn from Dewey's biography that he was plagued from his youth by eyestrains, back pains, and sore neck, which flared up whenever he was under special stress (Martin, 2002). In 1916 he was introduced to F. M. Alexander and did extensive work with him. Martin points out that not only did the treatments of 1916-1917 relieve Dewey from pain, but that he also found a practical confirmation of his own psychology (Martin, 2002, p. 286).

concupiscence, anger, pride, love of money and luxury, worldly ambition, result" (ibid.).

These dichotomies have shaped our thinking for more than two millennia, waiting for the right time when the notion of embodiment can take root.[3] The change of world-view from mind *versus* body, to body/mind, operates on two interrelated levels. 1. The macro level consists of new theoretical frameworks across a variety of scholarly disciplines in the Sciences, the Arts, and the Humanities. 2. The micro level relates to the lived experience, consciousness and awareness of persons. These two levels interact with and shape each other, affecting value, life-style and for an increasing number of people, career choices.

In my personal experience, it is my situatedness within the arts—a performer turned researcher and educator (both of whom have strong performance aspects)—that heightened my attention to the experiencing body within a community. In my early experiences, accompanying the singing of folksongs was an auditory/kinesthetic/affective experience where personal experiences were transformed into social ones and vice versa. Similar qualities of intellectual/affective/kinesthetic connection to others were present in my roles as a teacher and a speaker. I have been increasingly aware of the role of my body not only in the ways in which I communicate and project my "self," but also in the ways that I attend and listen—to music, to other people, to the world; of its centrality to my lived everyday experience, intensified and otherwise. If my training in Aesthetics and Musicology provided me with tools for analysis and conceptualization, it was my body that made these experiences meaningful and vibrant.

In orchestrating this collection of essays by a group of leading scholars in various disciplines, I aimed in this book to map new theoretical, practical, and methodological directions in educational research. Theoretically, the chapters represent a range of conceptual frameworks, including aesthetics, anthropology, cultural psychology, curriculum theories, and arts (dance, music, and visual art) education, illustrating the interdisciplinary nature of contemporary educational thinking and research. The generation of new theoretical clusters, like the coming together of psychology, kinesiology, and anthropology, or anthropology and aesthetics, has created new ways of theorizing, and new research designs.

The arts, unlike the traditional academic areas, are an arena in which the body is central to the process of inquiry and constitutes a mode of knowing. This makes dance, drama, music, and visual arts education a particularly rich place to explore what embodiment means for educational researchers and practitioners. The view of the arts in this book includes not only the practice of arts, aesthetic theory and arts education, but also encompasses cross-cultural notions of the body within the arts as well as popular media, and special forms of bodily instruction.

---

[3] For cutting edge thinking that opens new directions on the body in various disciplines, see, for example, the work of Abrams, (1996); Butler (1990); Csordas (1994); Damasio, (2003); Lakoff & Johnson, (1999), and Shusterman (2000).

Section I presents philosophical perspectives on the body, examining historical and institutional contexts and their educational implications. The chapters in this section offer theoretical reconstructions of our notion of the body, laying new foundations for the possibilities of the body in education. Traditions of bodily instruction include such forms as the Alexander Technique, Feldenkreis, and Pilates that have long been the domain of self-selected audiences operating outside of mainstream education. As embodied knowledge is absent from the central areas of schooling, these fields contain invaluable knowledge about the somatic domain—including pedagogies and structures for embodied knowledge. Additional contexts encompass perspectives of the body as it emerges from different cultural contexts in Africa and Asian cultures, and different traditions of bodily conceptualizations through formal and informal education. These cultural contexts are made more complex by the clash between traditional societies and a globalized world (Bresler & Ardichvili, 2002).

Section II provides examples of state-of-the-art, empirical research on the body in a variety of educational settings. Schools are sites of cultural complexity where notions of the body interact with levels of schooling and subject areas, as well as the custom and cherishing of the community. Various art forms, curricular settings, educational levels, and cultural traditions are selected to demonstrate the complexity and richness of embodied knowledge as they are manifested through the institutional structures, disciplines, and specific practices—be it early childhood settings in the United States or in Japan, elementary schools or prisons, relatively homogeneous institutions or, as is increasingly common in a globalized world, transposed value-systems and instruction such as Taiko clubs in the US. The body as it exists in the classroom and within the school is contrasted to the body as it exists in a specific disciplinary arena or beyond the confines of the school (Kushner, 2000). The body as it is present in the contexts of art worlds is juxtaposed with the body found in educational settings. The book aims to be provocative, rather than exhaustive, focusing on powerful, research-grounded examples of the ways in which the body is shaped within educational settings. The assemblage of perspectives aims to bring us closer to constructing an understanding of embodied knowledge that will serve researchers as well as practitioners.

REFERENCES

Abrams, D. (1996). The spell of the sensuous: Perception and language in a more-than-human world. New York: Pantheon Books.

Bourdieu, P. (1984). Distinction: A social critique of the judgment of taste (R. Nice, Trans.). Cambridge, Mass: Harvard University Press. (Original work published 1979)

Bourdieu, P. (1990). The logic of practice (R. Nice, Trans.). Stanford: Stanford University Press. (Original work published 1980)

Bresler, L., & Ardichvili, A. (Eds.). (2002). International research in education: Experience, theory and practice. New York: Peter Lang.

Butler, J. (1990). Gender trouble: Feminism and the subversion of identity. New York: Routledge Indent.

Csordas, T. J. (Ed.). (1994). Embodyment and experience: The existential ground of culture and self. New York: Cambridge University Press.

Csordas, T. J. (1999). Embodiment and cultural phenomenology. In G. Weiss & H. F. Haber (Eds.), Perspectives on embodiment: The intersections of nature and culture (pp. 143-162). New York: Routledge.

Damasio, A. (2003). Looking for Spinoza: Joy, sorrow, and the feeling brain. New York: Harcourt.

Dewey, J. (1918). Introduction. In F. M. Alexander, Man's supreme inheritance (pp. xiii-xvii). New York: Dutton.

Dewey, J. (1928/2002). Preoccupation with the disconnected. A reprint from a talk given to the New York Academy of Medicine. Champaign, IL: NASTAT

Dewey, J. (1929/1958). Experience and nature. New York: Dover Publications.

Dreyfus, H. L., & Dreyfus, S. E. (1999). The Challenge to Merleau-Ponty's Phenomenology of Embodiment for Cognitive Science. In G. Weiss & H. F. Haber (Eds.), Perspectives on embodiment: The intersections of nature and culture (pp. 103-120). New York: Routledge.

Eliade, M. (1973). Yoga: Immortality and freedom. Princeton, NJ: Princeton University Press.

Foucault, M. (1977). Discipline and punish: The birth of the prison. New York: Vintage Books.

Geertz, C. (1973). The interpretation of cultures. New York: Basic Books.

Hanh, T. N. (2000). The path of emancipation. Berkeley: Parallax Press.

Hocking, B., Haskell, J., & Linds, W. (2001). Unfolding bodymind: Exploring possibility through education. Brandon, Vermont: Foundations for Educational Renewal.

Hoy, D. (1999). Critical Resistance: Foucault and Bourdieu. In G. Weiss & H. F. Haber (Eds.), Perspectives on embodiment: The intersections of nature and culture (pp. 3-22). New York: Routledge.

Johnson, M. (1999). Embodied reason. In G. Weiss & H. F. Haber (Eds.), Perspectives on embodiment: The intersections of nature and culture (pp. 103-120). New York: Routledge.

Kushner, S. (2000). Personalizing evaluation. Thousand Oaks, CA: Sage.

Lakoff, G., & Johnson, M. (1999). Philosophy in the flesh: The embodied mind and its challenge to Western thought. New York: Basic Books.

Martin, J. (2002). The education of John Dewey: A biography. New York: Columbia University Press.

Merleau-Ponty, M. (1962). The phenomenology of perception. London: Routledge & Kegan Paul.

Nietzsche, F. (1960). Thus spake Zarathustra (T. Common, Trans.). New York: Modern Library. (Original work published 1886)

Sarason, S. (1990). The predictable failure of educational reform: Can we change course before it's too late? San Francisco: Jossey-Bass Publishers.

Sartre, J. (1966). Being and nothingness: A phenomenological essay on ontology (H. Barnes Trans.). New York: Pocket Books. (Original work published 1956)

Shusterman, R. (2000). Performing live: Aesthetic alternatives for the ends of art. Ithaca: Cornell University Press.

Turner, B. (1996). The body and society: Explorations in social theory (2nd ed.). Thousand Oaks, CA: Sage.

Weiss, G. (1999). Body image: Embodiment as intercoporeality. New York: Routlege.

MICHAEL PETERS

EDUCATION AND THE PHILOSOPHY OF THE BODY: BODIES OF KNOWLEDGE AND KNOWLEDGES OF THE BODY

"THERE IS MORE REASON IN YOUR BODY, THAN IN YOUR BEST WISDOM"

Friedrich Nietzsche, *Thus Spake Zarathustra.*

The body has recently become a desideratum for a range of disparate studies in the arts, humanities and the sciences for a philosophical rescue operation that aims — against the dualisms bedevilling modern philosophy elevating the mind at the expense of the body — to rehabilitate the body as a site for reason, perception, knowledge and learning. This re-evaluation has been driven by a range of factors: the attempt to overcome the dualism of mind/body metaphysics (Wittgenstein, Dewey); the re-surfacing of a phenomenology of the body (Sartre and Merleau-Ponty) in the continuing rapprochement of so-called analytic and continental philosophy; the movement within continental philosophy that emphasises the finitude, temporality, and corporeality of the self (Heidegger) and, also, the historizing of questions of ontology (Foucault); and, the development of feminist philosophy where embodiedness, especially in relation to sex and gender, have played a central role. This chapter provides a conceptual mapping of these discourses of the body, starting from the inspiration of Nietzsche, and begins the task of unpacking the consequences of adopting such views for education and the curriculum, with a particular focus on aesthetics and the arts.

INTRODUCTION: PLATONISM/ANTI-PLATONISM

The idea that the soul is distinct from the body has it roots in classical Greek philosophy and is found in Plato. For instance, in the *Meno*, Plato indicates that the soul acquires knowledge before it enters the body and thus all knowing consists in recollecting. Later, in the *Phaedo* and other dialogues Plato articulates the notion of Forms, which are considered eternal, changeless and incorporeal. The Platonic dualism between the world of Forms and the world of mere appearances becomes one of the problem-sets in the history of philosophy. Gilbert Ryle said that all Western philosophy consists in a series of footnotes to Plato and, indeed, one can detect in the history of contemporary philosophy the antagonism between Platonism and anti-Platonism as a dominant theme. For instance, the controversial neopragmatist, Richard Rorty (1999, p. xvi) suggests that

philosophers are called 'relativists' when they do not accept the Greek distinction between the way things are in themselves and the relations which they have to other things, and in particular to human needs and interests.

He goes on to argue that philosophers who eschew this distinction

Liora Bresler (ed.), Knowing Bodies, Moving Minds, 13-27.
©*2004 Kluwer Academic Publishers. Printed in the Netherlands*

> must abandon the traditional philosophical project of finding something stable which will serve
> as a criterion for judging the transitory products of our transitory needs and interests... We have
> to give up on the idea that there are unconditional, transcultural moral obligations, obligations
> rooted in an unchanging, ahistorical human nature. This attempt to put aside both Plato and Kant
> is the bond which links the post-Nietzschean tradition in European philosophy with the
> pragmatic tradition in American philosophy.

Whether Rorty is correct in making this assertion about the link between these philosophical traditions is less important than his characterization of such philosophers as "anti-Platonists," "antimetaphysicians" or "antifoundationalists." As Rorty (1999) explains in the Preface:

> "Platonism" in the sense in which I use the term does not denote the (very complex, shifting,
> dubiously consistent) thoughts of the genius who wrote the Dialogues. Instead, it refers to the set
> of philosophical distinctions (appearance-reality, matter-mind, made-found, sensible-intellectual,
> etc.: what Dewey called "a brood and nest of dualisms." These dualisms dominate the history of
> Western philosophy, and can be traced back to one or another passage in Plato's writings (p. xii).

Platonism, thus, in educational thought stands for the elevation and privileging of the mind or intellect over the body: it stands for a host of optional metaphors that serve to dualize or bifurcate reason and emotion, metaphors, in their application and formalisation, have become the substance of educational practice. Perhaps, the most culturally deeply embedded dualism with which educational theory and practice must come to terms with is the mind/body separation. This dualism historically has developed as an instrument of "othering": of separating boys from girls, reason from emotion, minorities from the dominant culture, and classes from each other. It nests within a family of related dualisms, as Rorty explains above, and remains one of the most trenchant and resistant problems of education in postmodernity.

Descartes gives the specifically modern form of the mind-body dualism. He maintained that the essence of the physical is extension in space and as minds have no such extension they cannot be considered physical substances. By contrast, their essence is to think. The history of modern philosophy is a history of the mind-body problem from various forms of epiphenomenalism (the doctrine that physical states cause mental states), parallelism (the view that the mental and physical realms run in parallel), monism (the rejection of the Cartesian bifurcation of reality), to materialism and especially "central state materialism," (where all mental states are considered contingently identical with brain states) and functionalism (a doctrine that characterises cognitive psychology and the research program known as connectionism).

My strategy in this essay is to follow one side of the ambiguous legacy of Descartes in French philosophy.[1] Eric Matthews (1996) explains that "Descartes was both an 'Augustinian' philosopher of subjectivity and a 'Galilean' advocate of modern science based on mathematics"[2] My pathway is to follow the heritage of the first Descartes and, specifically, to explore modern French philosophy as a philosophy of subjectivity, based on Descartes' subjective turn – a philosophy that, through, its manifold incantations as phenomenology, hermeneutics, existentialism, structuralism and poststructuralism, exhibits a progressive tendency to theorise the body as a source of consciousness, perception and reason. Under the heading "The End of 'Humanism,'" Eric Matthews (1996, p. 8) suggests that

The outstanding feature of the development of French philosophy in the twentieth-century has been the deepening crisis of the Cartesian synthesis of Augustine and Galileo, and of the rationalistic and humanistic view of the world which was based on it. The narrative of this book will thus be the story of the development of this crisis. It has affected above all the Cartesian concept of the human subject, as a universal being of pure reason divorced from its body and so from any position in space, time, and history.

If I begin with Nietzsche, it is because he considers himself a Francophile and an author who prefers both to write in the Romantic language of French than in his own native German, and for a French audience. We might also cite his influence on the French philosophy of subjectivity indirectly through Heidegger (and thence via Sartre) but also in terms of a direct influence on thinkers as diverse as Sartre, Lacan, Bataille, Deleuze, Foucault, Derrida and Irrigaray. My approach will be to provide a series of brief sketches of the importance of the body as a thematic in the work of postwar French philosophers as part of a sustained argument interpreting postwar French philosophy as "bodies of knowledge" that stand against Platonism in all its guises. In contrast to Platonism, contemporary French philosophy emphasises the enfleshed subject, sensuous reason, and the embodied and engendered subject — a subject, not timelessly cast as an abstract universalism, but one that emphasizes the everyday activity contingencies of the becoming self. In so doing these philosophers provide us with subjugated knowledges of the body.

THE PHENOMENOLOGICAL BODY

Nietzsche and the Body

Friedrich Nietzsche is a pivotal thinker for contemporary Continental philosophy both for the line of thinking that extends phenomenology via Heidegger into hermeneutics and the line of thinking springing out of phenomenology, clearly evidenced in the works of the French existentialists, especially Jean-Paul Sartre, Simone de Beauvior and Albert Camus. Nietzsche is also pivotal for the line of thinking that we might characterise or christen as poststructuralist. Nietzsche is pivotal in many different ways – his linguisticality, his genealogical inquiries where he cultivates a form of historical narrative, his critique of truth, his conception of "will to power," his biological emphases, above all perhaps, his critique of the Cartesian-Kantian subject and his substitution of genealogy for ontology. In this constellation of guiding motifs and ideas it is the last – the philosophy of the subject — which serves as a signpost for the movements of phenomenology, existentialism and poststructuralism. More than anything, the *problematique* of the body serves as the touchstone that, at one and the same time, signals the process of dismantling and unravelling the main articles of faith sustaining the Cartesian-Kantian and Hegelian subjects and points to alternative sources for philosophical inquiry. The body, which necessarily occupies a spatial-temporal location, both fixes the subject historically, breaking down its universalist assumptions of individuality, pure rationality and self-interest. I shall not pursue this suggestion at length here but simply point to some sources where Nietzsche talks of the body, rehabilitating a notion of "embodied reason" against the mind/body dualism of Cartesian philosophy.

In Part One ("Zarathustra's Discourses") of *Thus Spake Zarathustra*, Nietzsche (1961, p. 61–63) writes "*Of the Despisers of the Body*," contrasting two views, one maintaining "I am body and soul," and the other, more enlightened view, which maintains "I am body entirely, and nothing else beside; and soul is only a word for something in the body" (p. 61). He elaborates this position further in the following paragraph:

> The body is a great intelligence, a multiplicity with one sense, a war and a peace, a herd and a herdsman. Your little intelligence, my brother, which you call "spirit," is also an instrument of you body, a little instrument and toy of your great intelligence. You say "I" and you are proud of this word. But greater than this – although you will not believe in it – is your body and its great intelligence, which does not say "I" but performs "I" (pp. 61–62).

From this passage and others textually nearby we can see that Nietzsche is calling our attention to an embodied form of reason, a form of reason deeper than a superficial rationality and one that has the power to govern our passions and regulate ourselves. For Nietzsche only a reason allied with the passions can be true reason. Thus, he is not Darwinian in that he believes that the forces of biology rule, rather Nietzsche is suggesting a *restored* and embodied form of reason that is capable of regulating the passions, where the passions become an instrument of reason and, thereby, Man (or humankind) can redirect reason to focus on himself considered as a *work* that can be sculpted.

Nietzsche's talk of the body and of an embodied reason can be construed as part of his attack on Platonism. This much Heidegger (1991, p. 201) certainly sees when he describes the inversion of Platonism that takes place in Nietzsche's thought,

> For Plato the supersenuous is the true world. It stands over all, as what sets the standard. The sensuous lies below, as the world of appearances. What stands over all is alone and from the start what sets the standard; it is therefore what is desired. After the inversion – that is easy to calculate in a formal way – the sensuous, the world of appearances, stands above; the supersensuous, the true world, lies below.

Yet, Heidegger claims, that the inversion does not achieve what it was designed to achieve as overcoming of nihilism, that is, "an overcoming of Platonism in its very foundations" (p. 201). Heidegger interprets the eternal return of the same and the will to power as the fundamental thought of Nietzsche's philosophy. It is this thought that in Heidegger's view that reaches out to being as a whole and at the same time stands in opposition not only to the metaphysics of Platonism but also of the Christian tradition as well.

Being-in-the-World: Sartre and de Beauvoir on the Body

While in this essay I wish to concentrate on postwar French philosophy, it is important to mention in passing the philosophy of Henri Bergson whose work on becoming also stands against a Platonism that holds that beyond the world of appearances is a timeless and unchanging reality or world of being. Bergson's metaphysics was to emphasise the primary intuitive awareness of our consciousness of ourselves as flowing through time – time considered as inner experience (or "duration" as Bergson terms it) rather than the spatialized time in which we can locate objects. Bergson, as Matthews (1996, p. 27) points out, while still dualistic deviated in important respects from Descartes and prepared the way "for one of the most characteristic concepts of twentieth-century French philosophy that of human beings as necessarily 'embodied' or 'incarnate.'"

In *Existentialism and Humanism*, an essay published in 1946, Sartre (1980, p. 44) writes:

> Our point of departure is, indeed, the subjectivity of the individual ... And at the point of departure there cannot be any other truth than this, *I think, therefore I am*, which is the absolute truth of consciousness as it attains to itself.

In that same work Sartre articulates what was to become the dictum of existentialism: "*existence* comes before *essence*" (p. 26) by which he means "Man is nothing else but that which he makes of himself" (p. 28) a description which he fills out be reference to the moral faculty of choice and action. His emphasis on "becoming" and "being-in-the-world" is spelt out in his famous *Being and Nothingness* published in 1943 where, taking intentionality as the hallmark of consciousness, he defines it as necessarily consciousness *of* something. The human mode of existence implies a "being-in-the-world" where the objects of consciousness and consciousnesses themselves cannot exist without each other.

Sartre begins with a notion of pre-reflective consciousness. He argues that the "I am" in Descartes' formulation is not the consciousness, which thinks. Similarly, he argues that Descartes' *cogito* is not the consciousness that doubts but rather one that reflects upon doubting. Both arguments lead Sartre to posit the pre-reflective *cogito* as the primary consciousness. He then makes a distinction between unconscious being (being-in-itself) and conscious being (being-for-itself). In Part One of *Being and Nothingness* Sartre (1966) establishes a view of the for-itself as a pursuit of being in the form of selfness. The bridge between the for-itself and the in-itself is knowledge, which is not possible without a consideration of the senses. Thus we are referred to the body in Part Three. Sartre distinguishes between two complementary modes of being for the body, what he calls being-for-itself or "facticity" and the body-for-others. Sartre (1966, p. 460) goes on to talk of a third ontological dimension of the body:

> I exist my body: this is my first dimension of being. My body is utilized and known by the Other: this is the second dimension. But in so far as *I am for others*, the Other is revealed to me as the subject for whom I am an object.

The body, then, both "constitutes the meaning and marks the limit" of my relations with others. Sartre describes concrete relations with others in terms of a conflict perspective ("while I seek to enslave the Other, the Other seeks to enslave me" p. 475), starting from the *look* (or the *gaze*) which objectifies and possesses me and moving on to consider the first attitude toward others (love, language, masochism) and the second (indifference, desire, hate, sadism).

If anything, Simone de Beauvoir's philosophy, historically, may have been more important than Sartre's and is considered by some as ultimately responsible for ideas for which he is best known. Marshall (2001, p. 5–6) argues that de Beauvoir abandons the notion of the solipsistic self early in her life, coming to emphasise, by contrast, that the Other is necessary for the constitution of self.

> In *She Came to Stay* the body is not a mere object or thing but is always experienced reality – "my heart is beating – I am here." Elsewhere and some years later she is to say explicitly, in a passage reminiscent of Bergson: "It is not the body-object described by biologists that actually exists but the body as lived in by the subject" (Beauvoir, 1989, p. 38).

In *The Second Sex* de Beauvoir (1949) discusses the desire to be as concretely embedded in the everyday life. In this existential-historical situation being is both sexed and bodied. Beauvoir turns her attention to the ways in which the embodied desire to be is lured by the particular images of woman and man, and focuses on the ways in which the image and myth of woman marks the embodied consciousness of woman. With de Beauvoir being and the problem of the self receives its first systematic gendered treatment and with her work begins a tradition of feminist philosophy. As Diana Meyers (1999) writes:

> The topic of the self has long been salient in feminist philosophy, for it is pivotal to questions about personhood, identity, the body, and agency that feminism must address. In some respects, Simone de Beauvoir's trenchant observation, "He is the Subject, he is the Absolute — she is the Other," sums up why the self is such an important issue for feminism. To be the Other is to be the non-subject, the non-person, the non-agent — in short, the mere body. In law, in customary practice, and in cultural stereotypes, women's selfhood has been systematically subordinated, diminished, and belittled, when it has not been outright denied. Since women have been cast as lesser forms of the masculine individual, the paradigm of the self that has gained ascendancy in U.S. popular culture and in Western philosophy is derived from the experience of the predominantly white and heterosexual, mostly economically advantaged men who have wielded social, economic, and political power and who have dominated the arts, literature, the media, and scholarship.

Merleau-Ponty: The Body as Subject

Maurice Merleau-Ponty, a friend of and fellow founding editor with Sartre of the influential periodical *Les Temps Modernes* published his major work *Phenomenology of Perception* in 1945. Merleau-Ponty emphasises embodied perception and the notion of "lived experience." He rejects both Cartesian dualism and also extreme subjectivism. While he follows Husserlian phenomenology he gives the body a more central role in the lived world, moving away from Husserl's transcendental phenomenology to an existential phenomenology influenced by Sartre. Rather than Husserl's "thinking ego" Merleau-Ponty talks of the "body-subject" and emphasises the primacy of perception in our relations with the world. He argues against the empirical notion of the world and our perception of it. As Matthews (1996, p. 90) explains:

> For the world as we actually perceive it does not consist of a collection of discrete, atomistic, and fully determinate sense-data, which acquire unity only because it is imposed on them by our own minds. Rather, we perceive the world as already structured and unified: the way in which we perceive a quality, for example, is affected by the sort of background against which we perceive it, or the context in which we perceive it.

The body is not an "object" in the objective sense to be identified through its spatial properties and its location; neither is the body limited to cause and effect descriptions. Rather, the body is the subject of action: it is essentially a practical, pre-conscious subject in the lived world that possesses both "intentionality" and "knowledge." As he argues, the experience of things in the world is lived from an embodied point of view. Thus, the subject is a perceiving body, situated in time, and immersed in the living world. Merleau-Ponty treats the body as subject (rather than object) emphasising that our bodies are part of our subjectivity and the basis for our being-in-the-world.

Marjorie O'Loughlin (1998) makes central use of Merleau-Ponty as a corrective to some strands of postmodernist feminism and educational theory that has critiqued the Enlightenment "subject" while, taking the linguistic turn, regard the subject as merely an effect of discourse or as a "position within language." At the same time, she notes, "there has been a burgeoning interest in the notion of embodiment as a means of getting at the realities of 'difference' among a multiplicity of subjectivities." Her argument is that Merleau-Ponty provides "a means of enriching our understanding of human subjectivity in ways which avoid some of the pitfalls of postmodernism, and which remind us of the "lived engagement" of the embodied subjects of education with their environments." O'Loughlin (1998) further, writes:

Recent post-modernist moves and the interrogation of the tradition by feminist philosophers has begun to bring the body squarely into focus, so that for some educational theorists, issues of critical pedagogy are now central to the politics of the body. Feminist and post-modern critiques have begun to provide an understanding of the constructed and performative nature of subjectivities and (following Foucault) of the notion of a direct somatic discipline, of the inscription of the body, and of the embodied learning which occurs in daily life. Most significant is the recognition of the gendered body as subject to a multiplicity of gender regimes within education. Nevertheless, I want to argue here is that the gender dimension, though crucial, does not exhaust the discussion concerning subjectivity.

In an insightful essay she goes on to examine two aspects of embodiment, which are of importance to education. She continues:

The first concerns the claim that embodiment can be meaningfully talked about irrespective of gender; the second draws attention to a specific, complex notion of embodied subjectivity which I believe captures a sense of the human being's "immersion" in places, spaces and environs in which, as gendered subjects, they encounter the world as dwelling place.

I shan't interrogate her argument or take issue with her here except to say that there is an essential element of poststructualism that O'Loughlin (1998) does not seem to take on board: the critique of the subject of phenomenology as harboring vestiges of liberal humanism. While O'Loughlin may be correct to assert that the body gets discursively submerged as Western philosophy developed, she gives no acknowledgement to the critique of humanism, especially as it is invested in phenomenology.

The sources for scepticism concerning the possibility of a metaphysics of human nature – an a priori account of an unchanging human nature – gets its first inspiration from Nietzsche's anti-Platonism, followed closely by Heidegger's famous "Letter on Humanism," in which he was at pains to expose humanism as a naïve anthropomorphism, especially the traditional interpretation of humanism as a renewal of Platonism or Neo-Platonism and so of Western metaphysics. As Heidegger (1996, p. 225–226) writes in a now famous formulation:

> Every humanism is either grounded in metaphysics or is itself made to be the ground of one. Every determination of the essence of man that already presupposes an interpretation of beings without asking about the truth of Being, whether knowingly or not, is metaphysical.

This Nietzschean-Heideggerian line of thinking is picked up by Foucault (1970, p. 387) when he writes: "As the archaeology of our thought easily shows, man is an invention of a recent date. And one perhaps nearing its end." Foucault is not only making the Heideggerian point that the concept of human nature with which we currently operate is a product of an historical period, and, therefore, operates ideologically to disguise itself (masking its power relations) but also that all a priori accounts of human nature, even those that simply invert Platonism, substituting the body of the soul, are ideological. In *Remarks on Marx*, a series of conversations with the Italian Marxist Duccio Trombadori, Foucault (1991) compares phenomenology with the Nietzschean line of thought.

> The phenomenologist's experience is basically a way of organizing the conscious perception of any aspect of daily life, lived experienced in its transitory form, in order to grasp its meaning. Nietzsche, Bataille, and Blanchot, on the contrary, try though experience to reach that point of life which lies as close as possible to the impossibility of living, which lies at the limit or extreme...phenomenology tries to grasp the significance of daily experience in order to reaffirm the fundamental character of the subject, of the self, of its transcendental functions. One the contrary, experience according to Nietzsche Blanchot, and Bataille has rather the task of "tearing" the subject from itself in such a way that it is no longer the subject as such, or that it is completely "other" than itself so that it may arrive at its annihilation, its dissociation (p. 31).

(POST)STRUCTURALISM: READING AND WRITING THE BODY

There is far too much ground to cover under this theme to treat structuralist and poststructuralist thinkers individually. I shall, therefore, make some notes, so to speak, comment upon some broad themes and only mention some of the more prominent philosophers and thinkers. Judith Butler (1987, p. 175) in a penetrating analysis of contemporary French theory as a series of reflections on Hegel, begins her final chapter with the following interpretation:

> The twentieth-century history of Hegelianism in France can be understood in terms of two constitutive moments: (1) the specification of the subject in terms of finitude, corporeal boundaries, and temporality and (2) the "splitting" (Lacan), "displacement" (Derrida), and eventual death (Foucault, Deleuze) of the Hegelian subject.

Of these two constitutive moments we can say that the first is played out in a series of phenomenological engagements with the body, whereas the second can be read as a series of disengagements with Hegel and phenomenology.

Lacan exemplifies this thesis well when he transposes Freud's emphasis on the biological to the linguistic and argues that the formation of the subject takes place through a relation to something external. The *mirror-image* thus moves beyond the loneliness and individual isolation of the "I think" to reclaim a relational analysis of self, one for the child, furthermore, that is anchored in "play" and cannot be divorced from the child's awareness of its own body.

Butler (1987, p. 183) comments that for both Derrida and Foucault "the Hegelian theme of relational opposition is radically challenged through a formulation of difference as a primary and irrefutable linguistic/historical constant." The projection and recovery of the subject in Hegelian terms, thus, for Derrida and Foucault sets conditions for an exercise in self-deception. Butler (1987, p. 198) plots the growing instability of the subject in the work of Kojéve, Hyppolite and Sartre, and summarises the progression in French thought as a series of reflections on Hegel's "anthropocentrism."

> While the subject in Hegel is projected and then recovered, in Sartre it is projected endlessly without recovery, but nevertheless *knows itself* in its estrangement and so remains a unitary consciousness, reflexively self-identical. In the psycho-analytic structuralism of Lacan and in the Nietzschean writings of Deleuze and Foucault, the subject is once again understood as a projected unity, but this projection *disguises* and falsifies the multiplicitous disunity constitutive of experience, whether conceived as libidinal forces, the will-to-power, or the strategies of power/discourse.

Certainly, it is the case that Foucault, along with Deleuze and Derrida, rejects both the normalizing and totalizing tendencies of the Hegelian dialectic and its anthropological expression in foundational assumptions of the human subject.[3] Foucault (1983, p. 199) tells us that he begins to study Nietzsche (outside the academy) as early as 1953, and that Nietzsche, Blanchot and Bataille permitted him to free himself from the confines of a French university education which, in philosophy, was "a Hegelianism deeply penetrated by phenomenology and existentialism, which hinged on the theme of the 'unhappy consciousness'" (Foucault, 1991, p. 45). For Foucault Nietzsche represented an "invitation" to call into question the category of the subject. There was also an important relation between Foucault's theoretical work and his (local) politics – "politics" he suggests at one point became "a way of testing how much I was maturing in my theoretical reflections" (Foucault, 1991, p. 47). Foucault's Nietzschean genealogical critique aims at revealing the contingent and historical conditions of existence. In short, he historicizes questions of ontology, substituting genealogical investigations of the subject for the philosophical attempt to define the essence of human nature.

Both Foucault and Derrida in seminal essays ("Nietzsche, Genealogy and History"; "The Pit and the Pyramid: An Introduction to Hegel's Semiology") begin with Hegelian themes to suggest a radical departure. Foucault questions the unilinearity of an implicit and progressive rationality, and the way in which the dialectical explanation of historical experience assumes a single origin and cause. Narratives of historical experience which draw on the theoretical fiction of an immanent rationality disguise and attempt to rationalise an original multiplicity of events and forces which resist the demands of a unifying dialectic.

Historiographers have masked and rationalised this original and radical heteronomy of events and forces through the "imposition of orderly theoretical forms." Butler (1987, p. 180) suggests that Foucault's analysis of modernity "attempts to show how the terms of dialectical opposition do not resolve into more synthetic and inclusive terms but tend instead to splinter off into a multiplicity of terms which expose the dialectic itself as a limited methodological tool ..." While Foucault professes not to understand the problem behind postmodernism, his sympathetic critics certainly take him to be a poststructuralist/postmodernist thinker, who, along with other poststructuralist thinkers, teaches that the values of the modern era were essentially logo- and homocentric illusions. Certainly both Poster (1981) and Frazer (1981; 1983; 1985) understand Foucault's examination of "the philosophy of the subject" — by which he means a *problematique* dominating the modern *episteme* that privileges the subject-as-mind as the foundation of all knowledge, action and signification. Both authors argue that Foucault's genealogical analysis of modern power operates on the basis of a radical decentering that denies an epistemic or historical privilege to either the traditional Cartesian notion of a "centered" subjectivity or the humanist ideal of a rational, autonomous, and responsible self. Poster (1981, p. 138), for instance, writes:

> In place of the continuous chronology of reason . . . there have appeared scales that are sometimes very brief, distinct from one another, irreducible to a single law, scales that bear a type of history peculiar to each one, and which cannot be reduced to the general model of consciousness that acquires, progresses and remembers.

They understand that Foucault's method allows us to see power very broadly in the development of a plurality of incommensurable discursive regimes, each with its multiplicity of "micropractices," which ultimately directs us to study the "politics of everyday life" and the way power is inscribed upon the body. Such a Nietzschean approach suspends the problematic of legitimacy understood in terms of the standard modern liberal normative framework with its talk of rights grounded as it is in the "nature of persons."

In *Discipline and Punish*, Foucault (1977) describes and analyzes a political system with the King's body at the centre. Yet in the nineteenth-century, Foucault suggests that the "body of society" becomes a new principle. The social body is protected through a series of dividing practices involving the segregation of the sick, the quarantining of "degenerates," the schooling of boys and girls, and the exclusion of delinquents. As Foucault (1980, p. 55) in the early interview "Body/Power" (given in 1975) says: "the phenomenon of the social body is the effect not of a consensus but of the materiality of power operating on the very bodies of individuals." These relations of power do not obey the Hegelian form of the dialectic but rather take the path of a strategic development of a political struggle in involves both the mastery of the body, achieved through an institutional investment in the power of the body, and the counter-attack in the same body. Foucault (1980, p. 56) provides the example of auto-eroticism:

> The restrictions on masturbation hardly start in Europe until the eighteenth century. Suddenly, a panic-theme appears: an appalling sickness develops in the Western world. Children masturbate. Via the medium of families, though not at their initiative, a system of control of sexuality, an objectification of sexuality allied to corporal persecution, is established over the bodies of children. But sexuality, through thus becoming an object of analysis and concern, surveillance and control, engenders at the same time an intensification of each individual's desire, for, in, and over his body.

Foucault upsets the normal understanding when he claims that we should set aside the thesis that power in our capitalist societies has denied the reality of the body in favour of the mind or consciousness. He writes:

> In fact nothing is more material, physical, corporal than the exercise of power. What mode of investment of the body is necessary and adequate for the functioning of a capitalist society like ours?

In the period from the eighteen to the beginning of the twentieth century the investment of the body by power was "heavy, ponderous, meticulous and constant" as evidenced in the disciplinary regimes of schools, hospitals, barracks, factories and the like. Then in the 1960s, it began to be realised that "such a cumbersome form of power was no longer indispensable" and "that industrial societies could content themselves with a much looser form of power over the body." As he insists: "One needs to study what kind of body the current society needs" (p. 58).

Another way of recognising Foucault's statement is to focus not on the kind of bodies the current society needs but how societies, both capitalist and non-capitalist, organise the selection of bodies to legitimate various kinds of exploitation and enslavement. Central to the claims of the feminist poststructuralist thinkers is the examination of philosophy as the master discourse of Western culture and one that harbour a deep *phallo-logocentrism*. Luce Irrigaray in *An Ethic of Sexual Difference* (1982, p. 6) argues: "Everything, beginning with the way in which the subject has always been written in the masculine form, as *man*, even when it claimed to be universal or neutral." Irrigaray, Julia Kristeva, and many other feminist poststructuralist thinkers, have criticised the Platonism of the Western philosophical tradition, a tradition that posits universal and gender-neutral abstractions that, nevertheless, secretly harbor patriarchal interests, associating girls and women, on one side of a subordinated dualism, with the sensuous, nature, emotion, and irrationality.

Julia Kristeva has been influential in feminist discourse for bringing the body back into discourses in the human sciences, particularly through the importance of the maternal body (and the preoedipal) in the constitution of subjectivity and the notion of abjection. As Kelly Oliver (1998) remarks:

> Theories of the body are particularly important for feminists because historically (in the humanities) the body has been associated with the feminine, the female, or woman, and denigrated as weak, immoral, unclean, or decaying. Throughout her writing over the last three decades, Kristeva theorized the connection between mind and body, culture and nature, psyche and soma, matter and representation, by insisting both that bodily drives are discharged in representation, and that the logic of signification is already operating in the material body. In *New Maladies of the Soul*, Kristeva describes the drives as "as pivot between 'soma' and 'psyche', between biology and representation."

Kristeva uses the notion of the maternal body as means to critique Freud and Lacan, and insists that it operates between nature and culture. The maternal body, with its two-in-one, or other within, becomes a model for all subjective relations. As Kelly Oliver (1998) explains:

> Like the maternal body, each one of us is what she calls a subject-in-process. As subjects-in-process we are always negotiating the other within, that is to say, the return of the repressed. Like the maternal body, we are never completely the subjects of our own experience. Some feminists have found Kristeva's notion of a subject-in-process a useful alternative to traditional notions of an autonomous unified (masculine) subject.

The work of feminist poststructuralism has been taken further by a second generation of writers such as Judith Butler and many other feminist thinkers in the English-speaking world.[4] Indeed, one might argue that this is where the cutting edge of research is and it should come as no surprise given the interests of women at stake.[5] Hélène Cixous' notion of *écriture féminine* which is conceptualized through her insistence on writing the body, may be helpful in relation to working through the consequences of an embodied curriculum, especially her suggestion that language speaks through the body.[6]

Anti-Platonism and the Curriculum

In "Theatrum Philosophicum" Foucault (1998, p. 343) asked "Overturn Platonism: what philosophy has not tried?" Yet he goes on to explain that if we defined philosophy as any attempt to reverse Platonism, then it begins with Aristotle or even with Plato himself and so he asks, "Are all philosophies individual species of the genus 'anti-Platonic'?" It seems that modern philosophy is defined in terms of the rejection of Platonism, though not necessarily always the same Platonism. It is anti-Platonism that Rorty takes to unite American pragmatism with Continental post-Nietzschean philosophy. Yet from the perspective of Platonists, the inversion or overturning of Platonism has been seen to involve nihilism — both a nothingness and a devaluation of the highest values. To embrace the world of mere appearances, the world of contingency as all there is, and to renounce any transcendent realm of reality behind appearances that offers an absolute epistemological, ethical, or aesthetic guarantee, in the mind of Platonists, leads to nihilism.

Foucault's essay is directed at reviewing Deleuze's *Difference and Repetition* and *The Logic of Sense* and it is where he makes his famous pronouncement "perhaps one day, this century will be known as Deleuzian" (p. 343). He then defines Deleuze in terms of a multifaceted anti-Platonism:

> To reverse Platonism with Deleuze is to displace oneself insidiously within, to descend a notch, to descend to its smallest gestures – discreet, but moral – which serve to exclude the simulacrum; it is also to deviate slightly from it, to open the door from either side to the small talk it excluded; it is to initiate another disconnected and divergent series; it is to construct, by way of this small lateral leap, a dethroned para-Platonism. To convert Platonism (a serious task) is to increase its compassion for reality, for the world, and for time. To subvert Platonism is to begin at the top (the vertical distance of irony) and to grasp its origin. To pervert Platonism is to search out its smallest details, to descend (with the natural gravitation of humour) as far as its crop of hair or the dirt under its fingernails – those things that were never hallowed by an idea; it is to discovering the decentering it put into effect in order to recenter itself around the Model, the Identical, and the Same; it is the decentering of oneself in respect to Platonism so as to give rise to the play (as with every perversion) of surfaces at its border (Foucault, 1998, pp. 345–346).

In "Plato, the Greeks" Deleuze (1998, p. 136) explains Platonism as a selective doctrine which aims at judging the well-foundedness or legitimacy of competing claims or rivals, based on the Idea which has firsthand quality and thus universal and necessary status. Plato's doctrine of judgement thus consists in determining the extent to which things possess the quality secondhand, third hand etc. We might say that this is an original version of a kind of representationalism where the thing (or statement) in a world of appearances is validated only by its correspondence with the original Idea. Deleuze suggests that Platonism finds its enemy – both limit and double — in the sophist, who lays claim to anything and everything and thus risks scrambling the criterion and perverting the judgement. The problem, Deleuze argues, finds its source in the City that form fields of immanence, populated, as they are by free rivals whose claims enter into a competitive *agôn*, where opinion assumes decisive importance. Plato criticises this aspect of Athenian democracy and restores a criterion of selection among rivals that involves erecting a new type of transcendence (differing from the imperial and the mythical) that can be exercised from within the field of immanence itself – the theory of Ideas. Deleuze (1998, p. 137) writes:

> The poisoned gift of Platonism is to have introduced transcendence into philosophy, to have given transcendence a plausible philosophical meaning (the triumph of the judgment of God). This enterprise runs up against numerous paradoxes and aporias, which concern, precisely, the status of the *doxa* (*Theatetus*), the nature of friendship and love (*Symposium*), and the irreducibility of an immanence of the earth (*Timaeus*).

He goes on to suggest "Every reaction against Platonism is a restoration of immanence in its full extension and its purity, which forbids the return of any transcendence" (p. 137).

There are some suggestive lines of inquiry in Deleuze's work that might lead us to a kind of anti-Platonism that enables an embodied curriculum. As Paul Patton (1994, p. 141) as argued Deleuze not only seeks to develop a new conception of philosophy dedicated to the overturning of Platonism but he also explicitly aligns his new conception with the tendency of modern art to reflect upon its own nature. He cites Deleuze, thus: "The theory of thought is like painting: it needs that revolution which took art from representation to abstraction. This is the aim of a theory of thought without image." Deleuze's anti-Platonism is "above all a critique of the persistent representationalism in philosophy" (Patton, 1994, p. 142) in an inversion of Plato's hierarchy between copies and simulacra, which purports to abolish the distinction. The abandonment of representational theory in modern art and painting, as well as philosophy, leads directly to an accent on the sensuality of the body — to an agenda that focuses upon the expression of feeling and emotions and to the exploration of formal possibilities of aesthetic experience.

In this Deleuzian exploration, the body can be seen as mutable and articulate as culture. On this view the body is not a natural biological material or essence. It is the play of forces, both mutable and endlessly transformable. This shifts the emphasis away from *being* to *becoming* so important in the project of feminist thinkers where there is a sustained attempt to de-essentialize the body and sexuality while at the same time articulating new forms of female subjectivity (see Braidotti, 1994; Grosz, 1994).

An embodied curriculum especially in relation to aesthetics and the arts begins from an understanding of a philosophy of the body not conceived in opposition to a philosophy of mind but rather as the basis for a materialist social ontology that heals the Platonic and Cartesian dualisms of Western philosophy. A new philosophy of the body as an educational project will draw lessons from phenomenology and especially the work of Merleau-Ponty. It will also draw on Nietzsche's notion of embodied rationality, a rationality that does not attempt to abstract from our moods, our situatedness, our cultural belongings, our embodied selves and physicality, our animality that together help to comprise our linguistic and cultural identities. Insofar as the philosophy of the body is concerned with the *lived* body that entertains both physicality and bodily activity or action, we can also make connections to the surface of the body and the way that the flesh is symbolically decorated, exercised, trained, clothed and generally *stylised*. If we can talk in this way of an aesthetics of the body, relating it to its lived aspects requiring action and movement, whether they be habitual, ritualistic or dramaturgical, then we can also welcome the body as a site of desire – the *libidinal body* – and emphasise its productive and reproductive capacities. The body, then, could serve as not only a critique of educational rationalism – of mind over body and the series of related dualisms, including adult/child, rational/irrational, male/female – it may also come to serve as a basis for a reformed curriculum in health, sport, dance, drama, sexuality and the arts.

NOTES

[1] This is not to deny that there is an advanced literature on both sides of the dualism—consciousness and the body—in Anglo-American philosophy. See, for instance, the excellent collections by Gallagher and Shear (1999) and Bermudez et al (1998). For a recent account of the human self understood as subject and agent in discourse and action see Schrag (1997).

[2] Matthews notes Augustine's remark: "Return to yourself; truth resides in the inner man." See also the emphasis on the "inner human" in Lyotard's (2000) *The Confession of Augustine*, where he takes as a guiding motif Augustine's remark "Our body with its weight strives toward its own place." Lyotard sees the *Confessions* as a determining source for the Western notion of self and structurally akin to Descartes "cogito" and Husserl's "transcendental ego."

[3] See my "Poststructuralism and the Philosophy of the Subject" in Peters (1996) and Peters (2001).

[4] See, for instance, Suleiman (1986), Gallop (1988), Diprose & Ferrell (1991), Bordo (1995) and Butler (1993). In education see, McWilliam (1996).

[5] Diana Meyers (1999) comments on Butler:

Poststructuralist Judith Butler maintains that personal identity — the sense that there are answers to the questions "who am I?" and "what am I like?" — is an illusion (Butler, 1990). The self is merely an unstable discursive node — a shifting confluence of multiple discursive currents — and sexed/gendered identity is merely a "corporeal style" — the imitation and repeated enactment of ubiquitous norms. For Butler, psychodynamic accounts of the self, including Kristeva's and Chodorow's, camouflage the performative nature of the self and collaborate in the cultural conspiracy that maintains the illusion that one has an emotionally anchored, interior identity that is derived from one's biological nature, which is manifest in one's genitalia. Such accounts are pernicious. In concealing the ways in which normalizing regimes deploy power to enforce the performative routines that construct "natural" sexed/gendered bodies together with debased, "unnatural" bodies, they obscure the arbitrariness of the constraints that are being imposed and deflect resistance to these constraints. The solution, in Butler's view, is to question the categories of biological sex, polarized gender, and determinate sexuality that serve as markers of personal identity, to treat the construction of identity as a site of political contestation, and to embrace the subversive potential of unorthodox performances and parodic identities.

Meyers concludes her study of the "feminist self" with the following remark:

As this article attests, there is tremendous foment and variety within the field of feminist work on the self. Yet, in reviewing this literature, I have been struck by a recurrent theme — the inextricability of metaphysical issues about the self from moral and political theory. Feminist critiques of regnant philosophical theories of the self expose the normative underpinnings of these theories. Feminist analyses of women's agentic capacities both acknowledge traditional feminine social contributions and provide accounts of how women can overcome oppressive norms and practices. Feminist reconstructions of the nature of the self are interwoven with arguments that draw out the emancipatory benefits of conceiving the self one way rather than another.

[6] See Sellers' (1996, p. 6–9) useful discussion of Cixous' writing the body. I am indebted to Nicki Hedge for this lead.

REFERENCES

Beauvoir, S. (1988). *The second sex* (H. M. Parshley Trans. & Ed.). London: Pan Books. (Original work published 1949)

Bermúdez, J. L., Marcel, A., & Eilan, N. (Eds.) (1995). *The body and the self.* Cambridge, Mass., & London: MIT Press.

Bordo, S. R. (1995). *Unbearable weight: Feminism, western culture, and the body.* Berkeley & London: University of California Press.

Bradotti, R. (1994). Toward a new Nomadism: Feminist Deleuzian tracks; or, Metaphysics and metabolism. In C. V. Boundas & D. Olkowski (Eds.), *Gilles Deleuze and the theatre of philosophy* (pp. 157-186). New York & London: Routledge.

Butler, J. (1993). *Bodies that matter: On the discursive limits of sex.* New York and London: Routledge.

Diprose, R., & Ferrell, R. (Eds.). (1991). *Cartographics: Poststructuralism and the mapping of bodies and spaces.* North Sydney: Allen & Unwin.

Frazer, N. (1985, Oct.) Michel Foucault: A 'Young Conservative'?. *Ethics* 96, 165-184.

Frazer, N. (1983, Fall) Foucault's Body-Language: A Post-Humanist Political Rhetoric?, *Salmagundi* no. 61, 55-70.

Frazer, N. (1981, Oct.) Foucault on Modern Power: Empirical Insights and Normative Confusions. *Praxis International* 1, 272-287.

Gallagher, S., & Shear, J. (1999). *Models of the self.* Thorverton: Imprint Academic.

Gallop, J. (1988). *Thinking through the body.* New York: Columbia University Press.

Grosz, E. (1994). A thousand tiny sexes: Feminism and Rhizomatics. In C. V. Boundas & D. Olkowski (Eds.), *Gilles Deleuze and the theatre of philosophy* (pp. 187-212). New York & London: Routledge.

Heidegger, M. (1996). Letter on humanism. In D. F. Krell (Ed.), *Basic writings* (pp. 213-266). London: Routledge.

Lyotard, J.-F. (2000) *The Confession of Augustine.* Cultural Memory in the Present. Stanford, Calif.: Stanford University Press; Cambridge: Cambridge University Press, 2000. Translation by Richard Beardsworth *La Confession d'Augustin.*

Marshall, J. (2001, November). *Foucault, education and the self.* Paper presented at the University of Glasgow, Glasgow, UK.

Matthews, E. (1996). *Twentieth-century French philosophy.* Oxford: Oxford University Press.

McWilliam, E., & Taylor, P. G. (1996). *Pedagogy, technology, and the body.* New York: Peter Lang.

Merleau-Ponty, M. (1962). *Phenomenology of perception* (C. Smith Trans.). London: Routledge & Kegan Paul; New York: The Humanities Press.

Meyers, D. (1999). Feminist perspectives on the self. Online entry from S*tanford encyclopedia of philosophy.* Retrieved August 28, 2003, from http://www.science.uva.nl/~seop/entries/feminism-self/

O'Loughlin, M. (1995). Intelligent bodies and ecological subjectivities: Merleau-Ponty's corrective to postmodernism's 'subjects' of education. *Philosophy of Education.* Retrieved August 28, 2003, from http://www.ed.uiuc.edu/EPS/PES-Yearbook/95_docs/o'loughlin.html

Oliver, K. (1998). *Feminist theory website: Julia Kristeva.* Paper. Retrieved August 28, 2003, from Virginia Tech University: http://www.cddc.vt.edu/feminism/Kristeva.html

Peters, M. A. (1996). *Poststructuralism, politics and education.* Westport, CT., & London: Bergin and Garvey.

Peters, M.A. (2001). Heidegger, Derrida, and the new humanities. In G. Biesta & D. Egea-Kuehne (Eds.), *Derrida and education* (pp.209- 231). London: Routledge.

Poster, M. (1981) The Future According to Foucault: The Archaeology of Knowledge and Intellectual History. In Dominick LaCapra and Steven L. Kaplan, eds., *Modern European Intellectual History: Reappraisals and New Perspectives*, pp. 137-152.

Sartre, J. (1966). *Being and nothingness: A phenomenological essay on ontology* (H. Barnes Trans.). New York: Pocket Books.

Schrag, C. O. (1997). *The self after postmodernity.* New Haven & London: Yale University Press.

Sellars, S. (1996). *Helene Cixous: Authorship, autobiography and love.* Cambridge: Polity Press.

Suleiman, S. R. (Ed.). (1986). *The female body in Western culture: Contemporary perspectives.* Cambridge: Harvard University Press.

WAYNE BOWMAN

COGNITION AND THE BODY: PERSPECTIVES FROM MUSIC EDUCATION

There is not a word, not a form of behavior which does not owe something to purely biological being—and which at the same time does not elude the simplicity of animal life, and cause forms of vital behavior to deviate their preordained direction, through a sort of leakage and through a genius for ambiguity which might serve to define man.

Maurice Merleau-Ponty
Phenomenology of Perception

1. ORIENTATION

Appeals to multiple-intelligence theory have become common currency among educators in the arts, apparently because status as "an intelligence" is seen as vindication of the educational integrity of artistic undertakings. Unfortunately, ascendancy to the status of intelligence has not been accompanied by careful examination of what intelligence means. We have become assertive about its plurality, to be sure. But "it" remains more or less the kind of cognitive construct it always has been: abstract, mental, cerebral, disembodied. After years of unsuccessful urging that music's alignment with feeling made it an essential corrective to such one-sided cognitive activity, we appear to have decided in recent years that there is more strategic clout to be found on the rational side of the cognitive/emotional divide. What we have not done, precisely, is to question the nature of the divide itself: this stubborn dichotomy between knowing that counts and that which does not, in light of which musical and artistic endeavors invariably come up short. In this essay, I explore from the perspective of musical experience what cognition means—of what intelligence that is musical consists—on the assumption that there can be no genuine progress in our efforts to explain and justify the contributions of artistic endeavors to education until the meanings of things like intelligence and cognition[1] are reconstructed.

Let us begin with the provocative statement by Maurice Merleau-Ponty that appears above. Merleau-Ponty's close juxtaposition of terms like leakage and ambiguity with the idea of genius flies in the face of the conventional cognitive ideals of certainty, of truth as something with transcendent clarity, and of knowledge as non-contingent and unequivocal. To give a place of honor to things like leakage and ambiguity is, from such perspectives, to advocate irrationality. So deeply entrenched are our assumptions about mind's ideality and rightful governance over things vaguely sensed, felt, or intuited (and indeed, over things *done or enacted*) that the suggestion ambiguity may be more important to humankind than certainty

29

Liora Bresler (ed.), Knowing Bodies, Moving Minds, 29-50.
©2004 Kluwer Academic Publishers. Printed in the Netherlands

probably strikes most of us as nonsense. For thousands of years Western language and culture has regarded biological being as animal-like, and mindfulness as the distinctive source of humankind's superior achievements. On this view, the body reduces to a vague sensorium, a collection of viscera whose only cognitively worthwhile jobs are to transmit sense data to mind for processing and to do mind's bidding.

Merleau-Ponty's view challenges us to undertake radical reconstruction of our epistemological and ontological convictions, to construe ambiguity and leakage not as cognitive flaws but as potent cognitive assets: he speaks of a *genius* for ambiguity, after all. To accept ambiguity as a kind of genius rather than a defect, however, requires extensive revision to what we understand by things like clarity and certainty. For it is precisely where clarity is utter, and certainty absolute, that the alternatives take on such pathetically defective status. What Merleau-Ponty implies is that to whatever degree we are capable of clarity and certainty, our access to them is inescapably bodily—which is to suggest that they are neither purely rational nor absolute. All human knowledge draws its sustenance from corporeal roots. Mind is inextricably biological and embodied; and what it can know is always grounded in the material and experiential world.

Easy though it has become to pay such things lip service, the habit of treating body as the disavowed condition of knowledge (the subordinated counterpart of mind) is an extraordinarily difficult one to shake. Deeply built into our inherited languages are the remains of conceptual structures in which mind is separate from and superordinate to things bodily, [2] and teaching old words new tricks is extraordinarily challenging. Regardless of intentions, then, ambiguity sounds very much like something that requires, or would benefit substantially from, mental resolution and improvement.

The embodied and enactive view of cognition I want to explore here may help, I think, to advance Merleau-Ponty's important insights by offering alternatives to the unfortunately disparaging baggage carried by metaphors like ambiguity and leakage. Instead of ambiguity, I propose the more positive image of polysemy: of multivalence, or simultaneous multiplicity of meaning. To the extent it refuses to reduce plurality and diversity to attributes of some unified entity, polysemy is inherently ambiguous; and yet, polysemic constellations of meaning are no less vivid, rich, or potent for being multifaceted. They are what they are unambiguously, however deeply they confound propositional systems of expression. Embodied understanding is always the view from somewhere, and therefore always partial; yet it remains profoundly ours, the experiential ground all claims to know require as the fundamental condition of their possibility. Partiality, multiplicity, and complexity are its inherent phenomenological conditions, but fluency at navigating such rough ground[3] is precisely the heart of human genius.

What then of "leakage"? What kind of positive spin can be put on a condition that surely presages emptiness? A more useful characterization and one more directly applicable to cognitive theory is cross-modal (or intermodal) transfer—on which schemata from one experiential domain (recurrent dynamic patterns of motor and perceptual experience, for instance) function as structural and organizational templates for another. The human capacity to use experience from one domain to make sense of another is an extraordinarily potent cognitive resource. Taken together, polysemy and cross-modal transfer orient us to ways of construing cognition that embrace the facts of human embodiment and regard them as invaluable resources rather than contaminants to be purged.

Ambiguities and leakages are among the more salient characteristics of music and musical experience—embarrassments we have struggled to explain away in a variety of imaginative ways over the years. Chief among our conventional strategies has been to align these worrisome attributes with a "special" kind of knowledge: one that affords privileged understanding of the realms of feeling or of human sentience. Despite honorable intentions, however, such rationales for music tend to accept the inherent inferiority, in cognitive terms, of bodily-constituted knowledge. Since reason's superiority is granted without challenge, it remains for musical undertakings to show that they are mindful or at least mind-like—albeit in realms less than, or other than, rational.

At least since the time of Baumgarten, the notion of aesthetic experience has claimed metaphysical and spiritual qualities that, though important in their own ways, concede more substantive cognitive status to reason. The argument for music and the arts has been that just as reason reigns supreme in the rational realm of logic, the arts are superior in realm of feeling and emotion, domains that lie outside and therefore elude propositional meanings. Thus, music acts like thought does—rendering things orderly and comprehensible—only, within a domain of emotion and feeling rather than reason. Music does for feeling what logic does for thought.[4] On this view, clarity and distinctness, Descartes' twin criteria for trustworthy knowledge, remain the operant epistemic criteria; and the realms of thought and feeling, mind and body, remain mutually exclusive hierarchically related opposites.

The embodied, enactive account of cognition that motivates this essay, maintains (a) the inseparability of mind and body; (b) the material basis of all cognition; and (c) the indispensability of corporeal experience to all human knowledge. On this view, the bodily-constituted knowledge of which music is a prime and precious instance is not different in kind from intellectual kinds of knowing. Rather, the two are continuous, deeply involved in each other's construction, and each in turn ecologically situated in the social world. Music is a valuable cognitive resource not because of what it teaches us about the disembodied metaphysical realm of feeling, but what it shows us about the profoundly embodied and socioculturally-situated character of all human knowing and being.

2. ADVOCATING SCHOOL MUSIC

Conventional accounts of music as a purveyor of insight into feeling through "aesthetic" experience defend music's cognitive respectability by celebrating its primary alignment with emotion, as opposed to propositional thought. In so doing, the notion that knowledge consists in reason and material fact—to which music relates as "other"—are left unchallenged. While music's ephemeral character becomes the foundation of a special kind of understanding, then, it remains "understanding" of a distinctly secondary kind. The quest to explain music's significance thus resembles the perennial struggle to which Sysiphus was condemned, as again and again its apologists toil to roll their boulder up the mountain of cognitive respectability. This mountain, however, is not a natural phenomenon, but a cultural one: one in whose construction we have participated actively and extensively, when we should have been trying to level it instead.

These epistemic issues take on particular urgency and political significance for those anxious to justify music's place in public education, where cognitive value is both the prevailing currency and the primary determinant of curricular prestige. Schooling is about learning, after all; and learning, or so goes the assumption, is about transmitting and acquiring knowledge. To reserve a place for music at the educational table, then, it is necessary to establish an important place in the system of values that brings the various educational players together in the first place. Thus: music makes us smarter, music develops spatial reasoning, and music is a kind of intelligence. At the same time, however, music education must assure that it accomplishes what it does in ways that differ from and are neglected by other candidates for legitimate "subject" status. Failure to do this would make it redundant. So music is educationally significant in light of cognitive value of a "special" kind. But possession of cognitive value, even if granted, does not establish in itself that musical instruction warrants curricular time and resources—both of these being expensive and in chronically short supply. Why *musical* cognition in particular, then? Why *musical* knowledge? Of all the things with cognitive value one might teach in school, why is music among those that must be taught?

Because, continue our conventional explanations, music fulfils its cognitive educational obligation in ways no other subject does.[5] Music's educational contribution is feelingful, expressive, or emotional in character: attributes that impart to its study significant humanizing import as an educator of feeling.[6] Note carefully the enabling mechanism for this claim: because music shares common structural form with the realm of feeling (because music sounds like feelings feel) it has privileged powers of representation. It symbolizes, brings to awareness, and affords insight into areas of human import otherwise too fleeting and evanescent to be grasped and understood. Its special educational significance thus derives from its unique formal/structural properties, from their congruence with the forms of feeling, and from music's resultant capacity to teach us things about the "real world" that elude our intellectual pursuits—accomplishing, thereby, within the realm of feeling what language and reason accomplish within their own realm.

From a strategic standpoint, this is a precarious argument for several reasons. First, it is not immediately evident to non-musicians that the engagements and actions typical of music teachers and students are particularly mindful in their focus, whatever their emotional or expressive character. Much musical instruction looks more like recreation or training than it does education. And second, feeling, coded soft and feminine ("other" to hard-headed rationality), is not really education's concern. *Feeling*? Who really cares? But third, and perhaps most importantly, it leaves untouched the idea that mind and body are opposite and hierarchically related, with mindfulness the "real" determinant of educational worth, and with bodily traces in perennial (to some, indeed, urgent!) need of domestication, clarification, and discipline.

In our determination to substantiate the educational value of music and the arts, I am suggesting, we have accepted uncritically notions of "knowing" and "understanding" crafted in other domains: notions whose inadequacy as arguments for the arts stems from deficiencies equally profoundly inadequate to their domains of origin. As a result we find ourselves advocating music study for reasons that fit with prevailing ideological assumptions about the nature of knowledge and the aims of schooling, but on which we are ill-equipped to deliver, and that neglect what may be most distinctive about music: its roots in experience and agency, the bodily and the social. Our most revered justifications of music education are built upon deeply-flawed notions about mind, cognition, and intelligence.

The dominant paradigms of epistemology and of recent cognitive science—those that define the context within which music education has sought to explain its significance and justify its existence—are linguistic and propositional in nature. Their neglect of non-linguistic behaviour, experience, and cognition is profound.[7] They reduce "legitimate" cognition to rational thought processes, paramount among them things like problem solving, deductive reasoning, logical inference, and so-called critical thinking.[8] Only, thought so construed is ghostly, disembodied, and attached to the physical body only by the thinnest of threads, if attached at all. Indeed, to be properly knowledgeable is to repudiate transience and flux, the personal and the subjective, here-and-now experience: the very things most phenomenally distinctive about musical experience.[9] In other words, what matters about music on cognitive models is formal unity of apperception, not process, not action, not embodied experience or agency. Music's purest manifestation lies in the contemplative appreciation of stable, abstract verities like pattern and structure: Kantian aesthetic experience. And outside such verities lies the realm of "mere" experience—irrational, felt, and vaguely sensed.

If the inadequacy of Cartesian dualism has become a commonplace in contemporary discourse, why is its vestigial influence so potent? Why do our protestations in music and the arts continue to take the form given them by such deeply-flawed language and its attendant baggage? At least in part, I believe, because we have side-stepped the mind-body-reality issue instead of deconstructing it: we have attempted to walk around Descartes rather than through him. We "know" and have learned to *say* that mind is incorporated; but we have neither grasped fully the profundity of that claim nor the range of its implications.

The challenge is not just to bring body and mind together. Both idealism and materialism advance strategies for that project, strategies that are content to have established mind-body interaction of some kind and degree. But interaction does not unite, does not undo the epistemic and ontological assumptions that place mind hierarchically superior to and separate from embodied experience. Nor can mind-body interaction alone undo the conceptual damage exacted by the assumption that body's contribution to knowledge consists in the mere provision of sensory receptors, a collection of data input devices—a stance that leaves us profoundly cut off and alienated from the real, out-there world. The idealistic "solution" to un-separating mind and body reduces embodied being to perception, and the body to a mental phenomenon. And the materialistic alternative presumes that "bodily surface irritations . . . exhaust our epistemic repertoire"[10]—presuming to ground successful negotiation of reality in determinate physical biology. Where the mindful, the emotional, and the merely physical apparently exhaust available educational alternatives, it is small wonder that music and the arts (not wholly any of these) must struggle for a foothold.

Breaking free of Cartesianism requires decisive action, not casual denial. We must somehow confront and neutralize the assumptions at its core: that, on the one hand, sensation and agency (sensing and acting in the world) are not cognitive achievements; and that, on the other, the higher-order abstractions characteristic of language comprise the quintessential (ideal) core of cognition. We need theories that grant both the necessity and the trustworthiness of corporeal experience, of bodily-constituted knowledge.[11] To settle for less is to trade away knowledge for mere certainty, and to reduce reality to an epiphenomenon.

In short, music educators need to resist having the terms and conditions of their presence in educational endeavors defined by systems of cognitive possibilities that preordain subaltern status for artistic undertakings. Our understandable eagerness to advocate for musical experience and education must remain grounded in accounts of music that are true to its bodily basis. We must cease making promises upon which we cannot deliver, just to get a foot in the educational door. Instead, we should be questioning more vigorously what is behind that door. We have accepted bogus notions that thought and feeling, mind and body (intelligence and skill?), are fundamentally opposed and hierarchically related, and have sought then to show how music (or at least music worthy of study) is suited in its own unique way to pursuit of rational ideals like clarity and certainty. Instead we should have used our intimate familiarity with the corporeal and enactive basis of reality to create a model of education in which music's role might be seen as a continuation and enhancement of precisely what makes all our intellectual achievements possible, and worth achieving in the first place.

3. TWO CONTRASTING MODELS OF COGNITION: REPRESENTATIONAL & ENACTIVE/EMERGENT

Music provides a fascinating and a compelling laboratory for the study and fuller appreciation of cognition: of what it means "to know" in the fullest sense of the term, and of what full recognition of embodiment entails. However, theorists and educationists have not taken seriously enough what musical experience promises to teach us in this regard, and as a result most of our claims and theories about music cognition and its significance sit on highly precarious foundations.

Most explanations of music cognition build upon information-processing models in which logical parsing is the operative mechanism. The accounts of musical perception and cognition they yield are mentalistic and abstract. Inspired by pitch and harmonic organizational tendencies in conventional tonal music, these theories reduce music perception and cognition to the mental manipulation of sets of syntactical implications (e.g. Meyer) or formal hierarchies (e.g. Lerdahl and Jackendoff). The body's role, to the extent it has one, is that of a conduit for conveying lower-order stimuli and auditory sense data to the brain, where the real work of music cognition (transformation, processing, representation) is done. Musical experience thus amounts to a sophisticated stimulus-response system, rendered musical by abstract mental pattern construction. The implicit assumption is that musical cognition is fully analogous to logical/linguistic cognition, where mouthy noises and their written representations serve as arbitrary signifiers of objective features in the out-there world. Without such symbolic intervention, experience would consist of little more than a booming, buzzing confusion. These are intra-musical models, yielding meanings that are modular, inherent, and unrelated to embodied or social situatedness in any musically-interesting way.

On these views, music's meanings are non-discursive; however, they are accomplished by the same cognitive mechanism as (linguistic, propositional) discourse. So music's cognitive function is, like language's, to represent aspects of reality that otherwise elude us: to render the world clearer, more comprehensible, more compatible with cognitive ideals of control and certainty. And the body's role remains subservient to that of mind. Where music's distinctive origin in sonorous bodily experience is explicitly acknowledged, such experience is reduced to sets of acoustic signals that become musical in virtue of their rule-governed combination into extended patterns or events. The bodily basis of sonorous experience, then, has to do primarily with low-level auditory processing—and is of cognitive significance interest only to the extent it feeds into and enables higher-level, language-like, rational/inferential processes. The body (in particular, the ear) works as a sound receptor; the mind refines raw sense data into high-order meanings—a mechanism precisely analogous to that wrongly presumed to mediate the construction of rational or propositional linguistic meanings.

I have described these accounts in ways that highlight the *subordinate* role each assigns to corporeality. Equally noteworthy is the implicit *separation* of the corporeal from the cognitive, their relegation to discrete ontological plains or processing modules. An embodied account of musical cognition, in strong contrast, seeks to retain a prominent place for the body, even at the highest levels, and resists the assumption of modularity. The body is not something to be transcended in musical experience, something whose presence serves us as a kind of inverse index of musical value. It is not only indispensable in, but constitutive of all experience and cognition that rightly claim musical status.

The failure of conventional models of musical cognition to accommodate matters like these compromises seriously their explanatory validity for the range of musical practices they are intended to illuminate—primarily the Western European artistic tonal tradition. For musics outside that limited range, however, this failure and its effects are much more profound. The attribution of universality to cognitive models based on tonal musical grammars has led their adherents (including many musicians who should know better) to characterize pronounced differences in musical-cognitive *priorities* as differences in musical complexity and *sophistication.* In particular, a marked contrast in the predominance of bodily elements between tonal- and groove-based musics (jazz, funk, and numerous others of non-European derivation) is wrongly taken as a difference in musical value in virtue of which the latter musics, because cognitively primitive (more predominantly corporeal), are inferior to the former.

Accounts of musical cognition in which embodied experience is marginal do not just develop *ex nihilo*. They follow almost inevitably from flawed epistemological theory and from the *cognitivist paradigms* that have long dominated cognitive science. As we have seen, cognitivism construes mind as a manipulator of abstractions wrought from raw data conveyed to it by a sensing body; mind as an entity that generates internal representations of external reality by means of mental symbols that mirror the "real" world; mind as a device for storing and manipulating symbols. However, such cognitivist theory fails to account adequately for (a) the emotional component of human intelligence,[12] for (b) intelligent action, for (c) creativity, or for (d) the intuitive resources that guide them all. From the standpoint of music and music education, these are profound shortcomings.

In contrast to cognitivist theories, *embodied accounts* construe mind as an activity emergent from, structured by, and never wholly separable from the material facts of bodily experience.[13] As such, they disavow the metaphysical propensities and universalist predilections of cognitivist theory. Bodies are grounded, concrete, and situated. Their views are always perspectival (the view from here), never the kind of "objective" orientation that is free of perspective (the view from everywhere). On embodied accounts, human conceptual capacities arise from sensorimotor actions[14] and experiences. And since all such processes are grounded in contextually situated bodies, theories of incorporated knowledge insist on biological, psychological, and cultural dimensions for all human cognition.

On the specifically *enactive* version of the embodiment paradigm,[15] the one I advocate here, human conceptual, sensory, and motor processes have coevolved with each other, and are indissolubly linked in each of us. Cognitive capacity emerges from reinforced neural connections between one's senses and motor system. In this way, sense, perception, action, and conception are mutually informative, and structurally linked to one another in important ways. The incorporated mind executes its cognitive processes using epistemic resources that emerge from and remain grounded in patterns of action: the actions of a body well-attuned to its needs, goals, and interests. To the extent that higher-level cognition and lower-level motor control share basic neurological mechanisms with each other, "mind" is a profoundly distributed entity:[16] the mind is *not* in the brain, but in the vast network of neural interconnections that extend throughout the body. In this way, the *body is in the mind*.[17] Mind is rendered possible by bodily sensations and actions, from whose patterns it emerges and upon which it relies for whatever intellectual prowess it can claim. At the same time, the *mind is in the body*, in the sense that mind is coextensive with the body's neural pathways and the cognitive templates they comprise.

Further still, to the extent that these neural pathways and cognitive schemata arise from a body's interaction with an experience-shaping environment *mind extends beyond the physical body* into the social and cultural environments that exert major influence on the body and shape all human experience. Thus, both body and culture are implicated in and constitutive of mind. The body is minded, the mind is embodied, and both body and mind are culturally-mediated. Incorporated cognition is thus a complex socially-mediated phenomenon, one that is "stretched over," as Lave suggests, "not divided among ... mind, body, activity, and culturally organized settings."[18] The boundary between "mind" and "world" is at once much less problematic and far more multi-facted than cognitivist theory allows.

The significance of these points for our understanding of music is momentous. For they suggest musical experience is about much more than symbolic representations of feeling, or perceiving and following syntactical patterns whose primary function is to represent. Music affords fields for bodily action that exercise and extend our cognitive capacities and fluencies: but not in the direction of the supposed clarity and distinctness of propositional knowledge, and not in the direction of rational certainty. The "smarter" that music "makes us" lies rather in its corporeal basis, and in the remarkable "genius for ambiguity" that affords. On an enactive embodied account of mind and knowledge, most of our questions about the adequacy or veracity of mind's representations of reality are wrong-headed: for embodied intelligence is not after all about representing; it is about acting and agency. On an enactive embodied account of human cognition, mind, culture, body, and action partake each of the other, *co-constructing* the only "realities" available to human experience. An enactive approach to cognition seeks, as Evan Thompson explains, "to avoid reified versions of the inner-outer metaphor by studying cognition ... as *embodied action*."[19] The term *embodied* entails two fundamentally important points: (1) that all cognition results from perceptuomotor capacities and achievements that are part of our bodily hardware, whether innate or acquired; and (2) that these capacities are invariably both "embedded in and constituted by their biological, psychological, and sociocultural contexts." The term *action*, in turn, maintains that "sensory and motor processes, perception and action, are fundamentally inseparable in all cognition."[20]

4. MINDFUL BODIES, EMBODIED MINDS, AND CULTURE'S IMPRINT

Considerable time has been devoted here to developing context: to explaining why words and theories about mind, body, and knowing should matter to music educators and educationists. Our explanations, arguments and promises make an enormous difference, both in how we conceptualize what we do and in how we go about doing it. In this section I want to elaborate more concretely on distinctions introduced above; to suggest briefly some of the ways body and social experience give rise to and sustain the possibility of music; and to suggest several ways enaction and embodiment offer to alter our understandings of musical cognition and praxis.

It is important to begin, I think, with the sonorous roots of music and musical significance: with the way the human body is hardwired for sound, and the potential relevance of such phenomenal facts for musical experience. The world of the ear is one we first inhabit three months before birth. Well before we have begun to explore (or create?) the world with our eyes, imparting to it the clarity and objectivity characteristic of visual experience, we experience and interpret our world through the polyvalence of sound. The intrauterine symphony, as it has been called, is where we first begin to discover the world around us and our place within it—a world dark and ambiguous, yet filled with vivid sound. The special relation between sound and the body is evident even at this early stage, detectable in things like association between sound and fetal heart rate, and the early presence of the startle reflex.

But throughout the human lifespan, sound (whether musical or noisy) and the body are linked intimately to one another. Sound puts us in the world as no other sense does. It is a distinctly bodily sense that asserts itself with peremptory immediacy and urgency. Seldom a take-it-or-leave-it kind of affair, sound can caress, grip, or violate the body. It is experienced with an inwardness typical of no other sense, such that the boundary between sound and self is quite porous: sound seldom respects the periphery of the body. It circulates in, around, and even through us, both individually and collectively. Nor is there any sonic counterpart to the constancy and objectivity so characteristic of vision: sonorous experience is invariably the experience of process and change—change of place or direction, of quality, of intensity. Sound is our most intimate sensory modality, one for which the body is wired to resonate and respond in ways unlike any other,[21] and one in which ambiguity, polysemy, process, and change are always salient features.

Even at the sensory stage, then, the body's relationship to sound is far more extensive and intensive than a mere act of aural reception. To hear is always to participate, to be corporeally involved, engaged, positioned. And since a given sonic "stimulus" may be constructed variously as noise, speech, or music, ambiguity, potential slippage, and unpredictability are always part of sonorous experience. At the same time, hearing involves what Shepherd and Wicke describe as a "technology of articulation": bodily-constituted linkages such that the signifier-signified relationship is never simply arbitrary or habitual.[22] Sonorous experience is invariably corporeal, and is distinguished from other semiotic experience by its links to muscle, movement, and action.[23] Phenomenal facts like these are what lead Shepherd to declare that timbre, the way sound touches the body, constitutes the essential core of all sonic events. Timbre is the "very vibratory essence that puts the world of sound in motion and reminds us...that we are alive, sentient, and experiencing."[24]

Probably the most conspicuous and oft-cited evidence of linkage between music and body comes from music's temporal or processual character, a character that manifests itself in things like pulse, tempo, rhythm: a cluster of phenomena often described as movement or time-feel. Music atrophies when it strays too far from dance, when it fails to engage the body in imagined sympathetic movement. The theories of Dalcroze have long stressed the importance of bodily experience to musical perception and aptitude, and movement is a major consideration in many if not most pedagogical approaches to rhythm. Humans hear and respond to rhythmic pattern prenatally; neonates are helped to achieve regularization of bodily processes by certain musics;[25] and toddlers respond to rhythmic music with spontaneous movement. Phenomena like our imposition of rhythmic pattern on repeated pulses and our entrainment to recurrent patterns are musical commonplaces. Tempo markings in music often implicate bodily actions like walking or running, and phrasing generally implicates human respiration. Thus, to claim a bodily basis for tempo, rhythmic subdivision of pulse, phrasing, or groove is unlikely to create controversy. I would go further, though, to assert that entire range of musical action is grounded in the body: perception of musical gesture is invariably a fundamental part of what "the music," fully perceived, is. And indeed, the ability to enact musical-bodily gesture is a central part of the conductor's art.

But why the body? And more importantly for our purposes here, how the body? I have gone to some length to deny that music functions as a stimulus to which the body simply (or even not so simply) responds. As well, I have urged that cognition (and therefore music cognition) is not about generating representations—of feeling, or of anything else for that matter. Even the familiar term "expression" seems ill-suited to the bodily facts I have in mind: for music doesn't really *express* the rhythmic character or the groove that seems to insist that my body dance. Rather, these are qualities the music *has,* attributes it *possesses.*[26] How does something like music come by such obviously human qualities features and qualities? Surely these are as much attributes of the perceiver's experience as they are properties of the music?[27] Or even more? T. S. Eliot speaks movingly of music heard so deeply that it is not really heard at all—rather, "you are the music while the music lasts."[28] Thomas Clifton describes musical experience as a state of mutual possession, such that music is, ultimately, "what I am when I experience it."[29] Barthes suggests we think in terms of the "body in a state of music."[30] DeNora writes of a kind of "latching" in which listener's bodies engage in movements that are "in some way homologous with music's properties, its ways of happening . . ."[31] And Feld suggests we think of music as "a special way of experiencing, knowing, and feeling value, identity, and coherence."[32] Descriptions like these are testimony to a relationship between body and music that is constitutive—more akin to identity than to things like stimulation, representation, or expression.

Perhaps this intimate relation between music and the body involves a kind of sympathetic reaction or resonance, of experienced similarity between beat's imagined movement and those of the body. But how does such "imagined movement" arise in the first place? And how are we to allow imagined or imaginary similarity without slipping back into troublesome mentalistic connotations that once again privilege mind over body, or encapsulate body within mind? What is needed is an account on which *similarities between musical and bodily movement are not imaginary or ideal, but actual and material.* That is what enactive accounts of cognition offer. Research on individuals with localized brain lesions suggests that perception of the rhythmic component of auditory images depends upon activation of the neural systems involved in motor activity.[33] If it is indeed the case that rhythmic/temporal features in musical perception/cognition arise from activation of substantial parts of the same neural circuitry involved in bodily movement and action, the bodily dimension so often evident in acts of musical listening (and music making) is not just a function of fortuitous resemblance, representation, or association. If listening and music making activate and deploy the same neural circuitry as bodies in motion, we have a material basis for the claim that bodily action is an indelible and fundamental part of what music, qua music, is. And if music requires bodily motion as a precondition of its being, so too may music shape and inform other possibilities for embodied being.

These comments demand immediate qualification, however, if we are to avoid committing to biological determinism. Talk of "technology" and of neural linkages might otherwise suggest connections that are dictated by sonic pattern, thus dividing correct from incorrect experiences (the "properly musical" from the unmusical or the primitive) in ways contrary to the constructivist intentions of enactive accounts. We began this essay, recall, with an interest in elaborating more fully the human genius for *ambiguity*. So it will not do to think of a body, constitutive though it may be of the time-feel dimension of music for instance, that merely responds to the dictates of a musical stimulus. What likely happens is considerably more complex and nuanced, a situation in which corporeal experience assumes a place of import in giving musical *possibility* to the phenomenally-experienced features of sound. Seen this way, music and the body extend each other "affordances,"[34] options, invitations to possible ways of embodied being that lie within certain ranges. There are multiple ways to "latch onto" sound in order to make it musical, and these ways are constrained by, among other things, hardwired linkages between sound and the body. At the same time, musical experience dramatically extends the range and quality of ways such "latching" or articulation can occur. *The way* the body finds its way into the music is a matter of personal propensities and possibilities. *That* the body find its way into the music, however, is not. For music's audible motion is invariably bodily motion, and bodily motion is a constitutive part of musical motion.

The inescapable conclusion is that music's motions are neither wholly objective nor merely subjective—that its meanings are neither (to use John Shepherd's words) "immanent" nor are they "arbitrary." "The sounds of music enter the body and are sensed, felt, and experienced inside the body in a way that, on the whole, the media of other artistic and cultural forms are not. And if one accepts the notion of affordance, then it is not a big step to realizing that there is an element of direct material leverage in the manner in which the sounds of music serve to construct and position individuals in their embodied, everyday lives."[35] This distinction between material leverage and biological determination is a useful on for thinking about the mechanisms operative in music/body linkages. Their simultaneously ambiguous yet vivid and compelling character, and at the same time their remarkable reliability and trustworthiness (who among us doubts the actuality of musical experience, or the veracity of musical movement and gesture?) stems from a human capacity for cross-modal transfer: a natural gift for mapping structures, patterns, and gestures from our embodied existence and actions onto inviting sonorous materials.[36] In this way, we deploy bodily-acquired schemata to transform intriguing patterns of sound (itself bodily-mediated and vested with distinctive "material leverage") into measured and metered musical movements, gestures, actions, and postures. This cross-modal or inter-modal transfer is neither wholly arbitrary, nor is it wholly immanent or dictated. Yet it is invariably neurally-mediated and bodily-constituted in the sense that the ability to experience such actions, movements, and events musically is a function of our having experienced and enacted things like them elsewhere, in non-musical realms. Musically moving experience, then, entails a kind of sympathetic resonance between and among neural pathways activated in bodily experience and those activated by sound claiming to be or seeking to become music, even though the particular ways such "resonances" eventually become manifest as music is very much a personal matter.

Again, these relationships, these sympathetic resonances, are inter-modal affairs. The practical significance of this point lies in its rejection of the notion that these relationships are intramusical, inherent, or modularly confined. This works in both directions: the construction of music using bodily and cultural resources, and the construction of bodily and worldly realities using musical resources. The embodied templates that constitute and permeate musical experience become in turn embodied resources for further constructive action, other acts of world-making. Thus, as Middleton suggests, music and musical experience extend us "way[s] of thinking relationships"—both within music and between music and the non-musical world. Musical patterns, Middleton elaborates, are saying: "as this note is to that note, as tonic is to dominant, as ascent is to descent, as accent is to weak beat (and so on), so X is to Y."[37] Music is thus both an embodied construction and a semiotic device for constructing/enacting further possibilities and ranges of embodied experience. Not only is music constructed both by those who engage in acts of performing it and listening to it, it is significantly implicated in constructing the broader realities in which those acts of performing and listening occur. Music is thus not just a source of "aesthetic" meaning and gratification, but a vital constructive agent in the lives of all who engage in it. It is at once an indispensable tool for "making things happen" in the human world and a vital part of "the action."

Music's cognitive significance does not depend on its capacity to represent or express. Music is not the middle, mediating term in the symbolic process envisioned by conventional semiotic theory. Such quintessentially musical facts as groove or swing (or, for that matter, such qualities as tenderness or joy) are unmediated by symbolic representation: they are material realities, enacted qualities of embodied minds. Music's gestures are not representations of motion; they arise from and consist in the (re)experience of actual, lived motion, through cross-modal resonance. The sensorimotor couplings enacted in musical behaviour may at times be deployed representationally, but that is not their sole or primary significance. The act of making music, whether as performer or listener, is a constructive act: the creation of coherent constellations of cross-modal connections, rich in their capacity to align and realign experiential worlds.

5. MUSICIANSHIP, THE MUSICAL AND THE "EXTRAMUSICAL"

The bodily actions and experiences from which such resonance arises range from the specifically musical to the other-than-musical—a fact with interesting potential ramifications for the all-important (to musicians at any rate) concept of musicianship: the dispositions and capacities generally believed to constitute musically informed perception and production, and to distinguish them from that which is less "musicianly" in nature. In the first place, an embodied account of music suggests that an important range of musically informed perception draws upon one's ability to hear a performer's body in the music (to tell "the dancer from the dance," as Yeats would have it). Thus, musical perception builds on productive experience in ways that are not just musically relevant but constitutive. A violinist, for instance, hears violins in ways unavailable to a non-violinist. An individual with improvisational experience hears improvisation against an important range of interactive possibilities that elude those who have never engaged in such actions. People with ensemble experience are more attuned to discrepancies and convergences between and among performers of music than those without it. And people with extensive experience on a particular instrument can often identify pitches produced on that instrument with a specificity not transferable to other instruments—through, it seems, a kind of muscle-based kinaesthetic hearing.[38] Thus, and in ways like these, musicianship includes important corporeal dimensions, developed primarily or solely through experience playing or producing music.

On the other hand, however, a crucial part of what distinguishes highly imaginative musical performances from merely competent ones is a performer's ability to draw upon bodily and gestural resources *outside* the "purely" musical realm.[39] Competent or craftsmanlike performances draw on conventional ways of moving, orienting, and behaving, whereas highly musical ones draw deeply on other bodily resources, exploring new ways to move on the instrument, or finding in patterns of other embodied experience novel, imaginative ways to move musically. Non-musicians' capacity to hear and appreciate such gestures is probably a substantial part of what accounts for their sense of musical engagement, of oneness with the music, of being the music while it lasts. Their experience is hardly less musical for that.

It follows that musicianship extends well beyond the musical, and that musical perception and cognition draw importantly upon resources widely available to any embodied human. Musicianship in the narrower, specialized sense, then, can hardly be considered prerequisite to musically-valid experience and understanding. And that being the case, we need to concede the possibility that professional and amateur status in music are not so radically opposed as is often believed.[40] The musical experience of performers and listeners, of professionals and amateurs, doubtless differs in many important ways. However, they share crucial bodily dimensions, dimensions that suggest continuity or commonality between professional and amateur musical perception.

The ideas of action, embodiment, and articulation we have been exploring here are useful in understanding how individuals from different musical cultures are able to find meaning in unfamiliar musical practices and styles despite their syntactical novelty or foreign-ness. Radically divergent though musical practices often are in tonal, harmonic, rhythmic or syntactic terms, it is seldom the case that musics of different cultures are completely incomprehensible to their respective practitioners. Music is no "universal language," but musical behavior is almost universally recognizable as such, and can be appreciated on at least some level without formal tuition. It is as if, one might say, enough of the music usually manages to "get through" for listeners and participants to get a basic bodily sense of its affordances, of the ways the music offers to orient the body, and of the way the performer's body is oriented in its production. In this way, music is both universal and culture-specific at the same time: universal in terms of the way its musical sounds and gestures articulate with the body; yet culturally specific in many syntactical, formal, timbral, or technical respects.

The bodily basis of musical meaning offers some clarification to the murky musical issue of musical profundity as well: for clearly, experience that is musically profound extends well beyond intramusical attributes like structural complexity, technical refinement, or expressive beauty. What is distinctive about musical profundity is the depth, range, magnitude, and range of experience invoked. Music that is profound taps into and resonates deeply and richly with life experience, leaving us with a vivid and extraordinary sense of aptness. This sense is not a function of appreciating representational or structural similarity abstractly or ideally. Rather, it consists in a vividly experienced unity of sound, body, and the world as lived. Its resources are sonorous, corporeal, cultural, and experiential—which helps explain why profundity is usually associated with age and maturity, and so infrequently coupled with youthful technical virtuosity.

Before moving on, let us remind ourselves of some of the experiential evidence for the embodied connections that lie behind the many claims we have been considering. At the most fundamental level of musical experience, the body gives us the experience of timbre. Sound's tactile core, timbre is no secondary quality with which a sonic stimulus is optionally overlain. Its roughness or smoothness, its intrusiveness or warmth, are functions of the way sound touches and engages the body qualitatively. Indeed, there can be no coherent talk of timbre, of tone's "quality," without the body.[41] Similarly, references to movement and gesture are inconceivable without embodied agency. The structural or syntactical traces to which we attribute such experiential facts are invariably just that: mere traces, retrospective evidence of offers extended to the body for potential enactment. The list of bodily-constituted musical "properties" is an extraordinarily long one, inclusive of such diverse yet central musical features as: tension and release; dissonance and consonance;[42] volume and balance; accent, meter and syncopation; tonal center and modulation; texture and density; line and phrase; height and depth; advancement and recession; vital drive and groove; movement and gesture—to say nothing of the immense range of so-called expressive attributes like seriousness, whimsy, playfulness, tenderness, or violence. It is the body's presence in each of these, and their consequently intimate links to personal and collective identity, that account for music's remarkable capacity to affirm or offend, to confront or console, and that account for the fact people are so seldom diffident about their musical preferences.

None of these musical-experiential facts can be reduced to the objective-stimulus/ subjective-response or cognitive representation model without radical distortion. For each is constituted, in performer and listener alike, by a central auditory-kinesthetic dialectic.[43] Musical hearing is hearing-as, and the foundation of this "as"-dimension is the body—grounded, polysemic, and active. The roots of musical listening, performing, and creativity draw upon our bodily-constituted attraction to and appreciation for discerning courses of action, and equally upon our adept avoidance of sterile possibilities. The mechanism that guides the hunches and intuitions by which we negotiate such ambiguous terrain is not rational and calculating, but somatosensory[44] and culturally informed.

6. SKILL & TASTE, BODY & CULTURE

There is no general "body," of which our individual bodies are particular manifestations. Embodied experience is always concrete and individual. We know our bodies from first-hand experience, from the ways they act, react, interact with the particular environments in which they are situated. Yet, as Butler[45] and others have shown us, despite their material and biological being, bodies are also shaped by their actions, and influenced in turn by social practices.[46] Bodies are always both thoroughly natural and thoroughly social or cultural.[47]

This brings us back to the fundamental ambiguity of embodied being with which we began this essay. On the one hand, the body is a concrete material fact. And yet, on the other, it is seldom if ever lived or experienced that way. The body is the general medium of our existence. Despite its insinuation into any and all meanings and realities that are available to us, then, it is never wholly available to us for scrutiny.[48] And this unavailability is one of its more salient features: the body has for us an ephemeral, indeterminate quality—an ambiguity rendered still more ambiguous by body's simultaneously natural and cultural status. The body is neither obdurate matter, nor is it epiphenomenal: yet it is in a sense *always both at once*.

Experience that is musical partakes uniquely of this ability to be both nature and culture, and of the ambiguity and polysemy that music manifests so vividly. The body in a state of music is a body closely tethered to sonorous materials. The sounds of music grip one's body, affording distinctive ways of moving, of orienting, and of being. While these linkages are not deterministic (they afford rather than constrain; they suggest or enable as much as they limit or direct), there is in any skilful performance or bodily action a corporeal dimension with direct and indissoluble links to identity. Music's simultaneity of natural and social meaning and the potency of its grip on the body make it an undertaking with exceptional formative and performative significance.

Musical instruction has among its primary concerns the development of skilful performances, whether in the sense of producing musical sound, or constructing embodied musical imagery as a listener.[49] On the view that has been advanced here, nurturing musically-skilled performance consists in developing, refining, and enabling the deployment of corporeal schemata, schemata which students assimilate and subsequently use to guide or govern actions in the instructor's absence. Developing skilful musical agency entails assuming and assimilating embodied stances, postures, and movements. In becoming skilled musicians, students assimilate the corporeal postures and gestures of a teacher—making them their own, weaving them into the dense fabric of their own embodied identity. Music is as much a matter of who they become as what they do.

Thus, musical learning is not so much a matter of what one knows as who one becomes: musically skilled action consists in both schematic and somatic identification with an exemplary model—more a process of "becoming" than a process of becoming aware or of "becoming knowledgeable." The implications of this corporeally-rooted, culturally-constructed identity are momentous. Bodily-constituted identity is no take-it-or-leave-it affair, but a fundamental component of selfhood and cultural belonging. It is small wonder, then, that musicians so often tend to identify as players of particular instruments first and foremost; that among the most pressing questions student musicians have for each other is what instrument they play; or that the identity of music educators in training is so much more deeply linked to musical than instructional performance. Corporeal schemata extend to the very heart of who we are, both biologically and culturally. In the teaching and learning of skilled musical performance, the biological and the cultural are linked in potent ways.

The bodily basis of skilful musical execution or performance, however, is but half the picture. For skilful actions and performances[50] are always also cultural. The body is an organ for the acquisition and sedimentation of actions that are socially and culturally useful, and at the same time these actions are dependent upon corporeal technique for their realization. The construct that welds the bodily and the cultural together has a name that is quite familiar to musicians: *taste*.

It is through the specific and personal character of bodily skill that taste is rendered material, inculcated, and refined. And it is through the inculcation of taste that the linkage between a world of radical change and flux and the more stable, habitual dispositions of the body is forged. Through taste, culture is turned into nature, made natural; while through (embodied) skills, nature is transformed into culture. "In neither case," Casey urges, "do we have to do with the superimposition of cultural constructions on preexisting bodily givens, but, rather, with a circumstance in which the (biologically) given and the (culturally) constructed meet in the crucible of the body."[51]

Skill and taste, both central concerns of musical education, are forged from and build upon corporeally-grounded experience: ritualized patterns of action through which cultural possibilities become natural inevitabilities. Through (embodied) musical skills and the tastes they inculcate, possibilities that would otherwise strike us as merely arbitrary are transformed into momentous choices; mere physical entities take on the status of deeply meaningful signs; and what might otherwise strike us as mere social obligations become virtuous actions and behaviours. Skill and taste (and, I submit, musical skill and taste in particular) are the human domains where the material is rendered socially significant, where the cultural is rendered material—where, in short, meaning is rendered incarnate. In developing musical skills in particular, bodily proclivities and dispositions are manipulated, extended, and shaped to cultural ends. In developing musical taste, these skills are transmuted into indelible systems of values and preferences.

In addition to my obvious interest in highlighting the ways embodiment and enculturation are co-implicated, I hope to make a further point of direct relevance to the way we conceive of musical education and its significance. That point is a profoundly ethical one: that musical education is unique among the areas represented in formal education in its practices of body management and taste management. Both focus their efforts at the point of confluence between biology and culture, between corporeality and cognition, between the personal and the collective, between the individual and the social. Music education manipulates bodies, and through them tastes, like no other area of curricular or instructional endeavour: stand this way; move this way; hold your arms, chest, or shoulders (tongue, lips, etc…) precisely like this; inhale now and in this manner, now exhale. The musical sounds we produce and struggle to refine are, through music's unique bodily resonances and articulations, in equal part what we produce and who we are. And constraints upon the range of acceptable bodily/musical action are highly significant among the things imparted in musical instruction. Music and identity (individual and collective, embodied and social) are joined at the hip; and musical education is thus a profoundly ethical trust. A statement by Joyce Bellous vividly highlights these connections and their ethical implications:

The problem with talent and identity in the musical arena has to do with the totality of the teacher's involvement over the learner—body, mind, and spirit. To be musical, and to develop the gift, the child's body is taken over by someone else who knows how the body should stand, look, posture itself, move, when and where. The influence of the musical teacher over the musical student is far more intrusive than the math teacher over the math student. . . . I think it is fair to suggest that only music remains in the domain of body management in this sense, and to the extreme that it does. Surely this must be seen as radically intrusive. . . . [I]n addition to the body, the [music] teacher educates the child in how to express feeling. So there is emotional territory that the teacher invades. Spiritually the teacher invests himself or herself in the student's life in such a way that the learner comes to see the teacher's way of life as a model for his or her own. So the child has no place to hide. . . . But what else can one do with one's body, soul, and mind that unites these three the way music does? Where else does one find the satisfaction? What else is there to drape one's life around that so holistically demands a person's attention?"[52]

In short, the development of skill and taste, concerns at the heart of musical instruction, are as profoundly ethical in character as they are potent in effect. Skilful production, perception, and appreciation are embodied, performative achievements—actions with links to identity that may be among the most powerful known to humankind.

7. (IN)CONCLUSION

One of the central convictions behind this essay is that music's significance to human culture, experience, and awareness is considerably more momentous than most of our conventional explanations and attempts at advocacy allow. Educators in particular have tended to urge that music matters because it is cognitively substantive: a valid point of course, but one that requires far more elaboration and qualification than is generally attempted. Left on its own, this argument tends to buy into the prevailing notions that to be cognitively substantive is to be rational, that what minds do primarily is "think," and that the proper measure of such endeavour is its clarity, orderliness, and so forth. Music becomes a mind-centered and mind-contained, psychologistic affair, purged of things like muscle, blood, bone, struggle, power, politics—in fact, most of the things that make it momentous. This leaves the body in an awkward place, if any place at all, and neglects music's status as cultural action.

On the enactive, embodied account of cognition I have begun sketching here, knowing is inseparable from action: knowing is doing, and always bears the body's imprint. This is particularly evident in music—a fact with significant implications for what music is deemed capable of contributing to the process of education. Part of what I have been urging here is that we recognize the profundity of the somatic/corporeal moment in human cognition, generally, and that we recognize music in particular as a kind of special celebration of this moment—of our here-and-now, embodied, action-based mode of being. Foremost among the reasons music truly matters educationally is its participatory, enactive, embodied character—and its consequent capacity to highlight the co-origination of body, mind, and culture.

We need to develop accounts of cognition and philosophies of mind that incorporate in nontrivial ways things like experience, attitude, culture, community, and the body, and that illuminate the mechanisms by which things like body and culture function as constitutive, emergent attributes of cognition. I have suggested that music is an excellent place to begin because of its distinctive polyvalence and polysemiousness—both results of a fundamental synesthesic, cross-modal, and dynamic character—a character constitutive of all consciousness, but highly salient in musical experience. Musical experience is no mere response to an aural stimulus, nor is it in any straightforward sense an act of symbolic representation. Musical experience is, however, invariably an embodied practice. When we hear a musical performance, we do not just 'think', nor do we do just 'hear': we participate with our whole bodies; we construct and enact it. We feel melodies in our muscles as much as we process them in our brains—or perhaps more accurately, our brains process them as melodies only to the extent our bodily extended schemata render that possible. And people make or listen to music not for what they know through it, or for the experience of "mindfulness" it affords, but for the way it is experienced, bodily.

Because an emergent, enactive, embodied view of cognition implicates a view of subjectivity as fluid, transient, polysemic, and experientially concrete, we must strenuously resist suggestions that music's processual character and distinctive bodily sense be regarded as secondary or epiphenomenal in terms of their cognitive significance.

Music plays a crucial role in the creation, maintenance, and negotiation of identity—both individually and collectively. It acts powerfully on the body, activating, guiding, facilitating, enabling, and shaping. The boundaries between the body and its environments are porous, allowing and facilitating interactions that are important if not fundamental to the body's constitution. Musical materials and their properties provide resources for particular kinds of bodies and bodily states, states that become regularized and reproduced over time. In all these senses, musical experiences and their educational "management" warrant recognition as crucial elements in the important business of social construction and regulation.

For all its words and claims this essay must end inconclusively, stopping short of the definitive summaries customarily offered at such points as these. But that is not inappropriate given our subject matter and the assumptions that have guided us here. Our primary concern has been, after all, to explore such musical attributes as ambiguity, slippage, polysemy, intermodality, temporality, processual emergence, concreteness and particularity—the kinds of "genius" an embodied mind may afford, and of which an incorporated self is capable. That further recognition that music is always at once thoroughly cultural and thoroughly natural effectively eliminates the possibility of a definitive conclusion.

On certain key points, however, the position that has emerged here is unequivocal. Music is not just "within" culture; nor is it "about" culture, or feeling, or the felt life, or other such things. It is, rather, a fundamental part of the action—in all its ambiguity, fluidity, fragility, and unpredictability. The embodied "genius" at the heart of musical agency is one with the genius that enables imagination, creativity, and discovery in the human world. Judged by criteria like certainty and clarity, music's plurality and slipperiness of meaning are defects. What has been advanced and advocated here instead is the integrity and trustworthiness of action and its agent, the minded body. Knowing in any humanly meaningful sense is emergent from and grounded in bodily experience, and continuous with the cultural production of meaning.

NOTES

[1] I use intelligence and cognition more or less interchangeably here. Since intelligence is a manifestation of exceptional cognitive capacity, problems attending the latter attend the former as well. This essay will focus more on cognition than intelligence, however.

[2] This binary hierarchical opposition insinuates itself into our language and our thought processes at almost every turn. Not only do its offspring distort our understanding of almost everything to which they are applied, they are, as feminist theories show, deeply implicated in the perpetuation of social inequalities of all kinds.

[3] Here I allude to Wittgenstein, who suggests that logic's "crystalline purity" is ill-suited to making our way in the messy, practical world. Ludwig Wittgenstein, *Philosophical investigations*, trans. G. E. M Anscombe (New York: MacMillan Publishing, 1976) §107 (p.46).

[4] This is an argument that has been advanced repeatedly over the years by Bennett Reimer. See, for instance, Reimer, B. (2003). *A philosophy of music education: Advancing the vision.* Upper Saddle River, New Jersey: Prentice Hall, 93.

[5] This strategy is not entirely wrong-headed. In fact I will advance a variant of that claim myself. Only, I will reject the desirability, indeed the possibility, of education that is purely cognitive in nature—in contrast to which, music must be doing something not-quite or not-really cognitive.

[6] This goes back to Langer, Schiller, and others. See also note 4, above.

[7] Admittedly, there have been noteworthy historical efforts to stress the "non-discursive" nature of the knowledge music affords. Unfortunately, the definitions of discursiveness on which these were based were not very illuminating. Moreover, the representational, idealistic models of mind on which they have built draw distinctions between knower and known that more recent science and scholarship has shown to be mistaken.

[8] Much of the literature on "critical thinking" in music confirms my assertions about the limited range of what counts, implicitly, as "thinking" among musicians and music educators.

[9] "Knowing-in-action" unfortunately reduces, on this view, to "knowing-while-in-action"—an advance over "knowing inaction," to be sure, but hardly the enactive, bodily-grounded, experiential knowledge to which we should be appealing.

[10] Michael O'Donovan-Anderson, "In search of real bodies: Theories and/of embodiment" in *The incorporated self: Interdisciplinary perspectives on embodiment*, Michael O'Donovan-Anderson, ed. (Lanham, Maryland: Rowan and Littlefield, 1996) 2–3.

[11] Where, by contrast, the Cartesian attitude may grant the necessity of incorporation, but cannot escape the fundamentally sceptical stance created by a body whose sensations have to be sorted and sifted in order to separate those that are cognitively and ideally trustworthy from those (many) that are not. Thus, my choice of the term "bodily-constituted" rather than "bodily-mediated."

[12] Damasio and others make a strong case that emotion plays an indispensable role in cognition. Antonio Damasio, *Descartes' error: Emotion, reason, and the human brain* (New York: Putnam's, 1994).

[13] Steven Feld puts it this way: "The significant feature of musical communication is . . . that its generality and multiplicity of possible messages and interpretations brings out a special kind of "feelingful" activity and engagement on the part of the listener, a form of pleasure that unites the material and mental dimensions of musical experience as fully embodied" (C. Keil and S. Feld, *Music grooves* [Chicago: University of Chicago Press, 1994] 91).

[14] Note the parallels to certain important features of the genetic epistemology of Jean Piaget.

[15] See _, _, _, *The embodied mind: Cognitive science and human experience* (Cambridge: MIT Press, 1992).

[16] Oliver Sacks advances neither a theory of cognition nor a philosophy of mind, nor speaks of music at length, but his extraordinary case studies offer vivid, compelling examples of what it means to say that cognition is distributed. They also raise provocative questions about the links between things like musical experience and quite a number of other human capacities we are not usually inclined to regard as musical at all.

[17] This is Mark Johnson's way of putting the embodiment thesis. Johnson's work, and his collaborations with George Lakoff advance numerous examples of the way bodily schemata structure the workings of mind. See M. Johnson, *The body in the mind* (Chicago: University of Chicago Press, 1987), and G. Lakoff and M. Johnson, *Philosophy in the flesh: The embodied mind and its challenge to Western thought* (New York: Basic Books, 1999).

[18] Jean Lave, *Cognition in practice: Mind, mathematics, and culture in everyday life* (New York: Cambridge University Press, 1988) 1.

[19] Evan Thompson, "The mindful body: Embodiment and cognitive science," in *The incorporated self: Interdisciplinary perspectives on embodiment*, Michael O'Donovan-Anderson, ed. (Lanham, Maryland: Rowan and Littlefield, 1996) 128.

[20] Evan Thompson, "The mindful body: Embodiment and cognitive science" 128.

[21] Phenomenological accounts of these facts abound, of course. In my book *Philosophical perspectives on music* (New York: Oxford University Press, 1998) I explore phenomenological/experiential accounts of music in the sixth chapter. Many of the points made here in passing receive extensive elaboration in D. Burrows *Sound, speech, and music* (Amherst: University of Massachusetts Press, 1990).

[22] John Shepherd and Peter Wicke, *Music and cultural theory* (Cambridge: Polity Press, 1997). Among Shepherd's and Wicke's points are that this "technology of articulation" represents a significant contrast to the arbitrary signifier-signified relationships generally held to constitute semiosis.

[23] For these reasons, musicing is not just part of culture but of biology as well.

[24] John Shepherd, "Music and male hegemony," in *Music and society: The politics of composition, performance and reception*, R. Leppert and S. McClary eds. (Cambridge: Cambridge University Press, 1987) 158 .

[25] See Tia DeNora, *Music in everyday life* (Cambridge: Cambridge University Press, 2000) 79–82.

[26] Their corporeal correlates are things I may or may not embrace, may or may not be able to take up, depending on the circumstances.

[27] Nelson Goodman makes the claim that expression amounts to metaphorical exemplification—where, that is, something that functions symbolically shows forth and to that extent represents properties that it possesses, but has acquired metaphorically. See Goodman's *Languages of art: An approach to a theory of symbols* (Indianapolis: Hackett Publishing, 1976) 85–95.

[28] Eliot, T. S. (1988). "The dry salvages: 'V,'" in *Four quartets*. New York: Harcourt, Brace, Jovanovich.

[29] Thomas Clifton, *Music as heard: A study in applied phenomenology* (New Haven: Yale University Press, 1983) 297.

[30] Roland Barthes, quoted in Richard Middleton, *Studying popular music* (Philadelphia: Open University Press, 1990) 266.

[31] Tia DeNora, *Music in everyday life* 161.

[32] Steven Feld, in C. Keil and S. Feld, *Music grooves* 91.

[33] B. Carroll-Phelan and P. J. Hampson. "Multiple components of the perception of musical sequences: A cognitive neuroscience analysis and some implications for auditory imagery," in *Music perception* 13:4, 554. This "recruitment" of motor activity's neural systems for the rhythmic components of auditory imagery extends in particular, state the authors, to those involved in the planning of motor sequences.

[34] Tia DeNora takes up the idea of "affordance" from psychologist J. J. Gibson, by way of sociologist Juergen Streeck. See *Music in everyday life* 38–39.

[35] John Shepherd, "How music works: Beyond the immanent and the arbitrary," in *Action, criticism, and theory (act) for music education* 1:2 (http://mas.siue.edu/ACT/index.html) 14.

[36] By no means do I mean to suggest that this is a uniquely human capacity. In fact, its continuity with other forms of life is precisely among the strengths of this approach.

[37] Richard Middleton, *Studying popular music* 223.

[38] As a trombonist, for instance, I can aurally identify notes produced on trombone with considerable accuracy, but that ability does not transfer to pitches generated on other instruments.

[39] I use quotation marks here because the view I am sketching clearly discounts the possibility of a musically-pure realm.

[40] Here I would urge, with Thomas Regelski and others, that we attempt to recover the original sense of "amateur" engagements: actions motivated by love. Amateur perception and engagement is not simply a diluted or deficient version of the professional. Recognizing action and embodiment as musically-constitutive precludes ranking and sorting music in virtue of its corporeal qualities. If all music becomes musical in virtue of the presence of bodily engagement and action, we cannot segregate "ideal" music—music directed to the mind—from music with more conspicuously visceral appeal. The ideal and the bodily are differences in degree, not in kind or in value.

[41] John Shepherd writes eloquently about timbre's tactile essence in his *Music as social text*. Experientially, please note, timbre is not a function of *pattern*. Pattern is a structural thing—about abstract relations—whereas tone *quality* is an inextricably bodily affair—*concrete and particular, here and now*. Most of our accounts of music cognition seriously neglect quality, focusing instead on pattern and structure, and relegating the remainder to the unfortunately residual status of psychological "response."

[42] For me, at any rate, the experience of in-tune and out-of-tune is a dramatically corporeal event—never an idle or detached observation.

[43] Thus, to Steven Feld's diagram (Keil and Feld, *Music grooves*, 86) of the act of musical communication, which features a reflexive interaction between a dialectically-constituted sound object and a listener's "interpretive moves" on the other, I would suggest the addition of a specifically kinaesthetic dimension that conjoins object and action.

[44] I am reminded of an assertion by Charles Rosen to the effect that in successful improvisation the fingers develop an independent logic, one not dependent upon mental ratification.

[45] Judith Butler, *Bodies that matter: On the discursive limits of "Sex"* (New York: Routledge, 1993).

[46] Butler's interest and focus lies primarily with discursive practices; to these I am obviously anxious to add musical actions and practices.

[47] On this point, see Edward Casey, "The ghost of embodiment: Is the body a natural or a cultural entity?" in *The incorporated self: Interdisciplinary perspectives on embodiment*, Michael O'Donovan-Anderson, ed. (Lanham, Maryland: Rowan and Littlefield, 1996) 25. Casey invokes the phrase "ghostly" to describe this capacity to be both natural and cultural, yet neither: which should remind us of the long history of spirit/ghost metaphors associated with music.

[48] Like water to a fish.

[49] Among the points to which my previous remarks have alluded is that these differ in kind rather than degree: performing and listening are both skills, both active, both bodily, and both constructive.

[50] Perhaps we might call this musical "body building"?

[51] Edward Casey, "The ghost of embodiment" 31.

[52] "Talent and identity" in *Orbit* 31:1, 2000 (39). The brief quote is excerpted from a more extended discussion entitled "Thoughts on shaping talent and identity" by L. Bartel, J. Bellous, W. Bowman, and K. Peglar, in *Orbit*, 31(1) 2000 on-line edition (OISE, University of Toronto).

RICHARD SHUSTERMAN

SOMAESTHETICS AND EDUCATION: EXPLORING THE TERRAIN

1

In the pragmatist tradition of William James and John Dewey, I regard experience as a central concept of philosophy and affirm the body as an organizing core of experience. So in developing a pragmatist aesthetics and a theory of philosophy as an art of living, I proposed a more constructive and systematic philosophical approach to the body which I call "somaesthetics" and which I conceive as a discipline of theory and practice.[1] Somaesthetics is deeply concerned with important educational aims and may offer some interesting new perspectives and techniques with respect to learning. But it also presents some particular problems with respect to its teaching in the standard university curriculum. In this paper, after briefly outlining the aims and structure of somaesthetics, I examine its educational potential and problems, considering both historical sources and the contemporary situation.

Somaesthetics can be roughly defined as a discipline devoted to the critical, ameliorative study of the experience and use of the body as a locus of sensory-aesthetic appreciation (*aisthesis*) and creative self-fashioning. Somaesthetics is therefore also devoted to the knowledge, discourses, practices, and bodily disciplines that structure such somatic care or can improve it. When Alexander Baumgarten founded the field of aesthetics as a theoretical but also practical discipline aimed at "the perfection of sensory cognition, this implying beauty," he excluded somatic study and exercise from this enterprise, probably because of religious and rationalist influences.[2] But while ancient Platonism and modern Western philosophy have been mostly critical of the body, if we simply recall philosophy's central aims of knowledge, self-knowledge, right action, justice, and the quest for the good life, then the crucial value of somaesthetics should be clear.

1. Since knowledge is largely based on sensory perception whose reliability often proves questionable, philosophy has always been concerned with the critique of the senses, but this critique has been essentially confined to the discursive analysis and critique of sensory propositional judgements that constitutes standard epistemology. The complementary route offered by somaesthetics is instead to correct the actual functional performance of our senses by an improved direction of one's body, since the senses belong to and are conditioned by the soma. Socrates long ago insisted that the body be kept fit and healthy in order to augment the accuracy and range of our perceptions. "The body is valuable for all human activities, and in all its uses it is very important that it should be as fit as possible. Even in the act of thinking, which

Liora Bresler (ed.), Knowing Bodies, Moving Minds, 51-60.
©*2004 Kluwer Academic Publishers. Printed in the Netherlands*

is supposed to require least assistance from the body, everyone knows that serious mistakes often happen through physical ill-health."[3] Similarly, a person will be able to perceive less of his environment if a stiff neck or rigid rib cage prevents him from rotating the head to look behind him.

2. If self-knowledge is a central aim of philosophy, then knowledge of one's bodily dimension must not be ignored. Concerned not simply with the body's external form or representation but with its lived experience, somaesthetics works toward improved awareness of our feelings, thus providing greater insight into both our passing moods and lasting attitudes. It can therefore reveal and improve somatic malfunctioning that normally go undetected even though they impair our well-being and performance.

Consider two examples. We rarely notice our breathing, but its rhythm and depth provide rapid, reliable evidence of our emotional state. Consciousness of breathing can therefore make us aware that we are angry or anxious when we might otherwise remain unaware of these feelings and thus vulnerable to their misdirection. Similarly, a chronic contraction of certain muscles that constrains movement and causes tension and pain may nonetheless go unnoticed because it has become habitual. As unnoticed this chronic contraction cannot be relieved, nor can its resultant disability and discomfort. Yet once such somatic functioning is brought to clear attention, there is the possibility of modifying it and avoiding its unpleasant consequences.

3. A third central aim of philosophy is right action, which requires both knowledge and effective will. Since we can only act by means of our bodies, our power of will—the ability to act, as we will to act—depends on somatic efficacy. By exploring and refining our bodily experience, we can gain a better grasp of how our will works and a better mastery of its concrete application in behavior. Knowing and desiring the right action will not avail if we cannot will our bodies to perform it; and our surprising inability to perform the most simple bodily tasks is matched only by our astounding blindness to this inability, these failures resulting from inadequate somaesthetic awareness.

Consider a poor golfer who tries with all his might to keep his head down and his eyes on the ball and who is completely convinced that he is doing so, even though he in fact miserably fails to. His conscious will is unsuccessful because deeply ingrained somatic habits override it, and he does not even notice this failure because his habitual sense perception is so inadequate and distorted that it feels as if the action intended is indeed performed as willed. In too much of our action we are like the golfer, whose "strong" will remains impotent, since lacking the somatic sensibility to make it effective. For such reasons, Diogenes the Cynic advocated rigorous body training as "that whereby, with constant exercise, perceptions are formed such as secure freedom of movement for virtuous deeds."[4]

4. If philosophy is concerned with the pursuit of happiness and better living, then somaesthetics' concern with the body as the locus and medium of our pleasures clearly deserves more philosophical attention. Even the pleasures of pure thought are (for us humans) embodied, and thus can be intensified or more acutely savored through improved somatic awareness and discipline. As thinking also involves the body's muscular contractions, it is better served by somatic health.

5. Since the body is a malleable site for inscribing social power, somaesthetics can also contribute to political philosophy's interest in justice. It offers a way of understanding how complex hierarchies of power can be sustained without any need to make them explicit in laws. Entire ideologies of domination can be covertly materialized and preserved by encoding them in somatic norms that, as bodily habits, get typically taken for granted and so escape critical consciousness:[5] for instance, the norms that women of a given culture should only speak softly, eat daintily, sit with their legs close together, walk keeping head and eyes down, assume the bottom role in copulation, etc. However, just as repressive power relations are encoded in our bodies, so they can be challenged by alternative somatic practices. Michel Foucault joins Wilhelm Reich and other body therapists in advocating this message, though the recommended somatic methods often differ greatly. Even if we are not interested in large-scale social reforms but simply one's own personal liberation from damaging habits and attitudes, a systematic attention to and modification of one's body practices can be a path to greater freedom.[6]

Though there is much contemporary discussion of the body, somaesthetics offers a structuring architectonic to integrate these very different, seemingly incommensurable discourses into a more productively systematic field. It also offers a clear pragmatic orientation, something that the individual can directly translate into a discipline of improved somatic practice.

2

Somaesthetics has three fundamental dimensions. *Analytic somaesthetics* describes the basic nature of our bodily perceptions and practices and their function in our knowledge and construction of reality. This theoretical dimension involves ontological and epistemological issues concerning the body, but also includes the sort of sociopolitical inquiries that Foucault made central: How the body is both shaped by power and employed as an instrument to maintain it, how bodily norms of health and beauty and even the most basic categories of sex and gender are constructions sustained by and serving social forces. Foucault's approach to these somatic issues was typically genealogical, portraying the historical emergence of various body doctrines, norms, and practices. But analytic somaesthetics can also compare the body ideologies and practices of two or more synchronic cultures.

Pragmatic somaesthetics is the dimension concerned with methods of somatic improvement and their comparative critique. Over the course of human history, many kinds of methods have been recommended to improve our experience and use of the body: diverse diets, forms of dress, gymnastic training, dance and martial arts, cosmetics, body piercing or scarification, yoga, massage, aerobics, body-building, erotic arts, and disciplines of psychosomatic improvement like Alexander Technique and Feldenkrais Method. These diverse methodologies of practice can be roughly classified into *representational* and *experiential*: The former emphasize the body's external appearance, while the latter focus not on how the body looks from the outside but on the quality of its experience. Such experiential methods aim to make us "feel better" in both senses of this ambiguous phrase that reflects the ambiguity of the very notion of aesthetics: They aim to make the quality of experience more satisfyingly rich, but also to make our awareness of somatic experience more acute and perceptive. Cosmetic practices (from make-up to plastic surgery) exemplify the representational side of somaesthetics, while practices like Zen meditation or Feldenkrais's Method of Awareness Through Movement are paradigmatic of the experiential.

The representational/experiential distinction is useful for seeing that somaesthetics cannot be globally condemned as superficial, since confined to surface appearances. But the distinction should not be construed as rigidly exclusive, since there is an inevitable complementarity of representations and experience, of outer and inner. How we look can influence how we feel, but also vice versa. Practices like dieting or bodybuilding that are initially pursued for ends of representation often produce feelings that are then sought for their own sake. Somatic methods aimed at inner experience sometimes employ representational means as cues to effect the body posture necessary for inducing the desired experience, whether by consulting one's image in a mirror, focussing our gaze on a body part like the tip of the nose or the navel, or simply visualizing a body form in one's imagination. Conversely, representational practices like bodybuilding utilize improved awareness of experiential clues to serve its ends of external form. The bodybuilder must be able to distinguish the good pain that builds muscle from the bad pain that signals injury, just as he must feel when he reaches the full extension and contraction of a muscle, since going through the full range of motion is the only way to stimulate the entire muscle and every possible muscle fiber.[7] The experiential/representational distinction is also not exhaustive; a third category of "performative" somaesthetics could be introduced to group methodologies that focus primarily on building strength, health, or skill: such as weightlifting, athletics, and martial arts. However, to the extent that such performance-oriented practices aim either at external exhibition or one's inner feeling of power, they may be somewhat assimilated into the representational or experiential categories.

The methodologies of pragmatic somaesthetics need to be distinguished from their actual practice. I call this third dimension *practical somaesthetics*. It is not a matter of producing texts about the body, not even those offering pragmatic programs of somatic care; it is rather about physically engaging in such care— through reflective, disciplined, demanding corporeal practice aimed at somatic self-improvement (whether representational, experiential, or performative). This dimension, not of saying but of doing, is the most neglected by academic body philosophers, whose commitment to the *logos* of discourse typically treats the body in mere textual terms. But actual bodily performance is crucial to the idea that somaesthetics is practice as well as theory.

                                        3

The study of somaesthetics in its analytic and pragmatic forms provides a wide range of knowledge about bodily forms, norms, practices, and techniques. Such knowledge, of course, has some educational value in informing us about these matters. But since space is brief, let me concentrate on the more provocative question of the educational value of practical somaesthetics, whose activity is not the representation of discursive truths. The practical somaesthetics of performance seems useful for education, if we follow the reasoning of Xenophon's Socrates that the cultivation of a stronger, healthier, better performing body should result in better functioning of the senses and mind. Even when philosophers describe the body as merely the mind's instrument or servant, they generally recognize that the mind is better served when its instrument or servant is in better functioning order. Though idealist philosophers who denounce the body and its senses as dangerous distractions that imprison the mind have often resisted this insight, even Plato (whose *Phaedo* presents perhaps the first and most vehement of such arguments against the body) ultimately insisted in works like *Timaeus, Republic,* and *Laws* on the importance of gymnastics for the better balance or harmony of the soul.

Rousseau's *Emile* provides an excellent set of arguments for the mental advantages of developing not only health but also bodily strength and skill. "The body must be vigorous in order to obey the soul... A good servant ought to be robust.... The weaker the body, the more it commands," thus "a frail body weakens the soul." We therefore need to exercise the body to develop the mind, which it nourishes and informs through its senses: "It is only with a surplus of strength beyond what [man] needs to preserve himself that there develops in him the speculative faculty fit to employ this excess of strength for other uses. To learn to think, therefore, it is necessary to exercise our limbs, our senses, our organs, which are the instruments of our intelligence".[8] Practical somaesthetic needs to be distinguished from traditional forms of physical education that merely seek to develop strength by mechanical repetitions of exercises that are aimed at achieving standardized bodily forms and measurements or acquiring mere brute power. Somaesthetics (as the term *aesthesis* implies) is concerned with educating the bodily senses (including our kinaesthetic and proprioceptive senses) that are needed to properly direct the bodily powers we deploy. A good part of this exercise involves our reflective awareness and assessment of our sensory appreciation, and this is where the disciplines of experiential somaesthetics come especially into play.

The educational value of such disciplines is not adequately recognized. Important philosophers, moreover, have made assertions that cast doubt on the usefulness of experiential somaesthetics. Kant, for instance, recognizes the role of physical education. For him it includes not only physical exercise like running, jumping, throwing, wrestling, carrying weights and games that involve such activities, but also the more elementary matters of "feeding and tending" and of "discipline (which he conceives as the "merely negative" work of "restraining unruliness"). However, Kant seems strongly opposed to the sort of reflective examination of one's somatic experience that constitutes practical somaesthetics. "To listen to oneself and constantly direct attention to the state of one's sensations takes the mind's activity away from considering other things and is harmful to the head." "The inner sensibility, that one here generates through one's reflections is harmful. Analysts easily get sick.... One must be self conscious in observing one's own representations and sensations (one feels oneself completely). This inner view and self-feeling weakens the body and diverts it from animal functions."[9] In short, experiential somatic reflection is harmful to both mind and body, and the best way to treat one's body is to ignore, as much as possible, the sensations of how it feels, while using it actively in work and exercise.

Though I think Kant's argument is wrong, it rests on a grain of truth. In our normal activities, our attention is and needs to be primarily directed outside to the objects of our environment in relation to which we need to act and react in order to survive and flourish. Thus for excellent evolutionary reasons, we should be primarily devoted to examining these outside things, not our inner sensations. That is why, to borrow an image from Montaigne, nature positioned our eyes to be looking out rather than in. Kant's error, however, is confusing primacy with exclusivity. If our attention needs to be mostly directed outward, this does not mean that it is not sometimes or even often very useful to examine oneself and one's sensations. Life is not a monolithic affair, so attention must vary its focus according to our changing needs and interests. Though Kant is right that incessant attention to one's bodily sensations is harmful, the problem is not somaesthetic attention per se but rather extreme one-sidedness of attention.[10] Incessant attention to one's bank account, reputation, philosophical studies, or anything else would also be harmful.

How can experiential somaesthetics' sharpening of bodily awareness help reeducate our use of our selves and our senses in order to enable us to learn more and perform better? The answer is already implied in my earlier explanation of how somaesthetics advances the basic aims of philosophy, but let me now try to be still more explicit.

1. Experiential somaesthetics can inform us of our feelings and emotions before they are otherwise known to us, and thus it can help us better manage those feelings and emotions so that they do not interfere in our learning efforts. To return to the examples I gave earlier, by becoming generally more aware of my breathing through somaesthetic training, I can learn from changes in my breathing pattern that I am angry or anxious or uneasy before I would otherwise be conscious of such psychological disturbance; and, once aware, I can then do something to counteract its disturbing effects on my learning or action. For instance, I could realize I am now too upset or impatient to read this material properly and I could then either postpone my reading till I am calm or regulate my breathing to introduce the necessary calmness for reading carefully and enjoyably with understanding. Similarly, I may be reading in a posture that is uncomfortable or stress-producing (for example, if I am holding my neck, occipital muscles, back, rib cage, belly, or jaw too tightly) without really being aware of this discomfort. Yet though this discomfort now lies beneath the threshold of my consciousness (because of insufficient somaesthetic attention), it is disturbing enough to distract or diminish the quality of my attention to what I am reading. And such disturbing muscular contractions, when continued over time, will eventually break through to consciousness in the form of pain that is more obviously and powerfully distracting and that can be so strong as to prevent me altogether from concentrating on what I read or even from reading at all. But if we learn through somaesthetic discipline to become aware of these excessive muscular contractions in their initial and less consciously disturbing stage, we can do something to relieve them before they explode into consciousness as serious discomfort and pain.

2. The awareness achieved through experiential somaesthetics not only gives us better knowledge and management of our feelings (whether in learning or in other aspects of life) but also better control of our movements, hence our actions. As the golfing example makes clear, one cannot (except by blind luck) learn to correct one's bad swing into a good swing until one is aware in concrete experiential terms of what one is doing wrong with one's body in one's bad swing and how the body should feel when its parts are properly integrated in the good swing. The case is similar for learning to improve other kinds of movement: hitting a baseball, kicking a football, shooting a jump shot, playing the piano. Here again, heightened awareness to unnecessary muscle contractions in making (or preparing for) the movement can also alert us to problems that will bring eventual pain or injury if these movements are very frequently repeated in their presently stress-producing form instead of being retrained into less taxing styles of performing the same movement. If one swings a bat (or plays the piano) while holding the rib cage very tightly so that one's force of movement is only in the hands and arms rather than involving one's back and pelvis, the long-lasting success of such action is very doubtful while pain and injury are very likely.

3. Education is not so much a matter of working on particular emotions or movements, but of reorganizing or retraining *habits* of feeling and movement and habits of conduct to which feeling and movement contribute. This is also true of experiential somaesthetics. We might have a habitual reaction of anxiety with respect to mathematics or foreigners of a certain race (perhaps because of some traumatic event that was accompanied by rapid breathing and a "freezing" of the jaw muscles in tight contraction), a reaction that repeatedly emerges against our conscious rational will and that leads us to poor conduct, such as instinctively refusing attention to any foreigner or to any mathematical expression. But we can do little to reform this habit of bad feeling and the undesired misconduct that it brings by simply urging the rational will to assert itself more strongly, since the habitual bad feeling and conduct rest on habitual somatic reactions that lie beneath ordinary rational awareness and beyond mere rational control. Only by bringing these disturbing somatic sensations into clear focus through heightened somaesthetic awareness can we ever hope to isolate them sufficiently in consciousness so as to control them and prevent them from issuing in misconduct. Only through such heightened awareness of them can we go still further and work to transform the bad somatic feelings associated with the math or foreigners into more positive feelings that could then foster more positive attitudes and conduct.[11] Likewise, a person whose persistent humiliation has engendered a habitual posture of holding himself timidly and tightly hunched over with bowed head will never gain full confidence without learning to assume a more erect, self-assured body posture that allows feelings of greater confidence. This is not merely because of habitual associations, but also because the hunched-over posture impairs not only ease of breathing (by contracting the chest cavity) but facility of head movement for scanning the horizon, both of which are factors productive of anxiety on the most basic experiential level.

No matter how compartmentalized our institutional learning has become, we become educated as embodied wholes. As there is a somatic dimension to all our feeling, thinking, and behavior, so we can sometimes get a better handle on the education of our emotions, attitudes, and conduct by approaching things from the somatic side. This hypothesis is central to many systems of somatic education and therapy (from the Asian forms of yoga and meditation to the Western somaesthetic practices of Alexander Technique and Feldenkrais Method), and it has been confirmed by the success of these practices in educating the mental, physical, and spiritual powers of its practitioners.

4

There is not space here to develop my arguments fully, but I hope to have indicated how a good case can be made for the educational value of somaesthetics, particularly in its practical experiential dimension, which, at first glance, might seem irrelevant or (as Kant thought) detrimental to productive education. I invite you to supplement my arguments by performing some somaesthetic exercise of your own, perhaps examining your feelings in the experience of reading this text. It is not easy to maintain a focus on these feelings, if one is not already well practiced in such meditations; and it is still harder to describe these feelings in words, since they are, for the most part, what William James called "the nameless feelings" of our stream of consciousness. That is one reason why they are generally ignored by philosophical theory. So let me help you focus by some guiding questions:

What are you aware of on the bodily level as you read these lines, and can you become more aware of your bodily position and feelings? Does your posture feel maximally comfortable for reading, or are there any tensions in your jaw, eyes, neck, chest, belly, hands, or legs? If reading philosophy (or simply reading English) is not very easy or enjoyable for you, you are likely to have extra tension in some place because of the special effort of concentration you are making. In making a special effort, we usually contract muscles beyond those necessary for making that effort; for instance, we often harden our jaw when we lift or push a heavy weight or when we force ourselves to do hard mental work, even if we neither lift the weight nor think with the jaw. Similarly, your effort of concentration in reading may involve unnecessary contractions and hardening of your rib cage, which constrains breathing. So are you breathing easy and comfortably, or is your breath more shallow and perhaps hurried, expressing your impatience to finish this task of reading? Are both feet resting calmly and firmly on the floor while you are reading? Does one foot (or part thereof) or one side of your body feel like it is bearing more of your weight than the other? Which part or which side? Is there any change of posture or breathing you think would make you feel more comfortable, and what deters you from making that change?

If you have not lost your patience through this brief exercise in somatically reflective reading, then you can better appreciate the final question of this paper. In what manner or framework could practical somaesthetics be most effectively introduced into the school curriculum at the various levels of primary, secondary, and college education? This problem greatly puzzles me, so I look to experts in educational studies for guidance. Though convinced that somaesthetic addresses philosophy's basic goals, I do not see how practical somaesthetics can be easily incorporated into the standard philosophical curriculum or practiced in the typical philosophical classroom that I know from Europe and America. Its distinctive physical engagement would probably be seen as sensationalist provocation that flouts philosophy's established academic definition as purely mental and theoretical.

I can imagine how most colleagues and many students would be horrified if I introduced exercises in the Reichian orgasm reflex, which is crucial to the somaesthetic discipline of bioenergetics, even if this exercise does not require students to engage in sexual acts or touch each other or even touch themselves sexually. That students have to lie on the ground and undulate their bodies through rhythmic contractions would be more than enough to offend standards of decorum in philosophy instruction. And what of the practices of touching that are crucial to the Alexander Technique and the Feldenkrais Method of Functional Integration? Even though the teacher's touching here is gentle, non-intrusive, and non-sexual, the mere fact of touching a philosophy student in the classroom seems a shocking violation of the established limits of teacher-student relations. Not wanting to link somaesthetics with sensationalism and scandal, I have discussed it in my philosophy classes only in terms of its theories and so far have resolutely eschewed teaching it there as concrete practice. Those students who express interest in pursuing the concrete practices are given guidance as to where they can get the kinds of practical lessons they seek. But I am not satisfied with this solution, for somaesthetic theory cannot be fully unless one has the experiences that only concrete practice provides.

Should somaesthetic instruction at the university, then, be confined to classes of dance and physical education, where touching and thematized physical movement are accepted classroom practices? I worry that this solution will not adequately address the theoretical side of somaesthetics and may not even do justice to the intensely mental, reflective dimension of experiential somaesthetic practice. The standard gym or dance class format tends to reduce its subject matter to instruction in movement; when yoga is taught in such formats it is typically robbed of its philosophical dimension so that what remains is essentially an exercise class.

This problem of a curricular framework for somaesthetics points to a more general limitation of philosophical learning in today's educational system. In ancient times philosophy was practiced not just as an academic discipline but as a way of life, so philosophical instruction would include the inculcation of certain bodily practices (including diet and forms of dress) that were characteristic of the particular school of philosophy (e.g. epicurean, stoic, cynic). Such a holistic, embodied study of philosophy still survives in the monastic traditions of Christianity, Buddhism, and other faiths, where religious philosophy is learned and practiced as a comprehensive way of life. Can something of this holistic approach be achieved in contemporary philosophical education outside the monastic tradition and within the university framework of regular "course offerings" or special programs?

Such questions also arise outside of philosophy? In the traditional aesthetic education of ancient Japanese arts (Gei-doh), the model of learning is similarly embodied, holistic, and experiential – a comprehensive process of mimetic absorption and transformational self-cultivation. "Of what a pine tree is, learn from the pine; of what bamboo is, learn from bamboo", wrote the poet Basho (1644–94). Should our educational curriculum in the arts, then, include field trips through the woods or noisy nights at techno raves? And what about lengthy sessions of lying on a matt while somaesthetically monitoring the rhythm and shape of our breathing and the tension of our muscles?

What reforms of curriculum, institutions, and attitudes would be needed to introduce such embodied education? If something important is learned through the experiential practice of somaesthetics (or through other experiential forms of learning) that cannot be adequately learned by mere discursive means, then it is perhaps worth looking for good answers to these questions.

NOTES

[1]   I introduced somaesthetics very briefly in *Vor der Interpretation* (Wien: Passagen, 1996), but explain it in greater detail in *Practicing philosophy* (New York: Routledge, 1997), *Pragmatist aesthetics*, 2nd edition (New York: Rowman & Littlefield, 2000), and *Performing live* (Ithaca: Cornell University Press, 2000). For critical discussion of somaesthetics, see the symposium on *Pragmatist Aesthetics* in the *Journal of Speculative Philosophy*, 16:1(2002) with papers by Paul Taylor, Thomas Leddy, Antonia Soulez , and my reply to them; see also the papers on somaesthetics and *Performing Live* in the *Journal of Aesthetic Education*, 36:4 (2002), with papers by Martin Jay, Gustavo Guerra, Kathleen Higgins, Casey Haskins, and myself. Besides these critics, I wish to thank my Feldenkrais trainers, especially Yvan Joly, for helpful insights on somatic education. My four-year training program to become a certified Feldenkrais Practitioner (1998–2002) and my subsequent work as a practitioner have provided an important part of the experiential background for some of the views I formulate in this paper.

[2]   For details see, *Pragmatist Aesthetics*, ch. 10.

[3]   Xenophon, *Conversations of Socrates* (London: Penguin, 1970), 172

[4]   Diogenes Laertius, *Lives of the eminent philosophers*, Vol. 2 (Cambridge: Harvard University Press, 1931), 71.

[5]   See Wilhelm Reich, *The function of the orgasm* (New York: Noonday, 1973), Michel Foucault, *Discipline and punish* (New York: Vintage, 1979), and Pierre Bourdieu, *The logic of practice* (Stanford University Press, 1990), ch.4.

[6]   Judith Butler has adapted some of Foucault's insights to advocate tranfigurative somatic performances of gender parody (such as drag and cross-dressing) for purposes of feminist emancipation. Iris Marion Young has also argued for the somatic dimension of woman's liberation by drawing on ideas from Simone de Beauvoir and Merleau-Ponty. All these approaches fail to see the full spectrum of possibilities that somaesthetics encompasses, and they seem especially blind to the value and uses of experiential somaesthetics and its heightening of explicit, reflective body awareness. For a detailed discussion of these points, see Richard Shusterman, "Somaesthetics and *the second sex*: A pragmatist reading of a feminist classic," *Hypatia* 18:4 (2003); and "The silent, limping body of philosophy," in T. Carman and M. Hansen, *The Cambridge companion to Merleau-Ponty* (Cambridge: Cambridge University Press, 2003).

[7]   See Arnold Schwarzenegger, *Encyclopedia of modern body building* (New York: Simon and Schuster, 1985) 82,115.

[8]   Jean-Jacques Rousseau, *Emile* (New York: Basic Books, 1979), 54, 118,125.

[9]   Immanuel Kant, *Reflexionen zur Kritische Philosophie* (Hgr.), Beno Erdman 9tuttgart: Frommann-Holzboog, 1992, paras. 7, 19 (pp. 68–9). Kant later critically remarks that "man is usually full of sensations when he is empty of thought" para. 106 (p. 117).

[10] Kant had personal reasons for rejecting attention to somantic sensations. By his own confession, Kant sometimes suffered from huypochondria, so that heightened attention to inner somatic sensations seemed apt to result in "morbid feelings" of anxiety. See his book *The contest of the Faculties* (Lincoln: Universityof Nebraska Press, 1992), 187–189.

[11] I develop this point with much more detail and argument in Richard Shusterman, "Wittgenstein on bodily feelings: Explanation and melioration in philosophy of mind, art, and politics," in Cressida Heyes, *The Grammar of politics: Wittgenstein and political philosophy* (Ithaca: Cornell University Press, 2003).

PIRKKO MARKULA

EMBODIED MOVEMENT KNOWLEDGE IN FITNESS AND EXERCISE EDUCATION

As educators, we are intimately engaged with knowledge. When we teach, we deliver knowledge about the usual subjects in curriculum but also knowledge on our behavior and bodies or more broadly, knowledge on how to be a reasonable human being. We hope, then, that our students will let such knowledge guide them, not only through school, but also through the rest of their lives. Some of this education is not necessarily explicit and if asked, we might not be able to pin point the origin of our knowledge. It might a book, a television program or a magazine article, in fact, any type of media that today so effectively distribute knowledge. In this chapter, I focus on a type of bodily knowledge, fitness, that is not necessarily part of the school curriculum, "the official knowledge," but seems to shape our lives and the lives of our students beyond the school environment.

What do we know about fitness? Quite a lot. We know that staying in shape, keeping fit, exercising regularly is good for our health. We can also list such physical activities as aerobics, weight training, walking, running, and cycling as ways of getting fit. Or we might recommend a health club as a place to exercise. How do we know all this? Well, positive effects of exercise are constantly emphasized by medical doctors and various fitness experts. In addition, there are plenty of specialized fitness magazines, self help fitness books, and exercise videos offering advice on how to become fit. Or we attend exercise classes and learn from our instructors and fellow exercisers about a fit body. It is also clear that fitness and exercise are physical and therefore, our fitness knowledge concerns our bodies. We could even say that exercise provides us with bodily experiences and sensations that are lost in the modern, sedentary lifestyle. Therefore, in the realm of fitness, where the body is the dominant way of knowing, we have a possibility to sense the world around us holistically through physical and mental. But is all that we know about our fit bodies the type of knowledge that promotes unification of the body and mind into an integrated self?

In this paper, I look at how fitness knowledge constructs our understanding of our selves. Through this analysis, I aim to conceptualize whether a fit body provides us with embodied ways of knowing about ourselves and the world, not as minds separate from and independent of our bodies, but as integrated human beings. To analyze the meanings embedded in current fitness knowledge, I derive from Michel Foucault's concept of a truth game to detail a construction of the fit body in the contemporary fitness industry. I conclude by examining the meaning of knowing about fitness for educators.

Liora Bresler (ed.), Knowing Bodies, Moving Minds, 61-76.
©2004 Kluwer Academic Publishers. Printed in the Netherlands

DISCOURSES OF COMMERCIAL FITNESS CULTURE

For Foucault, knowledge embeds much more than mere useful information. As a matter of fact, knowledge for Foucault is one of the most important ways of using power. To illustrate this link, he developed his theory of discursive power. Foucault's starting point was that no knowledge is neutral, no knowledge is "true" but is rather constructed as a particular way of knowing in certain circumstances and certain contexts. He labelled this process of knowledge construction, discourse: "Discourses…are ways of constituting knowledge, together with the social practices, forms of subjectivity and power relations which inhere in such knowledges and the relations between them" (Weedon, 1987, p. 108). Foucault, however, believed that no knowledge is harmful or bad per se, but it will become a tool of power that objectifies humans to the control of and dependence from someone else when we become convinced of its absolute truth value (Foucault, 1983). In contemporary society, Foucault maintained, much of our knowledge stems from objective scientific research. It is not, however, a guarantee of truth but has, during specific circumstances of western society, become to dominate over other ways of knowing. Consequently, "scientifically proven" practices and behaviours become privileged in our society. For example, health practices based on scientific research are considered more beneficial than practices deriving from so called alternative medicine or mere testimonials. Similarly, scientifically based fitness practices are recommended over experiential or common sense fitness practices.

Foucault argued that there is no one truth to be discovered by scientific methods, but merely different types of knowledges, all created within relations of power. However, when science is made the objective indicator of truth, the link with knowledge and power is disconnected, because the origin and meaning of knowledge as socially constructed is masked in this process. As a consequence, people follow the scientific truth unquestioningly and knowledge turns into a dominant discourse that dictates how we lead our lives. Foucault demonstrated that a particularly effective way to inscribe power is by disciplining the body. The "body" here does not mean merely the biological aspect of the body, but a body that is an object of control and manipulation. He labelled this type of power as "bio-power." One well known example of bio-power is schooling that has been used as a way of instilling bodily discipline to pupils who are taught to control the space, behaviours and appearance of their bodies. To further illustrate how dominance through bodily discipline is possible in today's society, Foucault used the concept of a truth game.

By participating in every day practices, like exercise, we enter into a game with truth, in this case, truth about fitness and the fit body. This truth is defined by knowledge (what we know about correct or best ways to achieve the fit body) that is again defined by dominant discourses. For example, fitness knowledge is predominantly based on medical, psychological and physiological research and this knowledge, thus, dominates various fitness practices. Based on this knowledge, practices of fitness are developed and in Foucault's theoretical schema, these practices discipline the body to achieve the scientifically measured fitness level. Again, following Foucault, this develops into an endless game that cannot be won: the body is never disciplined enough to entirely achieve the desired goal. Arthur

Frank (1991) uses a vivid example of how a dieter, by desiring a thinner body, enters into a truth game. In this scenario, "the thin man inside is the truth, the scale becomes the daily truth game and the diet the disciplinary regime" (p. 57). Similarly, the fit body becomes the truth to achieve and the exercise program the disciplinary regime. In this endless game, the self becomes dominated through the discipline imposed on the body by the scientific truth about fitness: we do not question the meaning and the origin of the fitness knowledge and turn into docile followers of discourses. Foucault found disciplinary discursive power a particularly effective means of control as we, after a while, take its truth so for granted that we begin to discipline ourselves by carefully monitoring our own behaviour without ever wondering why such control is necessary.

Foucault did not, however, advocate that all knowledge disciplines the body or that entering into a truth games necessarily means accepting dominance of the self. Rather, the idea is not to get rid of truth games, knowledge or power, but to re-consider how these are used (Foucault, 1988). Consequently, different fitness discourses also represent a different deployment of knowledge and power and what matters, then, is how they are used. Therefore, the possibility of re-creating the discourse always exists: while knowledge can govern us by turning us into docile bodies, Foucault also pointed out that knowledge turns us into subjects: while bio-power can effectively discipline us into docile bodies, there are also active practices through which "a human being turns him- or herself into a subject" (Foucault, 1983, p. 208). In what follows, I aim to detect how some discourses shape commercial fitness culture and detect whether these truth games, by disciplining the body, lead to the domination of the self.

To organise my discussion, I distinguish between three ways of knowing about the fit body—the fit body as a healthy body; the fit body as an ideal body; and the fit body as "a mindful" body—that I believe underline current fitness practices. I will locate each one of these into Foucault's concept of the truth game and detail what truth we seek by playing each specific fitness truth game; what disciplinary practices are involved in fitness truth games; and whether, by entering into such fitness truth games, our selves are likely to be dominated through the bodily discipline. I will begin by discussing how health related physical fitness engages us into a truth game.

THE FIT BODY IS THE HEALTHY BODY

The most widely accepted justification for promoting fitness is its health benefits. Therefore, it is possible to treat knowledge regarding health related exercise programs as a type of truth game. In this game, the healthy body becomes the truth to discover and exercise programs the practices to achieve it. Now, the next task is to determine whether this truth game disciplines the body and thus, leads to the domination of the self. To begin this task, it is useful to examine the type of knowledge that defines the link between health and exercise.

One of first researchers to popularise the notion of health related fitness was Dr. Kenneth Cooper in his 1968 book "Aerobics." Cooper, at the time a medical doctor for the United States Air Force, became concerned with men's lack of fitness: Americans had become sedentary and overweight. Consequently, Dr. Cooper believed, the prevalence of heart disease escalated. He set to develop a scientifically based aerobic fitness programme, adjustable based on the exerciser's gender, age, and fitness level, to improve the condition of lungs, cardio-vascular system and the heart. Cooper now leads his own research institute, the Cooper Institute in Texas, devoted to scientific research concerning the health benefits of physical fitness. Cooper's legacy is important: a large proportion of current fitness knowledge focuses on proving the link between the absence of illness and physical activity through scientific research. For example, medical and physiological research has provided strong evidence that improved physical fitness can prevent coronary heart disease and related hypertension (high blood pressure), type II diabetes, some types of cancer, osteoporosis, depression and anxiety (Blair, Brill & Barlow, 1994; Haskell, 1994; Paffenberger, Hyde, Wing, Lee & Kambert, 1994; Pollock, Feigenbaum & Brechue, 1995; Shephard, 1995). This knowledge now dominates the way fitness practices are sold to the consumers and shapes the way scientifically "correct" fitness programmes are prescribed.

While improved health has been used as a powerful motivator to exercise, it is interesting to analyze more closely what is meant by health in scientific research on physical fitness. It seems that often, when referring to health benefits, the scientific research is actually focusing on the ability of physical fitness to prevent illness. As mentioned earlier, increased physical fitness has a proven, strong link with illness prevention. Information from the website of the prestigious and influential President's Council on Physical Fitness and Sport (www.fitness.gov/physical_activity_fact_sheet) can serve as a case in point. In an informative fact sheet titled Physical Activity and Health, the authors emphasize how physical inactivity causes cardiovascular disease, obesity, diabetes both in adults and children and how physical activity can prevent these diseases. They also refer to a report by the U.S. Department of Health and Human Services titled "Physical Activity Fundamental to Preventing Disease" (U.S. Department of Health and Human Services, 2002). This report begins by stating that "Regular physical activity, fitness and exercise are critically important for the health and well being of people of all ages" (p. 1) and then continues to demonstrate how regular physical activity can reduce morbidity and mortality from many chronic diseases. In this way, they advocate that health equals the absence of illness. However, according to the World Health Organization (WHO), this is a limited view of health. The WHO defines health more broadly as a state of complete physical, mental and social well-being (Crawford, 1980). Despite the WHO's view of health, the focus on illness prevention, yet in the name of health, strongly shapes physical fitness practices (Markula, 1997).

In general, scientific research postulates that the better our physical fitness, the better our health is predicted to be. Therefore, it is crucial to continually improve what is labelled as health related physical fitness. This is seen to consist of four components: cardio-vascular fitness, flexibility, muscle strength and endurance, and body composition. Exercises have been designed specifically to improve each of these components of physical fitness. For example, to improve cardio-vascular fitness and body composition, one has to regularly engage in aerobic exercise such as running, walking, cycling or swimming. To improve muscle strength and endurance one should do resistance training and regular stretching improves one's flexibility. In addition, exercise consists of increasing amounts of physical activity and exercise prescriptions are, thus, based on the need for continual improvement in physical fitness. This continual improvement is labelled the training effect. Because one's body gets used to the current exercise load, one needs to regularly "overload:" to increase the amount of exercise to continue gaining a training effect and the subsequent health benefits. It is, therefore, important that the exerciser regularly monitors the exercise amount. To know how exactly to do this, the American College of Sports Medicine (ACSM), for example, publishes guidelines for recommended exercise doses. Following a program that ensures a training effect, or a continual improvement of physical fitness, requires commitment, discipline and continual surveillance of the body for any symptoms of plateau. All of this sounds unmistakably like a disciplinary body practice that leads to the domination of the self. Does seeking an illness free body always produce a disciplined, docile body?

In the health related fitness truth game, like in any truth game, we partly influence the outcome. For example, we can choose in what exact activities we participate, where we exercise, and with whom. However, the overall reason to exercise and the premise of our exercise regime is determined by the discursive construction of health related physical fitness. It is important to emphasise here that, according to Foucault, no knowledge is innately good or bad, but the way it is used can turn it into a discourse: a tool of power in the truth game. Therefore, the scientifically proven link between the absence of illness and physical fitness is not itself discursive. Indeed, it is definitely appropriate to exercise in order not to become ill. However, a singular focus on this exercise benefit can mask other, multiple reasons to be physically active and other, multiple ways of maintaining one's health. I ask now: Why has illness prevention become the dominant fitness discourse? Why haven't researchers focused on a more embodied and holistic notion of health and well being?

In many ways, the governmental web site provides us with a clear answer: taking care of ill people is expensive. Their report states: "A physically inactive population is at both medical and financial risk for many chronic diseases and conditions" (U.S. Department of Health and Human Services, 2002, p. 2). The financial risk is a combination of health care costs and the costs associated with the value of lost wages by people unable to work. For example, in 2000 heart disease cost the United States $183 billion, cancer $157, diabetes $100 and arthritis $65 billion. These are powerful statistics. Obviously preventing disease by exercising will result in substantial monetary savings and is, therefore, an entirely justifiable reason to promote physical fitness programs. While this is an important aspect of illness prevention, Foucault (1973) argued that a singular emphasis on medical benefits places the problem on the individual body. Medicine, he continued, has become a science of the individual: Medical problems are biological and physical manifestations of the individual, diseased human body. Therefore, the cure for these problems calls for individualized treatment, not the reordering of social, political, and environmental circumstances. For example, the focus on economic benefits can result in an extreme focus on an individual's responsibility to become fit and healthy despite societal constraints such as pollution, unhealthy, processed food production, increasing demands of work life, or insufficient child care support that can hamper even the best efforts to stay illness free. Consequently, categorising physical fitness as an individual's responsibility can attribute social problems to individual people. For example, it is very well to campaign for walking, running or cycling, but ignore the fact that most people have to exercise in polluted, traffic infested urban environments without sufficient lighting or safety. Andrew Sparkes (1991) elaborates that while individuals can take some responsibility for their health, "many groups in our society have less freedom of choice than others to pursue a healthy and active lifestyle and that their lives and experiences are structured in such a way as to increase their chances of suffering illness" (p. 214). This means that social causes for ill health might be ignored, if we assume that individuals are solely responsible for their freely made health choices. Richard Crawford (1980) adds that assigning illness prevention purely as an individual's responsibility can lead to victim blaming and moral judgements, because by falling ill we fail to make the required commitment to health. As Crawford explains: "the failure to maintain health is ascribed to some kind of unwillingness to be well or an unconscious desire to be sick, or simply a failure of will" (p. 379). Therefore, individuals are blamed for catching an illness, because they have been, for example, too lazy to maintain a regular exercise program and thus needlessly burden the healthcare system by increasing the public spending on health.

It is no doubt that it is important to stay illness free and that improved physical fitness has an important role in the battle for a "healthier" nation. But does this approach to the body promote the domination of the self? The body is disciplined through a carefully designed, scientific exercise plan and constantly monitored for a continually improved fitness. While the body is an object of control, there is very little concern about other aspects related to exercise, such as enjoyment or the social benefits. Therefore, this way of knowing about fitness focuses on a free willed, responsible self and a body that turns diseased without careful attention and discipline. Instead of a more embodied self, physical fitness seems to contribute to a troubled self. For example, keeping illness free requires continually improving one's fitness level and the exercise regime becomes gradually more demanding. This means hard work and many people fail to maintain regular exercise schedules or do not exercise at all and end up feeling guilty for not measuring up to the requirements of a scientific exercise regime. Indeed, the disciplinary requirements of physical fitness prescription have failed to increase people's physical activity levels. In 1998, for example, almost 40% of American adults remained inactive (U.S. Department of Health and Human Services, 2002), while others go overboard and engage in excessive exercise or exercise compulsively, even when injured.

Such failures to confirm with the bodily discipline hint to a practice that acts as a tool of dominance by imposing an unnecessary bodily discipline based on a rather narrow definition of health. While physical fitness might save in health care costs, there are other factors causing illness that might need even more attention (e.g., the junk food industry and pollution). There are, however, other ways to motivate people to exercise and the commercial fitness industry is well aware of alternative strategies. Their definition of fitness benefits is based on a different premise.

THE FIT BODY AS THE BODY BEAUTIFUL

While governmental web sites and health officials emphasize the need to exercise for an improved physical health, in the popular media—fitness magazines, exercise self help books and exercise videos—understand fitness in a different light.

For example, in its December 2002 issue *Shape*, a popular women's fitness magazine, offers advice on how yoga can beat stress, but also boasts fast results from its "3 moves a day" exercise program that results in flat abs, a better butt and toned arms. In this popular consciousness, the boundaries between health (how to beat stress), beauty (better butt) and fitness (an exercise program consisting of 3 moves a day) are blurred. In addition, we get the impression that beautiful people are also healthy people. The December cover of *Shape* portrays supermodel Christy Turlington who, in revealing exercise clothing, poses in a yoga asana. In popular culture, health ideals and physical beauty ideals have become congruent as health has increasingly become inscribed on body shape (Featherstone, 1991; Spitzack, 1990; White, Young, & Gillette, 1995). In this truth game, where we seek first and foremost a beautiful body, health is not a forgotten goal but rather than being illness free we long to look healthy: when one looks beautiful, one is also healthy. This emphasis on looks has evolved into exercise regimes that target particularly women with a promise of creating a perfect body (e.g., Eskes, Duncan & Miller, 1998; Markula, 1995).

Sandra Bartky (1988) summarises the characteristics of today's feminine body ideal: "The current body of fashion is taut, small-breasted, narrow-hipped, and of a slimness bordering emaciation; it is a silhouette that seems more appropriate to an adolescent boy or a newly pubescent girl than to an adult woman" (p. 64). Because an attractive female body is thin, borderline emaciated, many women who according to the available body composition measures are considered "normal" or underweight diet and exercise to lose weight because they perceive themselves as being fat. In addition, Susan Bordo (1990) observes that it is no longer enough to eliminate excess fat, but healthy bodies, in addition to appearing thin, are to look tightly toned. While muscle tone is an important aspect of the women's body ideal, too much muscle mass is considered repulsive (Markula, 1995). The ideal male body differs somewhat from the feminine ideal. While thinness is a highly valued feature for both genders, the male ideal seems to centre around muscularity and particularly, abdominal and upper body muscularity (White & Gillett, 1994; White, Young, & Gillett, 1995). A myriad of exercise practices exist to shape the body closer to the ideal perfection.

Because a beautiful woman has to possess a thin, toned and young body, the majority of exercises designed to improve women's "body fitness" focus on fulfilling these three requirements. It is not surprising, then, that women exercise to lose weight (Markula, 1995) and our exercise practices have been transformed to maximise weight loss. For example, aerobic exercise was originally designed to improve one's cardio-vascular fitness. However, it also utilises fat as its energy source and is most effective in terms of weight loss. Consequently, it is common that a large part of women's exercise advice is devoted to aerobic exercise: walking, running, swimming or cycling. A typical aerobics class can serve as a case in point:

a majority of the time is spent doing an aerobics routine to burn fat. Women's resistance training ("toning exercises") is designed to improve muscle tone that refers to the looks of the muscle. Therefore, the benefits of resistance training are connected to women's improved appearance rather than improved strength. For example, the fitness industry offers special muscle conditioning classes advertised through catchy names like "New Body" or "ABT" (abs, bums and thighs). These titles clearly indicate that such classes are designed to reshape the body.

In popular literature, men's exercise programs center on improving upper body strength and size through weight training. In addition, exercises such as sit-ups for abdominal definition ("the six pack") feature prominently. Because men's body ideal is also lean to display maximum muscle definition, weight loss exercises, often running or cycling, are an important part of men's fitness programs.

Fitness magazines and videos offer new varieties of exercise in each issue to motivate us to enter into the reshaping game and we will gain visible benefits from physical activity, not only an assurance of an illness free life. Such exercise advice definitely seems more fun than the regimented and rigid health related physical fitness programs. Will these exercise practices lead to a domination of the self?

Through the commercial fitness discourse we are persuaded that it is necessary to spend time reshaping our bodies toward the required ideal, but the process of bodily transformation requires hard work. The body has to be disciplined if we aim to attain the desired results. For example, certain parts of the female body need concentrated attention. Often these parts—abdomen, bum, thighs, and the underarms—are labelled as "the problem spots" and they appear particularly resistant to manipulative toning, albeit they need it the most. Why are these spots so problematic? They appear especially prone to excess fat and flab and indeed, these are the natural fat storage areas for females. At the same time, these are the very parts of our bodies that identify us as females (Bartky, 1988; Bordo, 1993; Markula, 1995). These female parts are also the ones we hate the most and fight the hardest to shape into the current boyish ideal. Logically then, we hate looking like women. To add to the body work, women have to keep their bodies looking young. The aging process exacerbates the problems women have with their bodies. When aging progresses, women have to work incredibly hard to maintain the ideal figure. Particularly, the problem areas seem to get flabbier and more resistant to shaping. But with a well planned, regular exercise program one can obtain results. Aerobics queen Jane Fonda's body demonstrates how effective vigorous exercise can be. She, although over 60, displays the ideal young boyish body. Obviously, developing the feminine look demands increased control and discipline over one's body (Markula, 1995) and the body work has become a tool of dominance of the self as the constant advice for a better body acts as a discourse. The beauty of this arrangement is that we inflict the discipline on ourselves through surveying the defects on our bodies. We learn to monitor any changes in our bodies and consequently, spend considerable time worrying about our body shapes without really pondering why such an ideal is desirable or why we spend so much time on body shaping. To make body work even more justifiable, women's fitness magazines, such as *Shape* and *Self*, sell their exercise advice connected to psychological well being.

The characteristics of healthful beauty have now been expanded to include a psychological dimension: the attractive female body has come to signify a controlled mind and healthy self-confidence (Markula, 1995; 2001). Unattractive women, conversely, lack discipline, have low self-confidence and are, consequently, considered unhealthy (Spitzack, 1990). If women build self-confidence through the aesthetic, thin and toned body, men's self-confidence manifests in a muscular upper body and well defined abdominals.

Men's self-surveillance assumes a different form, because their muscular body ideal derives from a different premise. White and Gillett (1994) point out that upper body muscularity or strong abdominals are of little use for today's male as many men's work involves little physical strength. However, they add, muscles have increasingly important social value for men in today's changing society. Building muscles helps some men to re-define themselves as males in an environment where other opportunities for "traditional" masculinity have become increasingly scarce. These researchers claim that muscles are markers of embodied masculine power: muscles are used as a sign of dominance, control, authority, physical strength, and power.

The fit body seems, then, to embrace principles of holistic well being: fit body results in confident self. Clearly, exercise embodies a promise of bodily transformation. The healthy look is achievable if we actively and continuously work (out) towards it. As it is now possible to change from unhealthy and flabby to active and attractive, health has increasingly become a personal responsibility instead of an inherited destiny. The attractive, healthy body is a visible indicator of one's success to fulfil this responsibility. Following White, Young and Gillett (1995): the body now is a possession to display moral and physical health. Despite this promise, the quest for the body beautiful tends to result in constant self-surveillance and endless body discipline.

It is obvious that most people do not naturally possess the ideal body shape. Even with the strictest "body work" regimens most men and women will never look like the magazine models, because most of us simply do not have the biological make-up for the ideal body. For example, it has been estimated that only 5% of women are born with the right genes for the contemporary slim ideal. Obviously, the rest of us are doomed to fail our body shaping mission. The discrepancy between the ideal body and our own defective bodies has resulted in great body dissatisfaction, particularly among women and in the worst case this dissatisfaction can expand to a body-related psychological disorder. There has been a dramatic escalation of clinical disorders such anorexia nervosa and bulimia nervosa and sub-clinical disorders such as body image distortion, obsessive exercise and compulsive eating (Bordo, 1993; Markula, 2001; Wolf, 1990). In this sense, the emphasis on the body beautiful has created psychological problems rather than psychological well being and self-confidence. Consequently, this kind of body knowledge can be very damaging as it promotes an increased control of the body for a rather dubious cause. This truth game, a search of the perfect body, dominates the self through a needless and never ending body discipline.

It has become obvious that so far fitness knowledge focuses on the condition of the physical body: exercise as a means for producing an illness free body or a beautiful body. These forms of knowledge tend to lead to disciplinary body practices, constant self-surveillance and can be seen to serve as practices that increase the domination of the self. The problems of these fitness approaches— high inactivity rates, body-image disorders, excessive exercise, injury rates—have not gone unnoticed by the fitness industry. New forms of fitness practices with less emphasis on the body shape and discipline have emerged. The integration of mind and body through exercise has become a new fashionable fitness trend.

THE FIT BODY AS THE "MINDFUL" BODY?

When we engage in exercise practices that are designed to integrate the mind with the body into an embodied self, we enter into yet another truth game. We now search for an innate, integrated self dichotomized by our culture. Following Foucault, truth games themselves do not connote domination and therefore, the idea is not to get rid of the fitness truth games but to play it differently. This means that in order to avoid the domination of the self, we need to move away from practices that discipline the body. What kind of fitness regime, instead of promoting disciplinary body practices, aids in a discovery of the embodied self? The so called mindful fitness practices promise to guide us through such a process and have now become increasingly popular in the fitness industry. However, what exactly mindful fitness practices are, is a complex matter. As these classes have become more common in the industry, IDEA (Health and Fitness Association), the biggest association for the fitness industry in the United States, has established a specific mind-body fitness committee to create an industry wide definition for activities that can be offered under the umbrella term mindful fitness. In 1998, it defined mindful exercise as physical exercise executed with a profound, inwardly directed awareness or focus (Monroe, 1998). In addition, mindful exercise should include most of the following components (Monroe, 1998):
    focus on a mental component:
        noncompetitive, non judgemental, process oriented
    focus on proprioceptive awareness:
        low level muscular activity, mental focus on muscle
        and movement sense
    breath centric
        breath the primary centring activity
    focus on anatomical alignment or proper physical form
        particular movement patterns
        spinal alignment
    energy centric
        flow of one's intrinsic energy or vital life force (chi
        or prana)
This definition clearly promises a more integrated approach to physical activity: we move from fitness as a means to other goals such as illness prevention or beauty (product orientation) to a focus on the movement process itself. In mindful exercise, participants concentrate on observing their own movement patterns through proprioceptive awareness (proprioceptors are small organs that sense where the body

or individual body parts are located in space). This process is aided by the focus on breathing, proper bodily alignment and the use of intrinsic energy. In these classes, both mind and body work together to create a holistic sense of self. This definition allows for a number of diverse activities to be classed as mindful fitness. While all of the mindful fitness practices embed such important features as "being present" during the activity, process orientation, slowness, and embracing the activity itself, the most common practices classified as mindful fitness are yoga, Tai Chi and Pilates.

As generally acknowledged, yoga originates from India. While the western notion of yoga has come to mean physical exercise, the ultimate goal of yoga is to seek unity with the divine. Originally this meant an engagement with several different types of practices, only one of them physical. Westerners now practice several different types of physical yoga such as anusara, ashtanga vinuasa (also labelled as power yoga), Yyengar, Bikram, kripaly, and kundalini yoga (Hollingshead, 2002). While these differ in terms of style and execution of the movements, all yoga consists of separate physical postures (asanas) that are carefully executed with precision, slowness, concentration, proper breathing, and relaxation to increase general body control.

Tai Chi is also an "eastern" movement form that is based on the Taoist idea of health being a balance or harmony of the mind and body. Similar to yoga, Tai Chi consists of precisely defined movements, but instead of being executed separately, they flow together in round patterns of resistance against and compliance to force. In Tai Chi, the entire continuous movement pattern is performed standing up (certain yoga asanas take place on the floor) and initiated from the body's center. Therefore, movements (or power) cannot be forced or "muscled" but should be executed with "ease" supported by a relaxed mind. While the movement quality is quite different, yoga and Tai Chi both consist of pre-designed exercise routines which are carefully followed. Both also emphasize an internal focus and awareness during the movement and proper breathing that aids in the concentration. Both are movement practices that derive from "eastern" forms of spiritual and religious knowledge. However, these forms have changed with time and context and are often adapted to "western" cultural needs. For example, there are several variations of yoga that are modified to the safety precautions required in the American fitness industry. They have become what Edward Bruner (1996) labels as transplanted traditions and often aim to combine the best of both worlds: the western scientific knowledge with the eastern spirituality. However, a western movement form that derives from the eastern tradition, but without a religious connection, is Pilates.

Pilates is a movement form created by Joseph Pilates in the United States in the late 1920s (Gallagher & Kryzanowska, 1999). Originally, he titled his exercise program as "Contrology: The science and art of coordinated body-mind-spirit development through natural movements under strict control of the will" (Gallagher & Kryzanowska, 1999, p.11). From the eastern tradition Pilates assumed the idea of calmness, the importance of the body's center (that he titled "the Powerhouse") and the idea of limberness of the entire body. From the western tradition, he included strength training and developed a set of exercises to be performed on the floor or with different equipment he designed. Like yoga and Tai Chi, Pilates movements are performed with concentration, control, precision, slowness, proper breathing and relaxation. The goal of the exercise routine is to train the mind to master the body and thus increase self-confidence and courage.

In addition to yoga, Tai Chi and Pilates there are a number of hybrid or incorporated mind-body forms. For example, Ralph La Forge (1998) estimates that there are about 1700 mind-body exercise forms offered in the United States. A hybrid form can consist of a combination of two or more mindful fitness forms, such as yogalates that includes moves from yoga and Pilates. Hybrid forms are also born when mindful exercise components—attention to the movement process, correct physical form and focus on breathing—are added to other exercise forms. Step aerobics can turn into mind-body step, toning class to yoga sculpt, and aerobics to yogaerobics. While such classes can ride on the hype of mindful fitness fashion, they also potentially transform the focus on body discipline to an embodied activity where an integrated self is discovered in a physical activity. These classes can offer, then, a radical break from the previous never ending truth games of physical fitness in the name of health or the perfect body. While this premise sounds wonderful and in no doubt, many instructors who follow the principles of mindful fitness can create new experiences for their participants, has the fitness discourse changed with the emergence of mindful exercise? Have we finally stepped into a fitness truth game that can turn exercisers into subjects?

To analyze the impact of the mindful fitness truth game on the self, it is important to consider, again, how this type of fitness knowledge is used. This task is complicated by the notion of "eastern spirituality" and further by what is made of this concept in the western fitness context. As a westerner reading western fitness texts on yoga and Tai Chi, it is not immediately obvious that "eastern spirituality" refers to what we mean by mind-body integration. It seems rather that they advocate a control of the mind that is achieved when the body is controlled (Tai Chi) or evolution of the soul freed from the mind and the body (yoga). Pilates promotes a similar principle: exercises (and the body) are to be performed under strict control of the will. Apparently, the promise of the mindful fitness truth game is a strong, confident and controlled self; a notion not dissimilar to the idea that within each ugly, fat body a confident beauty is screaming to be let out—it only requires body discipline and hard work. Does the mindful fitness truth game dominate the self or create subjects of its participants? Is creating a controlled, willed self creating a subject that uses his or her power in the truth game, not only submit to the dominance of discursive construction of the self? I assume that it can be and it is definitely positive to focus on one's moving self in the mindful fitness classes, relax and concentrate, but that by itself is not creating a subject or reversing the dominance if we still buy into the discursive logic of the self. In addition to the problematic meaning of the integrated self, the western fitness texts are unable to disconnect mindful fitness from the fitness discourses of illness prevention and "body beautiful."

The link between physical activity and health is so central to the fitness industry that mindful fitness activities are also justified by their ability to improve health. However, the definition of health is now expanded. For example, Mary Monroe (1994) defines health as "physical, mental, emotional and spiritual—true health of each client may be a blend of all four" (p. 35). Knowledge on the physical body is no longer sufficient when we talk about health, rather health is a relationship between mind and body. Consequently, Monroe draws a parallel between mindful fitness and alternative medicine united with their focus on preventative practice: "We are not in the business of exercise. We are in the business of preventive medicine" (p. 37). Mind-body exercise potentially prevents or cures diseases connected to the mind (psychosomatic conditions), for example: stress, anxiety, depression, fatigue, eating disorders, substance abuse problems, cardiac rehabilitation, hypertension, blood lipid disorders, coronary disease, insulin resistance, immune system deficiencies, gastrointestinal disorders, accident prevention, and chronic pain. Despite a call for a broader understanding of health, mindful fitness, like the health related physical fitness, becomes a means for illness prevention. La Forge (1994) looks for more scientific research to a clearly established the link between illness prevention and mindful fitness exercise:

> Despite all the interest in and apparent benefits of mind-body exercise there is a lack of peer-reviewed, controlled research trials investigating its effects on physiology, behavior and health. Most existing research on mind-body exercise is statistically underpowered and/or lack valid comparison with research on more popular exercise programs. (p. 58)

Therefore, there is a similar need for an acceptance from the medical community that underlined the discourse of illness prevention and physical activity in general. In this sense, mindful exercise forms need the same verification from the bioscientific knowledge as other exercise forms to be taken seriously. As bioscientific knowledge tends to objectify the body to the gazing researcher, to seek for this link seems to disconnect mindful fitness from its embodied roots. Apparently, science and medicine are such strong discourses in our society that it is impossible to exist without their acknowledgement. It is more beneficial to align mindful exercise with these discourses than challenge the premise of medical knowledge as disembodied and unsuitable to judge the benefits of mind-body forms. Obviously, it is also crucial to the American fitness industry to be closely allied with the medical establishment to create a firm connection with insurance companies. By advertising its medically proven capacity to prevent illness, similar to alternative medicine, some of the health insurance money will be directed to the fitness industry as clients now can get their exercise classes reimbursed by their insurance companies. Therefore, the mindful fitness industry operates within the same discursive climate as the rest of the fitness industry: the medical discourse underlines the mindful fitness knowledge in the professional literature, but the popular literature has, as usual, taken a slightly different approach.

I discussed earlier how the popular knowledge defined exercise as a body shaper. It is now well publicized that celebrities such as Madonna or Christy Turlington are yoga devotees and the former Spice Girl, Geri Halliwell, has her own yoga video series. In the popular media, the mindful fitness forms operate in the same truth with the perfect body. I take two examples to illustrate how this game is played.

The first example is *Shape's* (2002) feature on Christy Turlington that introduces four of her favorite yoga poses. These poses, titled Unity, Openness, Grace and Harmony, are performed by the supermodel herself in revealing tight top and short "hot pants." The focus is mostly on improving flexibility and the article appears, thus, as a radical break from the usual exercise programs that target the "problem spots" (abs, bottoms and thighs). In addition, Turlington explains how yoga has unlocked her potential in life by helping her to overcome obstacles and by providing a way to relax, to de-stress, and to appreciate her body. It is a journey for self-discovery. The article, therefore, seems truthfully presenting the premise of mindful exercise. Simultaneously, however, Christy Turlington's perfect body promises that the uncomfortable looking yoga poses will produce a body like hers. In short, this feature "will help you achieve your own strength, balance and beauty—inside and out" (Latona & Shelton, 2002, p. 126). Therefore, while subtle, the message of body beautiful is still intertwined with the mindfulness of yoga in this article.

The second example is a *Men's Fitness* (November, 2001) feature on Pilates that provides men with strength, endurance, and flexibility. Pilates, according to the author, helps develop a strong mind-body connection by engaging a whole body and emphasizing the correct movement technique. These characteristics strongly establish Pilates as a mindful fitness form, something different from "your typical strength work out" (Fitzgerald, 2001, p. 102). However, the article focuses on very selected examples of Pilates vocabulary all designed to increase abdominal strength. In addition, the model displays very well developed, bare upper arms epitomizing the ideal male body.

While the message is subtle we still aim for that perfect body, but instead of toning exercises and aerobics, the readers are told to perform Pilates and yoga to obtain that sexy, perfect body. We still feel good only if we look good.

CONCLUSION

It is evident that the body can take several meanings when we engage in fitness truth games. While we seek different truths—health, beauty or an integrated self—through different fitness practices, it appears that we tend to turn into docile bodies in this endless quest for finding such truths; fitness knowledge easily turns into a discourse that dominates the self. What do we learn from this potentially depressing conclusion? What can this mean for educators?

First, we have to keep in mind that knowledge about the body is not necessarily embodied and the engagement in bodily practices or promotion of bodily practices does not alone guarantee the construction of an embodied subjectivity. On the contrary, the body is often disciplined to objectify the self under discursive construction. At the same time, this does not mean that all fitness practices are oppressive and all fitness instructors teach "bad" things. In the world of fitness, there are many good experts and many excellent ways to exercise, but it is crucial to be able to recognize such practitioners and practices. It is equally important to recognize that fitness, like other body related techniques, is indeed based on knowledge. What I mean by this is that too often fitness, as a bodily practice, is considered something anyone can do—no knowledge at all! Illustrative of this assumption is that many prominent fitness "experts" are celebrities that "look the part" but possess no fitness related knowledge or movement competency. Similar to fitness, Spitzack (1990) observes that another body related concern, obesity, is treated with a careless attitude: "Although most Americans would not solicit the aid of a movie star or a businessperson to correct a kidney malfunction, cures for obesity are often readily marketed and consumed, with little concern for expertise by consumer or governmental agencies" (p. 9). As demonstrated, fitness knowledge, like any knowledge, engages humans into truth games that are a part of the discursive construction of power and fitness has to be taken seriously if we long to create embodied subjects instead of docile bodies.

Second, because fitness knowledge so easily turns into disciplinary practices, it is absolutely pertinent that educators themselves become critical consumers of fitness knowledge. The trick is to consider what fitness practices and what kind of instruction will, instead of objectifying the body, allow for embodied subjectivity. The only way to do this is to know about fitness and critically analyze the bodily knowledge around us. How we turn into such critical consumers is, of course, difficult to establish. Fitness instructors, perhaps, need to provide "better" information about their practices and the fitness instructor education, instead of merely focusing on the physical aspects of fitness, should also include critical social and pedagogical analysis. A very difficult task is to change the way popular media promotes fitness and consequently, shapes the consumers' knowledge. At the moment, at least, we can aim for critical readings of their messages by analyzing the knowledge base of provided fitness information.

Finally, it is important to consider what kind of bodily knowledges we promote through educational practices. Do we, unquestioningly, advise students, friends or colleagues to lose weight and exercise in the name of a disease free existence? Do we suggest that girls go to aerobics and boys lift weights to look good? Do we tell students to exercise because, once they look better, they also feel better? What kind of fitness practices do we teach? Toning for trouble spots? Yoga for flexibility and long, lean muscles? If we draw others to fitness truth games that we unquestioningly accept, we will only produce more docile bodies, not holistic human beings. Only by knowing the premise for our practices, are we able to instruct others to take part in positive fitness.

Obviously, fitness knowledge can be read in multiple ways to produce multiple practices. It is also evident that bodily knowledge in itself is not embodied, but knowing our bodies can create a more holistic self understanding. However, it is necessary to critically read fitness information to engage in an embodied fitness practice.

REFERENCES

Bartky, S. (1988). Foucault, femininity, and the modernization of patriarchal power. In I. Diamond & L. Quinby (Eds.), *Feminism & Foucault: Reflections on resistance* (pp. 61–86). Boston: Northeastern University Press.

Blair, S. N., Brill, P.A., & Barlow, C. E. (1994). Physical activity and disease prevention. In H. A. Quinney, L. Gauvin, & A.E.T. Wall (Eds.), *Toward active living* (pp. 25–31). Champaign, IL: Human Kinetics.

Bordo, S. (1993). *Unbearable weight: Feminism, western culture, and the body.* Berkley & Los Angeles: University of California Press.

Bruner, E. (1996). My life in an Ashram. *Qualitative Inquiry, 2,* 300–319.

Cooper, K. (1968). *Aerobics.* New York: Simon & Schuster.

Crawford, R. (1980). Healthism and the medicalization of everyday life. *International Journal of Health Services, 10*(3), 365–388.

Eskes, T. B., Duncan, M. C., & Miller, E. M. (1998). The discourse of empowerment: Foucault, Marcuse, and women's fitness texts. *Journal of Sport & Social Issues, 22*, 317–344.

Featherstone, M. (1991). The body in consumer culture. In M. Featherstone, M. Hepworth, & B. S. Turner (Eds.), *The body: Social processes and cultural theory* (pp. 170–196). London: Sage.

Fitzgerald, M. (2001, November). Strength, endurance, flexibility: A Pilates home workout will leave you with all three. *Men's Fitness*, 102–104.

Foucault, M. (1973). *The birth of the clinic: An archaeology of medical perception.* New York: Pantheon.

Foucault, M. (1983). Afterword: The subject and power. In H. L. Dreyfus & P. Rabinow (Eds.), *Michel Foucault: Beyond structuralism and hermeneutics* (pp. 208–252). Chicago: The University of Chicago Press.

Foucault, M. (1988). The ethic of care for the self as a practice of freedom: An interview with Michel Foucault. In J. Bernauer & D. Rasmussen (Eds.), *The final Foucault* (pp. 1–20). Cambridge, MA: The MIT Press.

Frank, A. W. (1991). For a sociology of the body: An analytical review. In M. Featherstone, M. Hepworth, & B. S. Turner (Eds.), *The body: Social processes and cultural theory* (pp. 36–102). London: Sage.

Gallgher, S. P., & Kryzanowka, R. (1999). *The Pilates method of body conditioning.* Philadephia: BainBridgeBook

Haskell, W. L. (1994). Physical/physiological/biological outcomes of physical activity. In H. A. Quinney, L. Gauvin, & A. E. T. Wall (Eds.), *Toward active living* (pp. 17–23). Champaign, IL: Human Kinetics.

Hollingshead, S. (2002, April). Yoga for sports performance. *IDEA Health & Fitness Source, 20,* 30–39.

La Forge, R. (1998, July/August). Research case for mindful exercise grows. *IDEA Health & Fitness Source, 16,* 40.

La Forge, R. (1994, June/July). The science of mind-body fitness. *IDEA Today, 12,* 57–65.

Latona, V., & Shelton, L. (2002, December). Christy Turlington's top yoga moves to beat stress. *Shape, 22,* 126–131.

Markula, P. (2001). Beyond the perfect body: Women's body image distortion in fitness magazine discourse. *Journal of Sport & Social Issues, 25,* 158–179.

Markula, P. (1997). Are fit people healthy? Health, exercise, active living and the body in fitness discourse. *Waikato Journal of Education, 3,* 21–40.

Markula, P. (1995). Firm but shapely, fit but sexy, strong but thin: The postmodern aerobicizing female bodies. *Sociology of Sport Journal, 12,* 424–452.

Monroe, M. (1998, July/August). Mind-body fitness goes mainstream. *IDEA Health & Fitness Source, 16,* 34–44.

Monroe, M. (1994, June/July). Seeing our clients in a whole new way. *IDEA Today, 12,* 35–42.

Paffenberger, R. S., Hyde, R. T., Wing, A. L., Lee, I-M., & Kambert, J. B. (1994). An active and fit way-of-life influencing health and longevity. In H. A. Quinney, L. Gauvin, & A. E. T. Wall (Eds.), *Toward active living* (pp. 61–68). Champaign, IL: Human Kinetics.

Physical activity fact sheet. Retrieved October 9, 2002, from *www.fitness.gov/physical_activity_fact_sheet.html.*

Pollock, M. L., Feigenbaum, M. S., & Brechue, W. F. (1995). Exercises prescription for physical fitness. *Quest, 47,* 320–337.

Shephard, R. J. (1995). Physical activity, fitness, and health: The current consensus. *Quest, 47,* 288–303.

Sparkes, A. C. (1991). Alternative visions of health-related fitness: An exploration of problem-setting and its consequences. In N. Armstrong & A. C. Sparkes (Eds.), *Issues in Physical Education* (pp. 204–277). London: Cassell Education.

Spitzack, C. (1990). *Confessing excess: Women and the politics of body reduction.* Albany, NY: State University of New York Press.

U.S. Department of Health and Human Services (2002). Physical activity fundamental to preventing disease. Retrieved June 20, 2002, from *http://aspe.hhs.gov/health/reports/physicalactivity*

Weedon, C. (1987). *Feminist practice & poststructuralist theory.* Oxford, UK: Basil Blackwell.

White, P. C., & Gillett, J. (1994). Reading the muscular body: A critical decoding of advertisements in *Flex* magazine. *Sociology of Sport Journal, 11,* 18–39.

White, P. C., Young, K., & Gillett, J. (1995). Bodyworks as a moral imperative: Some critical notes on health and fitness. *Society and Leisure, 18*(1), 159–182.

Wolf, N. (1990). *The beauty myth.* London: Vintage.

Minette Mans

THE CHANGING BODY IN SOUTHERN AFRICA—
A PERSPECTIVE FROM ETHNOMUSICOLOGY

INTRODUCTION

Societies in southern African countries are increasingly burdened by crime and poverty, the uneasy aftermath of colonialism and apartheid, and growing neocolonialism. In the recent past racism in its strongest form was consolidated in apartheid policies, but permeated local societies in many more subtle forms, such as the missionary introduction of a form of Christianity in which God was partial to the white race. As a result, people live in racialized spaces occupied by racialized subjects (Elder, n.d.), both being embodied in their art, dance and music. "Race lives in the house of music because music is so saturated with racial stuff…" (Radano & Bohlman, 2000, p. 1). Notions of race, self perception and perception of "other" are closely linked, and are inextricably tied to the value system of the perceiver. Changes in any one of these will affect the others.

This essay sets out to (re-)address our understandings about the ways in which societies, histories and personal experiences are embodied in southern Africa, looking at changes occurring and how arts education may be involved. To begin, I ask: whose body are we looking at, and in which circumstances? Using dance in Africa as a means to understand body perceptions and images, I address some of the existing societal subtexts. Through dance I shall look mainly at feminine bodies in urban and rural, past and present circumstances. The discussion is initially placed within the generalized African context, investigating ideas, pre- and misconceptions surrounding "the African body," particularly the dancing body.

Within contemporary transitional societies of southern Africa, value systems are said to be rapidly eroding. How does this impact on society and how are these changes embodied? Specifically, how do women embody modernity, race, gender and beauty and how is this translated into dance? As arts education should be informed by reality, these matters should be investigated. Learning, especially arts learning, is often a corporeal learning—feeling, touching, sensing, experiencing. In Africa this corporeal learning, in dance, drumming, work and general demeanor, has traditionally been of great importance. In this chapter this form of learning is explored.

The idea of an African Renaissance brings the reality of transcultural and transnational education into play. Attempts to marry custom with development cannot ignore deeply embedded notions of race, ethnicity, power and class. I argue that contemporary southern African education (formal and informal) is transmitting

77

cultural memories in rapidly changing ways. The changes affect deeply held traditional values. Do arts curricula and the body concept embraced by schools inculcate traditional (African) values or contemporary African values? Are the issues surrounding racialized bodies addressed, so that the way may be paved for reconstruction and reconciliation to be embodied within education? Such fundamental issues cannot merely be rationalized intellectually. They need to be felt, sensed and experienced as learners do.

The research guiding this essay arises from my ethnomusicological and choreological field research of the past decade in Namibia.[1] This data is enhanced with contemporary urban views, emerging from a questionnaire given to a small sample of female students, service workers and lecturers at the University of Namibia, completed anonymously. Clearly this sample is not representative of the whole population, nor indeed the African continent, although respondents represent different ethnicities and regions in and around Namibia. The survey sought to provide a certain perspective that might not emerge from my ethnographic fieldwork. Questions were asked about body images, perceptions, their own dance experiences and how they perceived those of their mothers. Individual personal perceptions emerged quite clearly from the responses. Drawing together these responses with those of the mainly traditionalist rural groups encountered in my fieldwork, I hope to find a nexus of values that can inform arts education programmes.

A perspective from ethnomusicology poses a potential problem. The entire arena of anthropology has been subjected to suspicion and serious criticism, questioning field research in the light of political and social motivations and effects. The very nature of ethnomusicology is based on explorations of "otherness," and hence might be construed as an effort to continue to racialize the world. However, my arguments and interpretations should be seen as a projection of my experience of continuity and change in body knowledge, experience and perception in recent times. Remembering that every act of interpretation is implicated in the background of cultural practices which have formed the interpreter, what follows is informed by my own mixed cultural perspective. Interpretations and generalizations are always bound by processes of self-understanding and my interpretations are of themselves a form of cultural activity. Many of these are explicitly personal thoughts and intuitions formed and informed by my research and life in different southern African regions.

Secondly, there is a danger of dichotomizing information—expressing information in terms of rural/urban, traditional/modern, or African/Western dichotomies. In my text I have tried to avoid extremes of this kind, yet these myths of tradition[2] are firmly entrenched in local discourse. The discussion should not be read as a firm division between then and now, nor between tradition and change, but as a viewpoint upon a constantly evolving system of small adjustments and readjustments taking place on a relatively large scale. I do not want to reconstruct racialized imagery, but wish to convey an impression of the ways contemporary Africa expresses and experiences itself. This text therefore needs to be read as an individual's impression of a transitional society.

VISIONS OF BODY

To begin, the body is sketched from an African point of view, relating it to customs and values, because bodies in performance always enfold and reveal diverse histories of gender, social status, kinship, ethnicity and power as well as the bodily experience. Dance foregrounds cultural memory as "embodied practice by virtue of its predominantly somatic modes of transmission" (Buckland, 2001, p. 1).

I discard the dated image of "the African as noble savage," the paternalistic attitude of "reaching out to help the poor Africans," and the "real Africa." This is a vast continent of diverse, mixed and transient societies. "The African body" and "African dance" are in many ways idealized, romanticized and politicized constructs.[3] Indeed, the notion of "the African race" is an invention that is politically disabling and flawed. Given the understanding that we are dealing with myths, I am nevertheless compelled to use certain flawed terms for purposes of brevity.

The tendency to idealize the sensory and ideological filters through which we perceive the body and its relations is especially pertinent in terms of the cultural hegemonies that predominated in colonial times. Literature abounds with descriptions of the African body. "The image of Africans created by missionaries around the turn of the century, was not one single image, but consisted of a collage with the polarities of Light/Darkness, Christian/Heathen." (Mellemsether, 2001, p. 193). The physical strength, adroitness, beauty and "peculiarities"[4] of African bodies have long been deliberated by colonial adventurers, scientists, missionaries, and slave owners, as well as African artists[5] and scholars. The former perspective is evidenced in hundreds of photographic and "scientific" studies of nude and semi-nude black figures. Even as far back as the late 19th century black female figures in Namibia were portrayed in pornographic pictures (cf. Mail & Guardian, 1998). A polarity is often created between "dressed" white and "undressed" black bodies. In contemporary Sweden, at the 2002 Polar Music Prize-giving, Miriam Makeba's prize was celebrated, appropriately enough, by African drummers. They performed, however, in gleaming bare torsos, backed up by a symphony orchestra and audience (including the King of Sweden) dressed in furs and tuxedos. Larkin (1999, p. 2) describes how nineteenth and early twentieth century images of black women (cf. the infamous Baartman images) "were exotic shots of African women in tribal attire or were of slaves working in the fields or taking care of white children and babies." This image of the black woman as nanny or laborer indicates lack of self determination in the creation of the imagery. Clearly, the body is a site where social hegemonies are constructed, evaded or resisted.

Traditionalists describe the dancing body in Africa as a worshipping and worshipped body. It is a medium that embodies experiences of life, pleasure, enjoyment, and sensuality.

> The body of the African dancer overflows with joy and vitality, it trembles, vibrates, radiates, it is charged with emotions. Whatever the physical aspect of the dancer—thick or enormous, round or svelte, weak or muscled, large or small—as soon as his emotions are not repressed and stifled, as soon as the rational does not impose itself on him but accepts a collaboration with the irrational which is the true language of the body, the body becomes joyous, attractive, vigorous and magnetic. (Tiérou, 1992, p. 13)

This author-dancer clearly worships the dancing body as a fundamental part of an African culture.

PURPOSE, MEANING AND VALUE OF DANCE IN AFRICA

Despite the arrogance that mistakenly perceives this huge, diverse and constantly changing continent as a unified singularity, there is a certain pervading sense of "Africanness"[6] based on the "imagined community" of race and common aspects of history[7]. Within this murky mythical parkland studded with its political and ethnic traps, I shall describe some of the shared values and notions of African dance. My intention is to draw from that an understanding of changes in contemporary postmodern society.

The dancing body functions as a culturally mediated materiality. It embodies a display of the tensions and contradictions in society and its power structures, of history and the painful story of race. Through dance, history and heritage are carried across time. Given the understanding that the traditions and values that underpin dance are constantly in a state of change, the following general points might guide us against the backdrop of custom and tradition.

1. In the first place, the Cartesian dualism of mind versus, and controlling, body has never been an African understanding. Here in Africa mind and body are traditionally conceived as one and the same. One knows life through one's body. Life is embodied—felt and experienced ("erlebt") in all its sensory levels, and learning is situated in physical experience, not dissociated intellectual pursuits. Hence, the body and its ability to move in meaningful ways is more than just a vision of physicality. On a continent where dance has always been serious business, the body is a symbol and physical representation of value systems (Asante, 1996) and dance grew out of important societal needs. "The peculiarity of the African tradition (sic) is that it … gives primary importance to the body, the necessary intermediary without which spiritual life would be an abstraction." (Tiérou, 1992, p. 12). Whether this holds true for contemporary urban Africa remains to be seen.

2. The body individual and the body social are interwoven and mutually dependent. Hence, the embodiment of personal and social normative and aesthetic values can be seen in dance, dress, bodily shape, weight and tempo. These values form part of the ongoing and sustained construction of a society. "We cannot understand culture without reference to subjective meaning, and we cannot understand it without reference to social structure constraints" (Alexander quoted by Granqvist 1993, p. 5). The subjective meaning attached to a body and its movement within a particular society involves, for example, the temporal modality of dance and everyday movements, also the ways in which people (re)-create their own bodies over time and assess them in terms of beauty and appropriateness. Elder quotes Elizabeth Grosz who says:

> The body is a pliable entity whose determinate form is provided not simply by biology but through the interaction of modes of psychical and physical inscription and the provision of a set of limiting biological codes. [It is the human body's] capacity to open itself up to prosthetic synthesis, to transform or rewrite its environment, to continually augment its

powers and capacities through the incorporation into the body's own spaces and modalities of objects that, while external, are internalized, added to, supplementing and supplemented by the "organic body" that represents always the most blatant cultural anxieties and projections. (Elder, n.d., p. 10)

Consider the cultural anxiety exhibited through the role model bodies of middle-aged pop stars in North America, who blatantly reconstruct themselves to project a state of permanent slenderness and youth (cf. Cher, Whitney Houston or Madonna). Contrast this with singers such as Miriam Makeba, Oumou Sangare, or Sibongile Khumalo who embody the "traditional image" of African beauty and feminity. Which of these is the body that young African girls aspire to?

Notions of feminine beauty relate to female roles in society. Udegbe, in a recent research on sculptural art in Ibadan, found that artists continue to represent females as symbols of fertility, beauty and subservience (Udegbe, 2001, p. 142). Commonly, people in Africa prize a long neck with natural folds that create rings around it. Breasts are thought to be beautiful when rounded and full, but long drooping breasts "that begin to drink the cup of contentment" signify motherhood and are therefore respected. A rounded abdomen is well fed—whether in a child, woman or man. A flat stomach is "gutless." Legs should be shapely but not thin, and high, well-rounded buttocks are another sign of beauty. This is exemplified in popular African clothing designs that have become "traditional," where shoulders, hips and buttocks are exaggerated by folds and peaks created with the bold textiles. Custom dictates that curves and roundness are benchmarks of female beauty.

In Wodaabe culture in the Niger, where beauty and charm are of fundamental importance for men and women, the ideal young girl is not too tall, not too dark skinned, slender but "round," with big beautiful eyes and thick, long braided hair. Grace of movement in dance and when serving men is highly prized (Bovin, 2001, pp. 29-30). Male beauty is even more important. The three things that "make" a (male) Bodaado are movement in space with animals, following the Fulani moral codes, and dance—being beautiful and social (ibid., p. 70). Mette Bovin eloquently describes the importance of beauty and dance in Wodaabe culture, leading her to believe that in this society physical beauty represents order and the cosmos, while ugliness represents disorder and dirt. Women, because of menstruation, can never be as completely pure and beautiful as men can (ibid., p. 60). Aesthetics and dance are thus intimately woven into the entire cosmology.

The female body is objectified, romanticized and eroticized in terms its movement and rhythm—the walk, the bounce and sway—mainly by African men. This was memorably celebrated in a hit song by Jackson Kauyeua called "!Nubu !uwus" describing the sexy way the beautiful round buttocks of a girl move when she dances. This can be interpreted as a patriarchal image, where man looks with desire upon the "tasty" female shape and body,[8] but does it express feminine aesthetics as well? Do men consciously preserve this image as a means of confirming a woman's sexually empowered but socially disempowered position?

Many a traditionalist African man admires beautiful, heavy, dark-skinned women who have large, high buttocks, strong thighs and who move with a slow dignity and a certain heaviness. According to Okumu,[9] for example, a heavy woman is beautiful because she symbolizes womanhood and motherhood. The slow movement tempo is equated with social expectations, and seen from a male patriarchal perspective, the mature woman should project the image of wife and mother, not independence or "wildness." It is therefore not so strange that stories convey the idea that beauty is not necessarily equated with virtue. For example, in

In the picture left, Tjimbambi performs her customary daily chore of milking. She is an embodiment of traditional femininity and beauty. (Photo: M. Mans, 1999)

Previously very slim, young married women (twenty-somethings) in a rural community (M. Mans, 2000)

Somali folk tales (Hanghe, 1988) the cannibalistic Dhegdheer was initially a beautiful, shapely young girl, obedient, patient, clever and popular. However, difficult circumstances (a bad husband and/or drought) turn her into a (independent) cannibal who is tall and fat, but fast with red eyes and one long ear. These stories might be interpreted as a statement that an African woman who claims her own space and time, challenging the stereotype, must be "bad" (cannibalistic) and to be avoided.

The body social is revealed in the symbolisms of dance. The symbols of a society "reflect in a profound way something of the essence of the people who form the society" (Swantz, 1986, p. 50). Hence the importance of cattle symbols in Namibian dances. Dances are commonly genderized in terms of category, modality, aesthetics, symbols and icons. All convey messages which embody the most fundamental societal values relating to gender roles and stereotypes. For example, a woman's child-bearing potential, her role as reconciler, care-giver and binder of families is portrayed in movement components and gestures. This symbolism crystallizes in these wedding beer pots given to a bride in Ongali (see picture below). As Martin Stokes so powerfully states:

> Since gender is a symbol of social and political order, and the control of gender behaviour is a means of controlling that order, gender boundaries cannot be separated from other social and political boundaries. Gender boundaries articulate the most deeply entrenched forms of domination which provide basic metaphors for others, and thus constitute the most intensely "naturalised" of all our boundary making activities. (Stokes, 1994, p. 5)

Symbols are embedded within the formalized movements of dance and correspond with aspects of social reality, which is why dance is inclusive of so many forms. To understand the personal and social meanings of dance requires insight into value-laden symbols. An example is the body as procreative vessel, often symbolised in the drum or female mortar and male pestle (Tiérou, 1992). African dances can vary from an emphasis on beauty and grace to harsh, strong and threatening actions; from extreme athletic actions of great range to tiny and powerful repetitions of vibrations; from forms that are formalized expressive movement but cannot be called dance, to "pure" forms of classical dance, and to dance as social entertainment and recreation. In dance the body individual is a reflection and confirmation of the body social.

Society's levels and expressions of (or lack of) power and class structures are further revealed in play. The order in which one may take a turn to dance, who may play certain instruments, where the dancer's gaze directed, all indicate status (social or age class) of the dancer. In this way, dance constructs, supports and reflects levels of power. Within the dance therefore, individuals in society with its structures and cultural manifestations are embodied and enacted in many ways—conscious and subconscious.

The bride's beerpots at a wedding in Ongali. (Photo: M. Mans, 2001)

3. Thirdly, dance and its music provide a crucial connection to Life Force and energy. This is what makes dance such a fundamental philosophical and aesthetic factor in most traditional African cosmologies and why dance has permeated most religious practices, even that of Christianity. In dance the physical body has traditionally been meaningfully employed with a strong ritual and spiritual character and has been a major tool in shaping and responding to prevailing cultural systems. Therefore dance is often an embodiment of praise, spirituality, and rejoicing worship as a journey from the "known pre-liminal state of earthliness to the unknown liminal state of spiritual non-physicality and back to a spiritually enriched earthliness" (Ajayi, 1996, p. 187). Alphonse Tiérou describes the body–spirit–worship interrelationships as follows:

- The strength of the African tradition is that it draws its resources from the universe and not from the narrow cult of reason.
- To dance in the African manner is to recognize that man is inseparable from the universe and that he is fundamentally a divine spark.
- It is the desire to know one's body, to live in the body, to obey it and its natural experiences, in full awareness, without recourse to drugs.
- It is also to have the courage to respect laws which are not always those of logic, the irrational being one of the privileged languages of the body.
- It is also to have the courage of accepting pleasure. In African dance, relationships are automatically charged with new meanings (Tiérou, 1992, p. 12).

The idea of vital force is fundamental to much Bantu[10] ontology. Dance informs the very concept of existence and the body can be seen as a spiritual home and force (Dagan, 1997; Asante, 1996; Ajayi, 1996; Blacking, 1985). Societies construct their concept of existence in the form of rituals as symbolic understandings of reality. Spirituality can and often should[11] be achieved through dance. It is through song and dance that San communities created the environment for their shamans to travel between spiritual and material realms.[12] In modern Africa many forms of spiritual dance have been replaced by recreational or entertainment dances.[13] Yet, while the employment of body to acknowledge and reiterate spiritual values has not yet declined in Namibia and Botswana's Ju/'hoan and !Kung healing dances in which the ritual body is totally submitted to the trance, the majority of spiritual dances have declined sharply in recent times.

4. Elders and ancestors in traditional African cultures hold a position of respect. Elders, even those who passed on to the spirit world, were considered sources of wisdom and experience. It therefore follows that in traditional society becoming older would be something one gladly anticipates. As an older person one is treated with respect, many chores are taken out of one's hands, and one has a certain measure of power within the family, community and society. In return, one is expected to behave circumspectly and with dignity. The value of age is clearly embodied in the slowed tempo of mature African women (even modern professional African women). They convey a sense of gravitas in their accumulation of weight as substance. Their connection to the energy of Life Force through dance remains important, but the interpretation becomes one in which the status of age is confirmed. A mature woman's dance movements may retain aspects of ephemeral[14] but within the frame of coolness and control. Small shoulder shrugs, subtle pelvic or buttock contractions, smaller amplitude of foot-to-ground actions performed with precision and style indicate this sought after coolness and exemplify age status.

5. The value attached to the wisdom and sagacity of elders leads us to a more comprehensive value—that of continuity. Continuation of the life-cycle is concretized in the importance of family. The larger familial linkages are formalized in (clan) systems, where age groups and lineages are tied together in complex vertical and horizontal matrixes. Implicated in clan systems are also various power structures and hegemonies. All of the above form a complex system in which societies and their philosophies are inextricably intertwined.[15] This system finds bodily form in dance. Thus the affinity between dance and ritual has facilitated the embodiment of traditional values such as fruitfulness (large families, good crops, good herds); society (communitas, sharing, synergy) and politics (class, gender, lineage and age hierarchies).

African cultures have long been said to value fertility—in crops, herds and families. Underlying much of the non-African discourse is the idea that Africans have an innate sense of and response to sex and rhythm, but have discarded reason. "Body, rhythm, race and sex are closely tied together in the romantic way of defining African culture as the body, the 'Other' of the bourgeois mind" (Brusila, 2001, p. 152). This implied negative relation between innate rhythm, sex and reason denigrates Africans. There is, however, truth in the value traditionally placed upon fruitfulness. Even in modern times large families are the norm and additional children almost always welcomed. Through children an unbroken line is maintained from birth through life and death to the spirit world. And dance is a means of symbolizing and securing potential continuation of life in all its phases. In traditional societies therefore, certain dances were metaphors for sexual intercourse and procreation, almost always within the confines of marital relationships or betrothal. Examples include dances during induction, presentation or agricultural (harvest) ceremonies. Uudhano, a north Namibian dance-play, was traditionally a way in which adolescents of both genders could meet, interact and flirt. Many of the present day movements are sexually very suggestive and may have had their origin in this kind of social circumstance where suggestiveness was acceptable although sexual intercourse among unmarried persons was taboo until after the girls had passed through their presentation ("traditional marriage") ceremony. Often, sexually suggestive dances are practiced only within the confines of all-female company, with humorous and ironic reference to sex and its social connotations. The fact that dance could relate to or imply sex might have been unacceptable to colonial missionaries, but was a way of expressing continuity of Life in many African traditions, and has been confirmed by informants in my research.

While the points outlined above have referred mainly to "traditional" values within the broader African context, it remains now to see whether and how they are undergoing change, and how this impacts upon arts education.

TRANSITIONAL SOCIETY

Southern African countries, including Namibia, South Africa and Zimbabwe, are caught up in a process of rapid cultural change, impacting upon societies and their value systems in as yet unknown ways. Wole Soyinka refers to people as agents of a continuum of experience, a result of "the layering of interactions and symbolic practices that link us as individuals with the history and society of a distinct place" (Granqvist, 1993, p. 6). Individual and societal experiences of history, culture, and future aspirations therefore necessarily inform the body perceptions of all population groups. Because we realize that reason is not disembodied, but arises from the integrated experiences of brain, body and feelings (as described earlier), it follows that when experiences undergo change, so does reason.

Over the past fifty years many changes in the region have been political: the end of colonial rule and apartheid—but not necessarily racism; the adoption of democratic systems of rule—but not necessarily equal rights for all. Placing these political changes within contemporary time and place, we see that they are accompanied by societal changes that relate to the adoption of Western (global?) aspirations of technological development and material comfort. More specifically one sees a quest for "modernization" as opposed to "traditionalism," nationalism as opposed to individualism, and changes in the status and expectations of women, youth and the aged.

Being modern

Namibia has undergone an interesting transition from very recent colonial occupation to independence with democratic rule. Becker (2000) and Winterveldt (2002) both stress that postcolonial discourse has been largely based on dichotomous distinctions between "old" or "traditional" and "new" or "modern." This discourse is confirmed in many conversations I have had with Namibian people—farmers, shopkeepers, housekeepers, musicians and politicians—who rationalize their own histories and motivations in terms of colonial or traditional versus independent, liberated and modern. Urban middle classes construct their identity by contrasting it with their rural peasant origins.

In embracing this very localized form of "modernity"[16] people strive to be seen as educated and knowledgeable, in touch with the latest trends, having escaped a "rural existence" and poverty. This generally involves relinquishing the so-called "traditional life." Modernity is embodied in many new and constantly evolving ways—in gestures[17], manner of dress, build, dance, denial—some of which I discuss briefly below.

Being black, being female

A powerful form of societal transition emerges in the current changes in feminine image and role models in most ethnic groups. In the past the public image of a white woman was that of "madam" and housewife, while the black woman was that of mother and servant. Contemporary women are constructing "new" embodiments of femininity, status, power and culture.

In South African apartheid's Bantu Education black women were only educated in certain fields, such as the preparation for employment as domestic servant, nurse or teacher. To break away from the image of black woman as worker and servant (even in her own home), I observe that young Namibian women are not encouraged, nor seek to become involved in physical tasks or sport. To "not" do brings status. Walking, moving or carrying heavy objects is seen as demeaning. There are of course exceptions, with women such as Agnes Samaria, who are fighting their way into male-dominated African athletics with "strong" bodies. Further, the involvement of black women in the liberation struggle meant that they joined the guerilla forces—in effect becoming "brave warriors." The lived experience of these women and the influence this may have had upon perceptions and conceptions of femininity, and upon understandings of the idea of bravery (which has always been one of the loci of masculinity) has yet to be investigated.

Women are increasingly seen to claim domains of empowerment. At the same time, the violence against them and powerless children is on the increase. Southern Africa has a horrifyingly high incidence of rape and physical abuse, depicting a bleak picture of women who are unable to enact a "no." While legal empowerment exists,[18] social empowerment is lagging. Gender roles in contemporary urban society are not clearly defined and there is a blurring of what is extolled as customary and traditional and that which the law allows. This is also evidenced in contemporary urban dances where gender and status lack traditional definition. This indicates a potential source of conflict and tension.

The dancing body and beauty

The purposes of dance have undergone fundamental change. Whereas dance in "traditional societies" often had therapeutic, spiritual or functional purpose, "modern society" has relinquished many of these. Has society found suitable replacements? How have cultural changes affected body experience of young women in southern Africa?

Our transitional societies, particularly those in rural areas, are experiencing rapid change as a result of development and modernization of infrastructure and education. Along with development and better education comes increased contact with global standards, values and ethics. Popular television, music and magazines exploit and pressurize women into "the" quest for beauty, individualism and materialism that characterizes many Western cultures. Rational contemporary Africans discard traditional healing and other dances as "primitive and backward" and ignore the therapeutic value of the participative and relatively non-judgemental play.

To understand the significance of the dancing body within a culture one must engage with a variety of discourses—the kinesthetic, somatic, visual, aesthetic and intellectual. Changes in dancing habits have led to other changes, notably a change in perceptions of feminine beauty. In modern urban society there is little sign of the implementation of traditional African criteria of beauty discussed earlier. The traditional values (respecting age and wisdom) that underlay the combination of gravitas and slow tempo resulted in an older appearance imparting greater status. This does not appear to hold true amongst the younger generation anymore. Namibian girls today[19] prefer a svelte look, with narrow waists, thin legs and arms, flat stomachs and small breasts. West African men complain that Namibian girls "having nothing to hold on to," being too thin. Namibian women, however, see "thinness" as a statement of empowerment—equating heaviness with tradition and lack of weight with modernity. No longer is the feminine stereotype with round, high buttocks, rounded stomach, and solid placement on the ground thought of as modern or beautiful. The new slim denim clad African girl and the resultant race after slenderness is evidenced in the marked increase in the incidence of anorexia.[20] While the majority of my youthful respondents perceived themselves as slender enough[21] several were concerned that they would become "big like their mothers" in later years. They also indicated that older men (fathers) preferred the look of bigger women like their mothers.

Not unexpectedly, survey respondents all indicated that their mothers' dance movements were slower, softer and smaller—but "nice." The music to which older women like to dance was described in similar terms—slower, softer, "old-fashioned" but "romantic." The young girls generally showed a preference for R & B and hip-hop music for dancing and they danced at clubs and parties. Older women danced "at home" or at occasional celebrations like weddings.

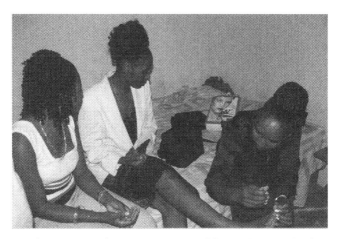

Contemporary beauty preparations (Photo: M. Mans, 2000)

The majority of my respondents indicated that they like to dance but were not good dancers. This creates an interesting juxtaposition. In the eyes of non-Africans, the myth of "African rhythm and African dancing" remains entrenched. In the eyes of youthful Africans, the notion that one needs special talent and instruction to be a dancer is similarly entrenched. Do they experience their lack of dancing ability in relation to "traditional dance" or to the images they see in music videos? Where do these views intersect? Can a general arts education find and utilize this intersection?

Looking at the body as a temporal interface between physical facts of existence and societal values, one perceives a tension created by the traditional concept of body as sexual and procreative vessel and the developing postmodern concept of the body as carrier of disease and unwanted impregnation.[22] This is compounded by cultural taboos pertaining to talk about sex (Fox, 2002; Talavera, 2002). In dance, it is understood that the body communicates, invites, and challenges within the framework of societal rules and hierarchies. In my survey, the young respondents indicated that they like to move fast and with energy in their dance, that they like to look sexy but not too intense, and that they want to look attractive when dancing. This seems to indicate that values of ephebism and "coolness" remain important. In addition, young women indicate that despite "liking to" use their bodies in dance to seduce, this does not lead to unwanted sexual intercourse or date-rape. What is unclear from my evidence, however, is whether sexual intercourse may follow but is not considered unwanted.

These are some of the issues that surround the changing female body in southern Africa. From the above the social body can at present be seen to form a continuum with perceptions and images that range from global and fashionable to customary and uniquely regional, while all the diversities are expressed in between. One should pose the question—how can the youthful urban culture relate to the values described as "traditionally African" when everybody yearns to move to the city and be seen as "modern"? How can this be married to the ideology expressed in Thabo Mbeki's call for an African Renaissance—a notion that conjures up a resurgence of African arts and systems of knowledge? It indicates that arts need to be interpreted in "new" African ways. It is my belief that correctly approached, arts education can be supremely effective in attaining this goal.

AN EDUCATIONAL PERSPECTIVE

Africa has many traditions of bodily instruction—in work, in dance and in daily life. While circumstances of living constantly change, the body remains an important tool for shaping societal roles. It remains an important source of knowledge of ourselves and others, and a means by which we are known. In itself, this clearly makes it a critical aspect of educational life.

Corporeal learning

In the past, much indigenous learning took place through bodily transmission and cultural immersion. For example, respect was demonstrated by touching one's hand to the opposite elbow, slightly inclining the upper body and lowering the eyes when giving or receiving something. Through practice this becomes such a fundamental embodiment of respect that a disrespectful attitude would have to be carefully cultivated. Drumming was taught by a master drummer physically demonstrating or even "working" the apprentice's hands so as to inculcate the right tension-release, energy input and timing. This embodied sense is eventually internalized and becomes a form of mindful body.

When the mind-body dichotomy is overcome and we utilize a thinking body, a whole realm of teaching-learning possibilities opens up to us. We all know that when children are having difficulties in learning or memorizing something, they almost instinctively revert to a bodily form of memory—tapping out a rhythm of a fact to be remembered, writing or drawing, even knocking on one's own head! The retention of corporeal learning is close to permanent. In schools, however, the proprioceptive sense is seldom fully utilized as a medium of learning. The reason why this important spatial sense remains undervalued and underutilized in education is a mystery. Especially considering the stress placed upon learning by means of visual and auditory senses. Like athletes, dancers carry corporeal learning very much further than memorizing movements. Dancers develop the link between bodily self-mastery in terms of their own movements, their anticipatory relation to others' movements, and control over their interior state (mental and emotional). An excellent dancer transcends the execution of steps to a level where she can 'play' not only herself but also the onlookers. Because traditional settings involved focus on the communal experience, dancers were expected to develop a level of communication, skill and self-control that would enable all participants to gain by the synergy of a good performance.

A dancer performs within the framework of an enculturated mental template or schema—knowing the correct movements, modalities, sounds and possible variations as well as the rules and meaning of the performance. A schema is "a cognitive structure through which interpretations about the world are made"

(Schwartz, White, & Lutz, 1992, p. 52), and is used as a procedural device to interpret the performance and its requirements. Understanding cognitive schemas involves interpretation of cultural symbols from the word and movement level to the level of large knowledge systems. To date, very little research has been done on the cognitive schemas involved in southern African cultures[23]. Knowledge of schemas works for us in two ways. Firstly, on a personal level one interprets one's own world by means of culturally informed schemas which include the templates relating to one's musical world. Secondly, it is useful for the educator to interpret the world of learners by means of the performed nature of their musical worlds. Dancers dance (and sing) their world with their bodies. In many African contexts and schemas the dance is aesthetically evaluated on several parameters, two of which are "goodness" and "tastiness." Goodness refers to the correct and skillful execution of the dance. Tastiness refers to the ability to add sweet (beautiful or exciting) moves, originality and variations. An individual adds "tastiness" to a performance within the societal parameters (rules) of the event. This is "goodness." Skilled performers can therefore play with both "tastiness" and "goodness." The schema is embodied in the performance dialectic between heart (emotion) and mind through a balance of self-mastery, "tastiness" and "goodness."

A further aspect of corporeal learning is identity formation. The body is one of the most important sites of identity construction and in dance it is an explicitation of personal as well as cultural (or group) identity. Not only does dance reflect identity but it also responds to changes in the socio-political environment. Hence, dance can serve as an impetus for change by making a statement and thereby negotiating and constructing identity. Contemporary southern Africa can be bodily renegotiated and reconstructed this way. Youthful dancers in my university class demonstrate this compellingly. Some of them come from a background of formal dance instruction, others imitate music video dancing or are very close to their cultural heritage, while yet others dance with an intuitive sense of self untrammeled by any specific style. In trying to practice my philosophy of using one's body to learn about oneself and others, students demonstrate noticeable growth in terms of mental and physical skills. But maybe more importantly in our multicultural transitional society, they express and demonstrate deeper understanding of themselves and their relations to others in an almost visceral physical way. They "feel" their blood, bones and muscles, something which is a shared human characteristic. They bump against others and "feel" their weight, impetus and influence. The bonds created by this form of corporeal learning might not necessarily be embodied in permanent friendships, but, according to the students,[24] are certainly embodied in a broader socio-cultural "mitgefühl."

Reconstructing racialized bodies

Education in many parts of the world has long embodied difference and exhibited race—even legitimized racism—in its academic discourse as well as practice. The very notion of studying "world music" for example, is based on the construction of "otherness." The invention of race (Radano, & Bohlman, 2001; Elder, n.d.) has informed the history of southern Africa and continues to do so in the form and shape of the media, tourism and education. Race is entrenched in curricula and educational materials. Illustrations in school books, for example, have only very recently started adapting from all white human images and homes to include black images and homes, although these often still embody racial stereotypes. Women are depicted in their "nanny" shape, homes are depicted as huts, and the working black person is depicted as farmer, labourer, or at best a desk clerk. Clearly one means of reconstruction should address the way people "image-ine" themselves. In isolated instances this happens, for example through a recent visual ethnography project[25] where people in rural areas were provided with cameras and instructions to picture themselves and their spaces. The honesty of their stories and imagery provided enlightening results. Similarly, visual artists and dancers are establishing their own bodily space with contemporary imagery, a space where race, gender and class are renegotiated. "Just as performativity assigns sex, gender, and sexuality to bodies, it also creates, maintains, and transforms a racialized body" (Wong, 2000, p. 62). In performance race and gender are articulated through one another. Through the body social relations of gender (hetero- and homosexual) and race traverse and re-map both private and public spaces. Music and dance act as mediating forces in the understanding and appreciation of "other," in effect, removing "otherness."

The contemporary "transnational mix"

Radano and Bohlman state pessimistically that "[w]orld music and postmodern hybridities have yet to eliminate racial barriers, and they show no sign of masking the conditions that give rise to racial factors" (ibid., 2001, p. 37). However, they argue that discourse on race and music acts as a means to face the issues directly, thereby "framing new territories of musical exploration and observing the dynamics of difference that so profoundly inform music's affective power" (ibid., p. 40.) Arts education has a role to play in the framing of these new territories.

In the dance class learners can be led to explore issues more fundamental than the movements or the history of the dance. They can explore bodily means of maintaining or changing the status quo and physical power. The shared southern African issues surrounding the AIDS pandemic, the empowerment of women, and the eradication of racialism and poverty should all be embraced as common challenges in arts education. Perception is an acquired cultural skill, and our perceptions of one another's and our own bodies are part of the cognitive process directly implicated in dance. Within the shared environment of a school culture, space can be created for an investigation into diverse embodiments of gender, power, and culture.

Is a sense of African Renaissance transmitted to classrooms in contemporary transcultural and transnational schools or do teachers remain parochial? In my experience in Namibia and parts of South Africa teachers tend to avoid celebration of African cultures, particularly in culturally mixed situations. They claim lack of cultural knowledge and skill when it comes to teaching music and dance. This appears to be due largely to pre-existing fears of inadequacy because they lack formal education in dance and, more importantly, they see "cultural dances" as backward and not 'modern'. In addition, there are even lingering notions of African dance as inappropriate for schools. In this way schools appear to embrace a puritan body that relates neither to modern nor traditional notions of Africanity.

Within the school culture African dances are seldom considered in terms of their qualitative and cognitive possibilities, but seen as unrefined although colorful expressions. A wealth of knowledge and aesthetic principles embedded within these dances remains unexplored. This knowledge is equal in human value to any other form of knowledge, including science and mathematics. After all, all mental processes are the action of a network of partially interconnected elements. Until these holistic modes of learning are reassigned the earlier values they carried, body as a means of learning and knowing is likely to remain underrated.

To properly blend custom and tradition into contemporary life, it is vital (for the curriculum) to identify which cultural values remain core values in society. Clearly there are inconsistencies and even clashes between certain customary and contemporary values inherent to women's dance, for example. Certain traditional dances promoted female subservience and the assignation only of roles as mother and sexual vessel. This does not sit well with the young women who emphasize their role as creators of their own destiny and power. Contemporary expectations and customary values need to be embodied compatibly, bringing a deeper understanding and re-valuing of fundamental life values.

Perhaps the idea of "new bodies" as a tool for shaping roles and others' knowledge of ourselves should become a critical aspect of educational life for both teacher and student. Deconstructing genderized bodies, for example, could be one way to do this—changing roles, exploring strength, discovering symbolism. While I support the notion of exploring new dance, we might also consider the use of traditional modes of dance to do this. In older dance traditions the individual entered the playing space and demonstrated personal prowess, but the freedom and expectation of performance was egalitarian. We can use the fact that "good" dancers are those who support one another—each providing performance space that makes the other look good. A balance of power between genders and age groups can be established. In this way a healthy and balanced body social can perhaps be renegotiated within the playing space.

The knowledge gained from understanding different body/mind constructions and experiences can contribute locally and beyond.

REFERENCES

Ajayi, O. S. (1996). In contest: The dynamics of African religious dances. In K. W. Asante (Ed.), *African dance. An artistic, historical and philosophical inquiry* (pp. 183-202). Trenton, NJ: Africa World Press.

Aparicio, F. R. (2000). Ethnifying rhythms, Feminizing cultures. In R. Radano & P. V. Bohlman (Eds.), *Music and the racial imagination* (pp. 95 - 112). Chicago and London: Chicago University Press.

Asante, K. W. (Ed.) (1996). *African dance. An artistic, historical and philosophical inquiry.* Trenton, NJ: Africa World Press.

Becker, H. (2000). 'Let me come to tell you' Loide Shikongo maps out power—gender identity and gendered subjectivity in colonial Ovamboland—Papers presented at the Public History: Forgotten History Conference, University of Namibia, August 22–25, Windhoek.

Blacking, J. (1985). The context of Venda possession: Music: Reflections on the effectiveness of symbols. 1985 *Yearbook for Traditional Music, 17,* 64–87.

Bovin, M. (2001). *Nomads who cultivate beauty. Wodaabe dances and visual arts in Niger.* Uppsala: Nordiska Afrikainstitutet.

Brusila, J. (2001). Jungle drums striking the world beat. In M. Palmberg (Ed.), *Encounter images in the meetings between Africa and Europe* (pp. 146-161). Uppsala: Nordiska Afrikainstitutet.

Buckland, T. J. (2001). Dance, authenticity and cultural memory: The politics of embodiment. *2001 Yearbook for Traditional Music, 33,* 1-6. International Council for Traditional Music

Butchart, A. (1998). *The anatomy of power. European constructions of the African body.* Pretoria: Unisa Press.

Collins, P. H. (1998). Mammies, matriarchs, and other controlling images. In E. C. Eze (Ed.), *African Philosophy. An Anthology. Blackwell Philosophy Anthologies, 5,* 346-354. Malden Massachusetts: Blackwell.

Dagan, E. (Ed.) (1997). *The spirit's dance in Africa: Evolution, transformation and continuity in Sub-Sahara.* Montreal: Galerie Amrad African Art.

Eboh, P. M. (1998). The woman question: African and Western perspectives. In E. C. Eze (Ed.), *African philosophy. An Anthology. Blackwell Philosophy Anthologies, 5.* Malden Massachusetts: Blackwell.

Elder, G.S. (n.d.). *The south African body politic: Space, race, and heterosexuality.* Paper. Retrieved June 3, 2002, from http://www.uvm.edu/~geograph/bodies.html

Eze, E. C. (Ed.). (1998). *African philosophy. An Anthology. Blackwell Philosophy Anthologies, 5.* Malden Massachusetts: Blackwell.

Fox, T. (2002). The culture(s) of aids—Cultural analysis and new policy approaches for Namibia. In V. Winterveldt, T. Fox & P. Mufune (Eds.), *Namibia society sociology* (pp. 317-331). Windhoek: University of Namibia Press.

Granqvist, R. (1993). Introduction: African culture—an estimate. In R. Granqvist (Ed.), *Culture in Africa. An appeal for pluralism.* Seminar Proceedings No. 29. Uppsala: Nordiska Afrikainstitutet (The Scandinavian Institute of African Studies).

Hanghe, A. A. (1988). *Folktales from Somalia.* Somali Academy of Sciences and Arts in cooperation with the Scandinavian Institute of African Studies, Uppsala.

Kober, G. D. (1997). *Articulating difference: Texts of identity in post-independence Namibia.* Unpublished doctoral dissertation, the University of South Africa, South Africa.

Larkin, A. A. (1999, Spring). Cultural history. Images of the black female body reflect and affect society's opinion. *Smithsonian Institution Research Reports, 69.* Retrieved June 3, 2002, from http://www.si.edu/opa/researchreports/9996/images.htm

Lash, S., & J. Friedman (Eds.) (1993). *Modernity and identity.* Oxford, UK and Cambridge, USA: Blackwell.

Lewis-Williams, D., & T. Dowson (2000). *Images of power. Understanding San Rock art.* Cape Town: Struik.

Hatano, G., & Miyake, N. (1991). What does a cultural approach offer to research on learning? Learning and Instruction, 1, 273-281. Holloway, S. (2000). *Contested Childhood: Diversity and Change in Japanese Preschools.* New York: Routledge.

Mans, M. E. (2002a). To Pamwe or to play: The role of play in arts education in Africa. *International Journal of Music Education, 39,* 50-64.

Mans, M. E. (2002b). Constructing cultural identities in contemporary musical traditions—strategies of survival and change. In V. Winterveldt, T. Fox & P. Mufune (Eds.), *Namibia Society Sociology* (pp. 253-270). Windhoek: University of Namibia Press.

Mans, M. E. (2002c). Okudhana nawa! (Play well). The talking drum. *Newsletter Issue, 17,* 2-7.

McClary, S., & Walser, R. (1994). Theorizing the body in African-American music. In *Transcultural Music Review, 3.* (Previously published in *Black Music Research Journal* Vol. 14 no. 1, Spring 1994, pp. 75–84.) Retrieved June 3, 2002, from http://www.sibetrans.com/trans3/mcclary.htm

Mellemsether, H. (2001). Gendered images of Africa? The writings of male and female missionaries. In M. Palmberg (Ed.), *Encounter images in the meetings between Africa and Europe* (pp. 183-194). Uppsala: Nordic Africa Institute.

Middleton, J. (1985). The dance among the Lugbara of Uganda. In P. Spencer (Ed.), *Society and the dance. The Social anthropology of process and performance* (pp.). Cambridge: Cambridge University Press.

Palmberg, M. (Ed.) 2001. *Encounter images.* Uppsala: Nordiska Afrikainstitutet.

Radano, R., & P. V. Bohlman (Eds.). (2000). *Music and the racial imagination.* Chicago and London: Chicago University Press.

Rohde, R. (1998). How we see each other: subjectivity, photography and ethnographic re/vision. In W. Hartmann, J. Silvester, & P. Hayes (Eds.), *The Colonising Camera. Photographs in the making of Namibian History* (pp. 188-204). Cape Town: University of Cape Town Press; Basler Afrika Bibliographien; Out of Africa; Ohio University Press.

Schwartz, T., White, G. M., &Lutz, C. A. (Eds.). (1992). *New directions in psychological anthropology.* Cambridge: Cambridge University Press.

Skotnes, P. (1996). *Miscast. Negotiating the presence of the Bushmen.* Rondebosch: University of Cape Town Press.

Soiri, I. (1996). The radical motherhood. Namibian women's independence struggle. *Research Report, 99.* Uppsala: Nordiska Afrikainstitutet.

Spelman, E. V. (1998). The erasure of black women. In E.C. Eze (Ed.), *African Philosophy. An Anthology. Blackwell Philosophy Anthologies, 5,* 355-359. Malden Massachusetts: Blackwell.

Stokes, M. (Ed.) (1994). Ethnicity, identity and music. The musical construction of place. *Berg Ethnic Identities Series* (pp. 1-25). Oxford & Providence: Berg.

Sullivan, S. (2002). How can the Rain Fall in this Chaos? Myth and Metaphor in Representations of the Northwest Namibian Landscape. In D. LeBeau & R. J. Gordon (Eds.), *Challenges for Anthropology in the "African Renaissance" A Southern African Contribution* (pp. 255 - 265). Windhoek: University of Namibia Press.

Swantz, M-L. (1986). *Ritual and symbol.in transitional Zaramo society.* Uppsala: Scandinavian Institute of African Studies.

Talavera, P. (2002). Sexual cultures in transition in the Northern Kunene—Is there a need for a sexual revolution in Namibia? In V. Winterveldt, T. Fox & P. Mufune (Eds.), *Namibia society sociology* (pp. 333 – 346). Windhoek: University of Namibia Press.

Thompson, R. F. (1974). *African art in motion. icon and act.* Berkeley and Los Angeles: University of California Press.

Thornton, R. (2000). Ethnicity and the geometry of power: The aesthetics of ethnicity in the imagination of the polity. *Critical arts. Ethnicity and identity, 14*(1), 16–43.

Tiérou, A. (1992). Dooplé. The Eternal Law of African Dance. *Choreography and Dance Studies, 2.* Switzerland: Harwood Academic publishers.

Udegbe, I. B. (2001). Gender dimensions in the images of Africans in commercial works of art. In M. Palmberg (Ed.), *Encounter images in the meetings between Africa and Europe* (pp. 135-145). Uppsala: Nordiska Afrikainstitutet.

Winterveldt, V. (2002). Traditionalism—social reality of a myth. In V. Winterveldt, T. Fox, & P. Mufune (Eds.), *Namibia society sociology* (pp. 227-238). Windhoek: University of Namibia Press.

Wong, D. (2000). The Asian American body in performance. In R. Radano & P. Bohlman (Eds.), *Music and the racial imagination* (pp. 57-94). Chicago and London: Chicago University Press.

NOTES

[1] This refers to my own doctoral research (1992—1996) and the project "The Living Musics and Dance of Namibia: exploration, education and publication" sponsored by the French Department for Cooperation and Cultural Affairs in Namibia and the University of Namibia (1998—2000). The research continues. Namibia is on the south-western coast of Africa.

[2] Within the Namibian context, people tend to interpret "traditional" as colonial and a nineteenth century phenomenon (Winterveldt, 2002; Becker, 2000). Being 'modern' tends to mean discarding tradition and negating rural origins.

[3] Consider, for example, the differences between Saharan African music and dance, West African drum-based dance, South African choral dance, San wordless songs and instrument-free dance, city club dance, and so on.

[4] In colonial times the "peculiarities" were described in racially derogatory "scientific" portrayals with particular reference to buttocks, penises and vaginas. For a discussion on this kind of portrayal, see for example Pippa Skotnes' book *Miscast. Negotiating the Presence of the Bushmen.* Rondebosch: University of Cape Town Press, 1996, and Bernd Lindfors' article "Hottentot, Bushman, Kaffir" in *Encounter Images,* edited by Mai Palmberg, Uppsala: Nordiska Afrikainstitutet, 2001.

[5] See for example Udegbe's article "Gender Dimensions in the Images of Africans in Commercial Works of Art." (2001); and in *African Philosophy. An Anthology* (1998) the essays by Eboh: "The Woman Question: African and Western Perspectives", Collins: "Mammies, Matriarchs, and other Controlling Images"; and Spelman: "The Erasure of Black Women". See also A. A. Larkin's report "Images of the black female body reflect and affect society's opinion." in *Smithsonian Institution Research Reports* (1999).

[6] This term is used in contrast to 'Africanity' which has defined philosophical and political connotations.

[7] Here I refer broadly to colonial occupation in all its shapes and guises which affected most of Africa.

[8] See "Ethnifying Rhythms, Feminizing Cultures" (2001) by Frances Aparicio for a discussion that traces the diverse meanings of the mulatta dancing figure in the Caribbean.

[9] C. C. Okumu, personal communications in Bergen, Norway, 2002.

[10] The term Bantu refers to the large language group originating in central Africa, who through many subsequent migrations established themselves in east, south, south-west and central Africa.

[11] Cf. for example the Masques de Sagesse of West Africa

[12] See Lewis-Williams & Dowson (2000) for a cogent explanation of this cosmology.

[13] New forms are constantly emerging e.g. in the shape of gospel and worship dances. The increase in popularity and performance of these dances in southern Africa is great, especially in Zimbabwe.

[14] See Thompson's (1972) well known discussion of ephebism in African dance.

[15] The *Ubuntu* idea confirms this.

[16] Postmodernist theory and its terminology has hardly made an impact in Namibia, where most people read modern as now.

[17] For example the American T-shaped hand gesture that denotes 'time-out' in Namibia is used as "Stop the car! I need a lift".

[18] Although in Namibia the Customary Property law of 1927, which does not allow women in northern territories to own property, is still in effect.

[19] All of the respondents in my survey—young and mature - indicated that they considered slender to be beautiful. Some contributed comments such as that about West African men.

[20] According to information provided to me in confidence by staff at the Student Clinic at the university of Namibia.

[21] They were! Most of these young women wore dresses size 28 - 32.

[22] I am referring to the spreading of the HIV infection through sexual intercourse. The incidence of HIV infection in South Africa, Zimbabwe and Namibia is frighteningly high. The incidence of teenage pregnancy is unacceptably high, causing large numbers of girls to leave school permanently. What happens when a society embraces the idea of dance with sexual connotations, but not the bodily consequences of sexual freedom? What role can arts education play in easing this bodily tension?

[23] Although this has been superficially addressed in my article "To Pamwe or to Play: the role of play in arts education in Africa" *International Journal of Music Education*, Vol. 39, 2002. My continued ethnomusicology research also investigates broad cultural cognitive schemas.

[24] These views have been expressed many times in informal conversations with students.

[25] See R. Rohde, 1998, p. 188 onwards.

DANIEL J. WALSH

FROG BOY AND THE AMERICAN MONKEY: THE BODY IN JAPANESE EARLY SCHOOLING

Below our apartment in Yashiro, Japan, was an exercise area with parallel bars, gymnastic bars, climbing ropes, a balance beam, and so on. Signs about 75 centimeters high explained how to use each one. My daughter, Scooter, a sixth grader, spent much time there climbing and swinging. She used the parallel bars to learn to ride a unicycle. One evening a fourth-grade boy from her school came by with friends. They ignored Scooter, as she did them. He stood in front of one sign, then jumped up and landed on the top of the sign. He hunkered there; buttocks on his heels Asian style, then jumped effortlessly down. He repeated the jump on two other signs before leaving. Awe struck, Scooter asked, "How does he do that? He's like a frog. He's a frog boy."

On the wall of the elementary school gym were mounted horizontal wooden bars used for climbing and exercising. Waiting for PE class to start, Scooter climbed up the bars. Using the bars, ropes pulled over against the wall, and window ledges, she climbed three-quarters of the way to the ceiling. Her teacher, Kikkawa-Sensei, looked up and shook his head. "Our American monkey," he announced, motioning for her to come down for class.

Working within the general framework of cultural psychology (e.g., Bruner, 1996; Cole, 1996; Shweder et al., 1998), I am particularly interested in how the self is differently construed and constructed across cultures (e.g., Kitayama & Markus, 1999, 2000; Markus & Kitayama, 1991). Markus, writing in Shweder et al. (1998), described the self as "where the individual, the biological entity, becomes a meaningful entity—a person, a participant in social worlds. Although the experience of self may appear as primarily individual creations, they are in several ways also cultural and historical constructions" (p. 895). This chapter explores the development of a physical self in Japanese early schooling.

I did not come to Japan to study children's physical development or ability. I came to study how cultural beliefs serve as a critical context for children's development (Walsh, 2002a). I soon concluded that cultural beliefs about children's physical capabilities and about the importance of physical development informed this developmental context. In Japanese culture young children are viewed as essentially and importantly physical—their physical development central to early schooling.

Many Japanese early childhood educators believe that intellectual development requires a balanced body and that physical play aligns the body (e.g., Harada, 1997). Harada argues that running games requiring children to change direction, like soccer

Liora Bresler (ed.), Knowing Bodies, Moving Minds, 97-109.
©2004 Kluwer Academic Publishers. Printed in the Netherlands

and tag, help align the body. He suggests that each preschool day begin with 100 minutes of outdoor physical activity. The preschools (described below) that were my main research sites all began with or had extended outdoor free-play periods.

I look at development of the young Japanese self from two perspectives: (a) my fieldwork, primarily in, but not restricted to, preschools, and (b) through the eyes of my two children, Buck, 5, and Scooter, 12, as they developed selves that became in their eight months in Japanese schools increasingly Japanese.

I had five primary research sites, in or near Yashiro, a town on 22,000 50 minutes northwest of Osaka: three yochien (kindergartens) and two hoikuen (day cares). Kindergartens in Japan are separate from elementary schools and can have three– to five–year–old children. One kindergarten was three to five; one, four and five: and one, fives only. The day cares had toddlers through five–year–olds. The kindergartens were half-day; the day cares, full day. I do not differentiate between the two in this chapter, referring to them generically as *preschools*. I also visited other preschools in Himeji, Osaka, Yao, Nagoya, Gifu, Tokyo, Nishinomiya, and Yokohama as opportunities arose.

I watched children in daily life—on the local playgrounds, in the shopping malls, and on the street. Both my children play ice hockey and joined a team in Kobe. I was able to systematically observe children in an organized sport—practices, games, and tournaments—from August through January.

Some cautions: I strive to remain critical, but I do admire much about Japanese early schooling. We lived in a small town, away from the restrictive pressures of daily life in Tokyo or Osaka. I describe good schools, schools that interested me. All were public preschools, which tend to be truer to Japanese early childhood traditions and less varied than private preschools, which predominate in big cities. My limited observations in urban preschools allowed me to calibrate my sites against urban ones. My descriptions were vetted by Japanese colleagues to ensure that they were identifiably Japanese, that is, within the range of normal practice.

Finally, my wife is Asian. Both children have dark hair and eyes and tan easily. The only *gaijin* (foreigners), Buck in a kindergarten of 180 children, and Scooter in an elementary school of 600, they did not stand out physically, merging relatively easily into their schools. They grew up in a bi-cultural home and had visited family in Thailand many times—both had been to Japan. They had an intuitive sense of Asian culture—they instinctively bowed, could use chopsticks, were familiar with Japanese food, and so on.

Each section of the chapter begins with a vignette then briefly explores one aspect of growing up physical in Japan. I conclude with a discussion of physical development.

GETTING PHYSICAL

I sat on a bench reading near a small playground in married student housing. Buck climbed on the jungle gym. Four mothers stood across the playground talking, occasionally glancing at their toddlers. One toddler climbing on the jungle gym slipped then caught himself, momentarily hanging precariously. His mother turned slightly then returned to her conversation. He repeated the maneuver three times, purposely losing his footing, hanging for a few seconds, and then regaining it. Each time he laughed elatedly. Later a different toddler, a boy about three, squat, square-headed with a crew cut and a mischievous grin, charged across the playground directly at me. I watched him uneasily—was he going to jump on me! I moved my book down to protect my genitals. At the last second he veered to his right and hopped, froglike, up on the bench next to me. He squatted there for 20 seconds, showing no awareness of me. Then he hopped down and ran back to his friends laughing.

On a beautiful day in May 1998, Buck, and I arrived in Yashiro. My wife and Scooter would come a month later. The rainy season had not yet begun, and the oppressive heat of summer remained a month away.

I was beginning a fellowship at the Center for School Education Research at Hyogo University of Teacher Education. I had been to Yashiro twice and was familiar with the area. I looked forward to eight months of full-time fieldwork. It promised and turned out to be a wonderful year.

The next day we shopped for Buck for kindergarten—the school year in Japan begins in April, breaks for vacation in August, and then resumes in September. We purchased a long list of necessary items—bento box (lunch box), washcloth, school hats, seat cushion, bathing cap, and jacket. He was ready for kindergarten.

I was *very* apprehensive about Buck's going to kindergarten. I had observed in many Japanese preschools. The last time I had been to his kindergarten, I had to protect my backside because some mischievous young boys repeatedly snuck up behind me and "goosed" me vigorously. They thought it great fun and laughed uproariously. I tried my sternest looks, threats, all to no avail. Eventually I kept close to walls. No one seemed to notice—the teachers, the principal who welcomed me, and the professor who brought me. I tried to imagine a Japanese professor visiting a kindergarten back home and no adult noticing kids goosing him. I couldn't. Later my children informed me that Japanese children are fond of goosing. Full disclosure: I was goosed on no other occasion, although, at one preschool, I was kicked in the genitals, and at another a sweetly smiling girl gouged a fingernail-full of flesh from the side of my nose.

Japanese preschools are, compared to contemporary American preschools, raucous places, filled with loud rambunctious kids who run, wrestle, hit, roughhouse, and climb on and over everything. Buck was a gentle soul. At his university preschool in Illinois children were encouraged to "use their words," as in "I don't like it when you hit me," fighting and hitting were forbidden, and rambunctiousness was constrained. Japanese children do use their words, but words of their *own* choosing—two of the first words that Buck learned were *baka*, fool, and *ochidi*, buttocks. But they are more likely to use their bodies. Would Buck be tough enough? Colleagues on sabbatical had packed up their families to the other side of the world, only to have the experience spoiled by one unhappy family member.

Would Buck, having been pushed around enough, refuse to go to kindergarten? Would I be doing fieldwork with an unhappy five-year-old in tow? American friends whose kids had been in Japanese preschool had described their kids being harassed and teased mercilessly. One told of his son taking a peanut butter sandwich from his Power Rangers lunch box to hear all the kids yell derisively, "Shit sandwich!"

I had told Buck what to expect, explaining that even if he spoke Japanese, "using his words" might not help. Scooter, as physical as her brother is cerebral, and about whose adjustment I had few worries, worked to "toughen and roughen" him up. She teased and pushed him around, urging him to fight back.

Each day I waited up for tears and tales, and none came. Each day he emerged happy and excited, eager to tell me about his day. After a week I asked if kids hit him or pushed him around. He shook his head emphatically, "A lot!" He continued admiringly, "The kids like to hit and fight, and the teachers don't make us stop." What did he do when the kids hit him? "I do this!" He crouched, feet wide apart, fists up like a boxer, growling and shaking his body—transformed. I was stunned. "What do the kids do when you do that?" I asked. "They run away, and then I chase them." Weeks later, teachers asked me to talk to Buck. They feared that he was being too aggressive and might hurt someone. Brave new world!

Buck did face subtle frustrations. His friends could climb the six-meter metal poles on the playground, and he could not. We returned to the empty playground in the evening for pole-climbing practice. First a half meter up the pole, then two. One evening he climbed to the top. The secret, he told me, was "sweaty sticky feet." His friends were still more agile and more confident about their physical abilities. Over the next eight months, however, with occasional tutoring and prodding, Buck became more confident physically. He ran, jumped, climbed, wrestled, and roughhoused with a new-found exuberance, reveling in his physical presence and developing abilities. Young children's friendships are profoundly physical. They develop their sense of a physical self in physical contact with others.

Then one day in early Fall, visibly upset, he stalked into my office. I waited for the worst. He stood shaking his head and staring at the floor. What was wrong? "It's just like CDL [his preschool back in Illinois]," he grumbled. I was puzzled. "The teachers said no more hitting and fighting. Just like CDL," shaking his head in disgust. I murmured sympathetically. "But we're going to keep on doing it," he said firmly. "We're not going to let it be like CDL!"

CONSTRAINING DEVELOPMENT

He was Japanese-American and had been working at an international company in Kobe for three years. She was Japanese and worked at the same company. They were engaged and visibly in love, sitting close on a warm day. They politely asked me about my research, and I described the physical precocity of young Japanese children. He was skeptical, sure that American children were more physically and athletically advanced than Japanese children. I explained how common unicycles were in preschools—that week some five-year-old girls had ridden unicycles across the playground swinging "hula hoops" over their heads then riding through them. He remained skeptical. Surely I was describing a rare event. He turned to his fiancée and asked confidently if she could ride a unicycle. She looked at him as though he were daft, "Of course, I can ride a unicycle! [Am I uncoordinated?]" He jerked back involuntarily; mouth and eyes opened wide, "You can ride a unicycle?" She looked at us, rolling her eyes. Just when you think you know everything about your lover.

Central to the idea of cultural contexts for development is the notion of *cultural constraints*. *Cultural constraint*s support some kinds of learning, making them easier, but at the same time make other learning difficult, even impossible. Hatano and Miyake (1991) pointed out that "cultural effects on learning are both enhancing and restricting. It is an important task for researchers in this area to specify how cultural constraints produce this double-sided effect" (p. 279). Constraints refer to how a culture enhances and restricts (a) what is possible and probable, (b) what is accessible, (c) what is valued, and (d) what is supported.

How, then, do preschools constrain Japanese children's physical development? What is seen as possible, and impossible, accessible and inaccessible, and so on? The constraints operating in preschool enhance children's physical development. Returning to the unicycle example: Unicycles are common in Japanese preschools—riding a unicycle is seen as possible. Children have access to them at school. Unicycles are readily available and relatively inexpensive in department stores, and children rode them in our campus neighborhood. School playgrounds often have long low bars that children can hold as they learn to ride. Being able to ride a unicycle is valued, by both children and adults. Being able to ride a unicycle in the U.S. is not seen as a possibility for young children; unicycles are not readily available and so on.

The culture values physical activity. The major fall event in schools is the Sports Festival, a daylong athletic competition of group rather than individual events. Families begin to arrive shortly after 8:00 a.m. and set up their tables, mats, and coolers. The competitions begin at 9 and continue until 3. All the children in the school are involved, including those with special needs. A most memorable experience was attending a sports festival at a school for children with mental and physical handicaps. The memory of children on walkers running short races and the cheers as the last ones crossed the line remains vivid.

In the Yashiro area, each town had a sports festival, with neighborhood teams. One event was a long relay race. Young children ran the first lap; the next by slightly older children, up through adulthood to seniors and back down again to a final lap run by young children. No runner dropped a baton during the entire race. I was astonished, then remembered the children in the preschools practice running relays. The runners had been running relays all their lives. Demure housewives sprinted around the track like experienced track and field athletes, which, in fact, they were.

The athletic activities in preschools reflect larger cultural constraints. At one preschool the children moved from 100 minutes of outside play to inside activities by slowly massaging each muscle group with towels, chanting, "Ichi, ni, san...(1, 2, 3,...)." A colleague explained that they were massaging each muscle group—the counting ensured that they massaged each one long enough. A few weeks later on a Tokyo subway, a business man in a well-cut suit was vigorously slapping his leg. No one appeared to notice. Done with one leg, he switched to other. Remembering the preschool kids, I realized he was massaging his muscle groups. After that I noticed this phenomenon often.

As a Japanese scholar friend explained to me, the body is central to the Japanese cultural narrative. The Western mind-body distinction was never part of the cultural view of self. As he put it, "We never accepted Christianity or Freud."

GROWING UP *GENKI*

One evening, when I returned home with a colleague, Scooter was practicing on the high bar. Envious of her classmates' proficiency on the school playground bars, she struggled to catch up with them. We watched and encouraged her. She grew increasingly frustrated. My colleague, in his early 30's, took off his sports coat and tie and joined her. He pulled himself up on the bar and performed series of flips. He showed her what do at each point in each move. I was astounded. I thought of him as a "techy," graceful, but not athletic. Maybe I saw all Japanese academics as pleasant bookish types, but not athletic. I should have realized that the little frog boys eventually grew up and some became academics. A few days later a friend complained to my wife and me about the scarcity of available and interesting unmarried men in the area—some topics cross cultures. We mentioned my colleague. She dismissed him—too bookish, not athletic enough, boring. Excitedly I described how he had transformed himself into a gymnast. She looked at me and my wife with the same look the young Japanese woman had given her intended, "All Japanese can do that." We had forgotten.

To be *genki*—an exuberant word meaning fit, strong, healthy, and physical—is highly valued. Kids respond to roll by jumping up and loudly announcing their presence, perhaps referring to a favorite cartoon character, **"Doraemon!!"** The teacher nods approvingly, "Genki!" Kids are expected to be tough and strong. Yashiro was unbearably humidly hot in the summer and bone-chillingly cold in the winter. On the coldest days, when I was shivering in coat and hat and unable to hold my video camera, kids ran around the playground in shorts, t-shirts, and unlined cloth jackets. Back in the classroom, heated by a portable kerosene heater in the middle of the room, I attempted to thaw my frozen fingers. The kids opened windows and asked the teachers to turn to heater off, "Too hot!" All part of being a Japanese self, kid-style.

The children's daring fascinated me. They appeared ready to climb to the top of anything. In time I understood that children appeared daring because the daring moment masked the gradual process of becoming daring. The daring of five-year-olds had begun when they were toddlers and had been developed slowly and with much practice. Price (1982) emphasized the importance for children's learning and development of "experiencing a prolonged, pressure-free period of familiarization" (p. 282). Extended periods of free play outside on playgrounds with challenging equipment and a sense of unrestricted space allowed children to push the limits of this equipment and of themselves. For example, they not only climbed the poles, at the top they climbed out on the bar connecting the poles and sat there.

Daring is defined by one's sense of danger, and *danger* is to some important extent constructed by expectations. The kids did not consider their actions dangerous, nor did the teachers, because the kids had been performing them in some form since they were toddlers. Developing a sense of daring is process of continual small steps over a long period of time. The young Japanese self is seen as, and accepted as, a physical self, developed on the playgrounds and in rambunctious interaction with others from an early age. Kids are encouraged to run, to climb, to fall, and to roughhouse. They are given the time and space to persist and practice.

Over the years I have watched too many ice hockey practices. Scooter has played for 10 years, Buck for five. American practices are rapid-fire affairs, with drills lasting a few minutes at time, driven, apparently, by a cultural belief in children's short attention spans. Move on to a new drill before kids get bored. As a result American kids' basic skills are often weak. One cannot develop good skills practicing them a few minutes a couple times a week. Their Japanese team's practices were more patiently paced. The same drill often continued 15 minutes or more, for example, kids in pairs passing to each other, back and forth, back and forth. The coaches accompanied the drills with explicit detailed instruction, squatting down, often kneeling on the ice, making small adjustments in the angle of a skate or stick blade, adjusting arm position, extending the follow through. Gaining mastery takes a long time and much practice.

Bordering the sidewalk up the hill to Buck's kindergarten stood a slightly sloped concrete wall that was about 4 meters high at the bottom of the hill, slowly diminishing in height as one climbed the hill. The wall was made of square pieces of formed concrete that allowed for toe and finger holds. For the kids on the way to school it became a climbing wall. The older more experienced kids climbed at the bottom where the wall was the highest and then walked along the top. The younger kids climbed closer to the top where the wall was not as high, slowly moving down the hill as they got more proficient. All jumped off at some point. I often saw kids jumping from heights of two meters, occasionally jumping over their mothers.

Both Scooter and Buck became more physical in their time in Japan. They became stronger—they had more hours of physical education than they had at home. They had more opportunities—all Japanese schools have swimming pools, and children swim every day in June and July. They sat still less and exercised more. They also learned the importance of being *genki*—aware of and confident in their physical capabilities.

A common culminating activity to elementary school is for the sixth grade to go to the sea and swim a kilometer or more. They swim as a group, with the fast swimmers in the back and the slow ones up front, teachers along the way urging them on and leading them in chants. Scooter arrived in Yashiro late June, less than a month from the planned trip to the Sea of Japan. She was not a strong swimmer, which her teacher diagnosed the first day. I anticipated that he would apologize profusely and tell me that given the late date, Scooter would have to maker the trip as an observer. I was completely wrong. He asked me for permission to keep her after school for additional swimming lessons and instructed me to take her to the university pool on weekends.

Scooter left for the sea apprehensive and nervous. She returned three days later changed. As she got off the bus, her smile transfigured her, and her feet seemed not to touch the ground. She had completed the 2-kilometer swim, and she came back more confidant than I had ever seen her, not only in her physical abilities, but also in her abilities in general. She was *genki*.

NATURALLY SENSIBLE

Scooter rushed into my office. "You won't believe what happened," she shouted. "You know how I've been practicing walking across the swinging structure?" It was a 20-meter-long narrow metal structure, ubiquitous on preschool and elementary school playgrounds—two parallel elongated inverted-u-shaped bars connected across the top by parallel metal bars at short intervals. Kids swing from one bar to the next from one end to the other. They soon master swinging and begin experimenting. "I finally got so that I could walk across the top without hesitating. I was so excited so I called Kikkawa-Sensei over and showed him. I thought he would congratulate me.

He just watched and asked, 'Can you run across it?'" She shook her head in total disbelief. "Can you believe that a teacher would encourage me to do something like that? Something dangerous? That would never happen in America." She was never able to run across the top; by the time she left she could move across it rapidly. She was, after all, only an *American* monkey.

In an earlier report of this research (Walsh, 2002a), I identified common Japanese cultural beliefs about children. Three are relevant to this discussion.

1. Children are naturally good and naturally sensible (e.g., Fujinaga, 1967). They can be trusted to make sensible decisions.
2. The "spirit" formed by early experience provide the basis for later life. A proverb states, "The spirit of a three-year-old [by Western counting, two-year-old] will last until 100."
3. Children are physical beings, and their physical development and expression critical to their well being.

I focus on the first two and how they inform the third. The belief that children are naturally sensible and can be trusted to make sensible decisions explains why children are given so much space, literally and figuratively, on the playgrounds for athletic and other activities. Teachers trust that children will not endanger themselves. Japanese parents and teachers are surely concerned about their children, but the concern starts from a trust in their ability to take care of themselves. People told me often that children were smart enough not to do things they weren't capable of. The most difficult adjustment we had to make as parents was giving Scooter and Buck more space than we did back home in Illinois.

Tobin (2003) wrote that

> The concluding argument of *Preschools in Three Cultures* [Tobin, Wu, & Davidson, 1989] is that the great strength of Japanese preschools is that they provide young children with the kind of social complexity otherwise lacking in these children's overly sheltered, narrow lives. This social complexity, in turn promotes *chiteki hattatsu* [difficult to translate—something like "intellectual development'] that occurs not so much because of how teachers interact with individual children as because of how they restrain themselves from interacting, by giving children space and time to interact with each other and with their environment. (p. 8)

Tobin is certainly correct that preschools provide a needed alternative to the home. But he does not argue that preschool completely breaks from the home. The constraints change, but the larger constraints of Japanese culture pervade both school and home. Even protected Japanese toddlers experience a physical freedom that, when seen on video, makes Americans uncomfortable (Walsh, 2001). The key is the space provided by teachers and parents who maintain a distance, again both figuratively and literally, from children. Children's interactions with each other are seldom directly mediated by teachers.

Preschools playgrounds are, by American standards, unsupervised. Teachers come and go, at times playing with children, but they do not "supervise," keeping the children and the playground under surveillance. A Japanese kindergarten teacher who had visited U.S. preschools asked me, "When American teachers are standing against the fence watching the playground," she leaned against the wall, arms folded across her chest slowing rotating her head from side to side, "what are they *doing*?"

What had I been doing all the times I had spent supervising playgrounds as a teacher? I replied that they were making sure that kids followed playground rules and didn't get hurt. "But can't the children do that themselves?" she asked. Good question.

In one kindergarten the kids liked to climb a tall tree behind one of the buildings. The tree was made for climbing with large evenly spaced branches. The older kids sometimes climbed quite high, at times making me nervous. The teachers paid little attention and seldom came into this area. I asked the teachers about the tree and how high the kids were climbing. By this time I knew that teachers cultivated an apparent inattention while almost clairvoyantly aware of every little thing happening on the playground and off. They had talked about the tree climbing at length in their daily meetings. They decided to ignore it because they didn't want to inhibit the children's explorations and because they were concerned that if they supervised the climbing in any way, the kids would become dependent on them and would, in this dependence become less careful. Further, they wanted the older kids to be responsible for the younger ones. Later, I saw older children helping younger ones climb and keeping them from climbing too high.

The first time I visited Japan, in the late 80's, our hosts took my wife, Scooter, then a toddler, and me to a zoo in Tokyo. As we got off the train, a class of third graders emptied out of the next car. The teacher, a young man, alone with his class, went to the front of the children, who more or less lined up three and four across behind him, and led them across the street to the zoo. I counted 30-some children. I asked my hosts if we could follow them for a while. The children were loud and spirited, and occasionally one or two would wander from the group. Each time they did, other kids ran out and pulled them back into line. The teacher *never* looked back. He continued straight ahead. I realized then, although I certainly did not understand how, that teaching in this culture was deeply differently defined from teaching, as I knew it. Children were to be trusted to make sensible decisions and to take care of themselves, not only individually but also as a group.

Japanese kids eventually develop into the polite quiet adults of the stereotype, which, in fact, they are when the context calls for quiet and politeness. But children are expected to be loud and wild—their spirit is not be quashed. Middle school and high school will do that, but by then the spirit will be fully formed. Exuberance in word and deed is valued. Children are seldom corrected. The typical strategy for dealing with behavior too troublesome to be ignored (ignoring is the rule) is distracting kids—something Japanese adults do well. My head often rang from the noise in the large playrooms on rainy days; more than once I got hit by objects being flung across the room. But, "They're kids, aren't they," teachers explained. Their words were more than explanation, they were encouragement. Spirited behavior is not an unfortunate fact of life, the noise and the chaos and the rambunctiousness are markers of the spirit needed to become the polite mature adult valued by the culture. A mature polite adult not informed by this spirit is an empty shell.

TRANSFORMING FROEBEL

We walked through a large park in Osaka with friends and their toddler. A large fiberglass dragon curled around part of the playground. From it protruded climbing and swinging apparatuses. The dragon was about 30 meters long, and the head; the mouth opened wide, rose about 7 meters in the air at its top. Many kids were playing on the dragon; most on the tail section, clambering over the triangular ridges that spanned the dragons back from head to tail. A boy, about 11, moved along the top of the dragon, stepping from the top of each triangular ridge to the next, balancing effortlessly until he came to the highest point on the head. Scooter and I were transfixed—the others had gone on down the hill. He stood balancing on the tip of the triangle—at this point about a quarter meter high with a rounded (I checked later), not flat, top. He stared off across the Osaka skyline for about 5 minutes then slowly turned and walked back the same way. In total envy Scooter rued, "I wish I could do that. I wish I could do that."

In 1837 Friedrich Froebel founded the institution that three years later he would name the *kindergarten*. The German word *kindergarten* can be translated in two ways, *a children's garden*, that is, a garden belonging to or for children, and *a garden of children*, that is, a garden where children grow like plants, and where, like plants, they are to be tended and nurtured. Both meanings can be found in Froebel. In fact, Froebel wanted each child to have an individual garden as well a larger garden tended by the class. In the history of American kindergarten the latter meaning eventually became dominant (Chung & Walsh, 2000). The Japanese prefer the former. Plants, after all, do not move. They cannot run and jump and climb.

As have many ideas imported from abroad, Froebel's ideas were made Japanese as they were interpreted through the lens of Japanese cultural beliefs. Japanese early educators take the idea of a garden for children literally. Plants proliferate. One sees the principal out weeding the flowers and the plants. Animals—rabbits, ducks, and chickens—are common, and the children's feeding the animals is an important activity.

The second way that the preschools are like gardens is that preschool is seen as an outside activity. A most visible difference between American and Japanese preschools is size of the playgrounds—Japanese playgrounds are generally large, even in the large cities. A second difference is materials. Classrooms have comparatively few puzzles, books, toys and so on. Playgrounds are elaborately equipped, not only with climbing structures and slides and so on, but also with unicycles, bicycles, tricycles, shovels, stilts, gymnastic equipment, hoses, troughs for diverting water, buckets, tools, and so on. Children do spend time inside, and in the large private urban kindergartens—I observed one with more than 700 children—organizational constraints keep kids inside more than in my five primary sites. But even there, the kids were outside many more than American preschool children. In my primary sites, children spent at least as much, and often more, time outside than inside, and until organized inside activity, usually late in the day, they moved freely from inside to out and back.

A preschool focused on outside activities will be more focused on the physical than one that emphasizes inside activities. Ironically, Froebel's *gifts*, which have generally disappeared from preschool education, emphasized the use of small muscles, as early critics of Froebel pointed out. These critics missed the importance that Froebel placed on nature walks, which he picked up from Pestalozzi, and other outdoor activities. In any case, American critics of Froebel replaced the small muscle activities of the gifts with limited large motor activities, for example, the circle games popular in early schooling.

The Japanese went from the gifts to unrestricted outdoor physical play. The emphasis on large muscle development was never limited to a circle games. Playgrounds encourage children to push themselves. Ayers (1993) argued that classrooms should be "laboratories for discovery and surprise, spaces where children can be active and experimental in following their own compelling goals, places where knowledge opens to future knowledge" (p. 58). Japanese preschool playgrounds are laboratories for physical discovery and surprise.

CONCLUSION

Japan is in transition—the long stagnant economy, the declining birth and marriage rates, changes in social structure have all had a serious and deleterious impact on early schooling. Enrollments in preschools have declined precipitously. Three of my primary sites had empty classrooms, and the birth rate has declined more slowly in small towns and rural areas than in large cities. Private preschools in big cities compete intensely for children. They must to survive. Japanese early childhood educators worry that traditional preschool values and practices are being lost in this competition. They worry about the appearance of societal problems they have never faced before.

I do not intend to romanticize Japanese early schooling. I note in passing Holloway (2000), who presents a bleak picture of Japanese early schooling. Her research is, at best, problematic (see Walsh, in press). Certainly one can find poorly run preschools and bad teachers in Japan. But they are not the norm.

Comparisons across cultures are tricky. The temptation to ignore the complexities and contradictions within in order to facilitate comparisons across cultures always beckons. I struggle with the temptation. I admire much about Japanese early schooling. A prominent Japanese professor told me that kindergarten is the high point of Japanese education. I certainly agree. I also believe that Japanese preschool is "a last best place" (Walsh, 2002b) in early schooling across the world. Early schooling in the U.S. has become increasingly restrictive, with children given little of the space and time needed for development. The dominant discourse of "developmentally appropriate practice" has contributed to the increasing restrictiveness (see, e.g., Lee, J-H, 2003; Walsh, 1991).

Focusing on the physical in early schooling, encouraging, supporting, valuing physical activities and development benefits children in profound ways. Whether physical and social development serve as the foundation of intellectual (and emotional) development, and I believe they do, young children can reach levels of physical and social expertise much more readily than they can equivalent levels of intellectual expertise. Intellectual development is a long slow process, constrained (hindered) by complex symbol systems and by well developed bodies of knowledge that take years, even decades, to master or to begin to.

Early on children can master climbing poles, riding unicycles, running fast, tumbling, walking on stilts, kicking soccer balls, and so on—if they have adequate space, time, support, and so on. American educators emphasize "self-esteem." Bruner argues (1996), however, that self-esteem is meaningful only within the context of agency and the ability to evaluate that agency.

A transformation occurs when young children begin to master a physical skill. Take, for example, ice skating. When kids can jump out on the ice without first steadying themselves on the rink door. Kids who are ordinary or even klutzy on dry land become graceful and in control on the ice, aware of their agency. Scooter, struggling with early adolescence, confided to me that no matter how bad her life was off the ice, how out of control and frightening, as soon as she stepped on the ice, she entered a world where she was in control, where she didn't worry about being awkward or accepted.

Children need rich opportunities to develop physically that give them many ways to excel. A dirty little secret about schooling is that one has to be good at only a few things to be wildly successful, and, one has to be bad at an only a few things to be wretchedly unsuccessful.

Not every child can be a dominant athlete, but every child can have an athletic self. Every child can be supported in this quest. I saw hundreds of preschoolers in Japan swinging themselves up and over bars. I also saw on playgrounds "scaffolds," not in the figurative Brunerian sense, but actual wooden devices that helped children get their legs up and over the bars. They walked up the scaffold and then easily swung over the bar. Again, what is possible, accessible, supported, and valued?

The developmental psychology encountered in the latest *Handbook of Child Psychology* (1998) is complex and systems-oriented. The developmental psychology encountered in everyday discussions within education, the folk psychology, is Piagetian stage-theory with maturationist underpinnings and that underestimates children's physical, social, intellectual, and other abilities. Development is viewed as *natural* and distinct from *learning*. Within developmental psychology, the longstanding distinction between development and learning was blurred years ago. Within American folk psychology, the distinction remains strong. If development is *natural* and *distinct from learning*, then norms for development can be determined by carefully observing children and establishing what children can do at a specific age. The *normality* of the individual child can then be measured by comparing the child to these norms. This approach, traceable back to G. Stanley Hall and his Child Study Movement and to Arnold Gesell, underlies the idea of *mental age* and IQ.

This limited discourse on development ignores the reality that what children can do at any given historical and cultural moment depends a great deal on cultural constraints—what is accessible and not accessible, valued and not valued, and so on. The norms themselves become constraints that both enhance and restrict as society sets strong expectations about what children can and cannot, and should and should not do.

Missing is the sense of the possible. Today's female athletes differ markedly from their often ground-breaking predecessors. They runs faster, jump higher, skate faster, and so on. The advances have not been the incremental ones that mark men's athletics over recent decades. Women's basketball or ice hockey or soccer is different sports from 20 years ago. Why? The cultural constraints have changed. Women's athletic development, once restricted, has been enhanced. Women have been able to begin to explore the bodily possible.

Enough said.

REFERENCES

Ayers, W. (1993). *To teach: The journey of a teacher.* New York: Teachers College Press.

Bruner, J. (1996). *The culture of education.* Cambridge: Harvard.

Chung, S., & Walsh, D. J. (2000). Unpacking "child-centeredness": A history of meanings. *Journal of Curriculum Studies, 32,* 215–234.

Cole, M. (1996). *Cultural psychology: A once and future discipline.* Cambridge: Harvard.

Fujinaga, H. (1967). *Early childhood education in Japan* (in Japanese). Tokyo: Kodansha.

Harada, S., & Saito, T. (1997). *Ashi karano kenkou zukuri: Okaasan to kodomo no tameno kenkou zukuri.* Tokyo: Chuou Houki. (in Japanese)

Hatano, G., & Miyake, N. (1991). What does a cultural approach offer to research on learning? *Learning and Instruction, 1,* 273-281.

Holloway, S. (2000). *Contested Childhood: Diversity and Change in Japanese Preschools.* New York: Routledge.

Kitayama, S., & Markus, H. R. (1999). Yin and yang of the Japanese self: The cultural psychology of personality coherence. In D. Cervone & Y. Shoda (Eds.), *The coherence of personality: Social-cognitive bases of consistency, variability, and organization.* New York: Guilford.

Kitayama, S., & Markus, H. R. (2000). The pursuit of happiness and the realization of sympathy: Cultural patterns of self, social relations, and well-being. In E. Diener & E. M. Suh (Eds.), *Culture and subjective well-being* (pp. 113–161). Cambridge, MA: MIT Press.

Lee, J-H. (2003). *The quest for quality: Evaluation and early childhood programs.* Unpublished doctoral dissertation, University of Illinois at Urbana-Champaign.

Markus, H. R., & Kitayama, S. (1991). Culture and self: Implications for cognition, emotion, and motivation. *Psychological Review, 98,* 224–253.

Price, G. G. (1982). Cognitive learning in early childhood education: Mathematics, science, and social studies. In B. Spodek (Ed.), *Handbook of research in early childhood education* (pp. 264–294). New York: Free Press.

Shweder, R. A., Goodnow, J., Hatano, G., LeVine, R., Markus, H., & Miller, P. (1999). The cultural psychology of development: One mind, many mentalities. In W. Damon (Ed.), *Handbook of child psychology, volume 1, theoretical models of human development* (pp. 865–937). New York: John Wiley.

Tobin, J. (2003, April). *Some thoughts on the "intellectual development" of young children in Japan and the United States.* Paper presented at the annual meeting of the American Educational Research Association, Chicago.

Tobin, J., Wu, D., & Davidson, D. (1989). *Preschool in three cultures: Japan, China, and the United States.* New Haven: Yale University Press.

Walsh, D. J. (1991). Reconstructing the discourse on developmental appropriateness: A developmental perspective. *Early Education and Development, 2,* 109–119.

Walsh, D. J. (2001, April). *The cringe factor: Cultural differences in beliefs about young children.* Paper presented at the annual meeting of the American Educational Research Association, Seattle, Washington.

Walsh, D. J. (2002a). The development of self in Japanese preschools. In L. Bresler & A. Ardichvili (Eds.), *Multiple paradigms for international research in education: Experience, theory, & practice.* New York: Peter Lang.

Walsh, D. J. (2002b, April). *A last best place: The strengths of Japanese preschools.* Paper presented at the annual meeting of the American Educational Research Association, New Orleans.

Walsh, D. J. (in press). Dimensions of Japanese early schooling [Review of the book *Contested childhood: Diversity and change in Japanese preschools*]. *Contemporary Psychology.*

JOSEPH TOBIN

THE DISAPPEARANCE OF THE BODY IN EARLY
CHILDHOOD EDUCATION

The body is disappearing in early childhood education. Once a protected site within the larger world of education in which the body could flourish, preschools are now a battle-zone in the war against the body, sites where the bodies of children and the adults who care for them fall under increasing scrutiny and discipline. The decline of the body in early childhood education takes many forms: compared to a generation ago, young children are spending less time in the sandbox and more at the computer; they are less likely to sit on their teachers' lap or to be given a hug, to finger-paint, dance, or run naked through a sprinkler, or to engage with their peers in physical interaction—of either the affectionate or rough-housing varieties.

My analysis will focus on what's happening to the body in preschools in the contemporary United States, but not because I believe this is a uniquely American phenomenon. Given that the discourses and pressures I suggest are causes of this process of disembodiment circulate globally, there is reason to believe that the same things are happening elsewhere, and where it's not happening yet, that it will soon.

I will attempt to explain the disappearance of the body in early childhood education by presenting six root causes. In reality, these causes overlap and are difficult to disentangle. But for heuristic reasons, in this essay I will deal with them one at a time. If some of my arguments sound familiar, it may be because I draw on theories and narratives, including those of Michel Foucault, that many of you know very well (even if you haven't seen them applied to early childhood education) and also because I borrow from some earlier published writings of my own, including *Preschool in Three Cultures* (1989), "The Irony of Self-Expression" (1995), "The Missing Discourse of Pleasure and Desire in Early Childhood Education" (1997a), "Playing Doctor in Two Cultures" (1997b), and "Childhood Sexuality after Freud (2001)." The invitation to contribute an essay to this volume has provided me with an opportunity to look across this series of studies, moving the problem of the body to the center of analysis.

Moral Panic: The Preschool as a Site of Sexual Danger

In the late 1980s and early 1990s, a series of cases of purported sexual abuse of children by caretakers in childcare settings received extensive news coverage. These cases, which typically included allegations that multiple children in a childcare setting were systemically abused by more than one staff member, sometimes in ways

111

Liora Bresler (ed.), Knowing Bodies, Moving Minds, 111-125.
©*2004 Kluwer Academic Publishers. Printed in the Netherlands*

that included satanic rituals or the production of child pornography, in the end crumbled in the courtroom. But although the high profile legal cases turned out to lack merit, they had the effect of establishing in the consciousness of the nation the twin characters of the pedophilic preschool teacher and the sexually vulnerable preschooler.

I am not suggesting that young children are never sexually abused by the people who care for them. I am suggesting, however, that the way our society approaches this danger has taken the form of a moral panic which, in it's mixture of fantasy, displacement, and projection, fails to protect young children while it diminishes the quality of their lives. While children's fathers, step-fathers, uncles, other family members, and mothers' boyfriends prey on young children in the home, tens of thousands of early childhood educators are being defined by the society at large, by parents, and by themselves and each other as potential pedophiles who cannot be trusted to act in the best interests of the children for whom they care. Unwilling or unable as a society to confront sexual abuse within the home, where it is epidemic, we instead impose draconian measures in preschool settings. In this climate of panic and accusation, not only teachers but also young children are criminalized: play that in other eras and other cultures would be considered normal and unexceptional becomes evidence of them being victims or perpetrators of sexual crimes. Viewing the actions of early childhood educators and young children through a lens of potential sexual abuse leads to the imposition of draconian, wrong-headed solutions which themselves create new problems, impoverishing the lives of children and teachers.

A chief effect of this moral panic has been a curtailment of bodily pleasures in early childhood educational settings. The most dramatic example is the emergence in the 1990s of safe touch workshops for the staff and the children in preschools and guidelines that prescribe how teachers can touch children (Johnson, 2000). Childcare workers are now routinely prohibited from changing a toddler's diaper without a second adult present, from helping children in the bathroom (pulling down their pants or wiping their behinds) or even from assisting them to change their underclothes and clean off after having a bowel movement in their pants. In safe touch workshops staff are advised that they should limit physical intimacy with children by, for instance, discouraging children from sitting on their laps. Some experts allow some lap sitting, but with the proviso that the child must sit side-saddle.

Even in situations where bodily contact with young children isn't explicitly forbidden, the climate of suspicion and panic has the effect of curtailing physical intimacy between caretakers and children. In situations where a generation ago a caretaker would have picked a crying child up and held her, there is now likely to be just a quick hug; where there once would have been a hug, there is now just a pat on the head; where there once would have been a pat on the head, there is now just a warm smile and words of praise or encouragement. And thus, step by step, but inexorably, the world of the preschool becomes disembodied.

This is unfortunate not just for children, but also for the adults who care for them. One of the great pleasures of being with young children is their physicality. By projecting our fears and desires onto the figure of the pedophile, we preclude the possibility of talking honestly to each other about the pleasures we find in work with children. Are pedophiles and perverts the only adults who desire children, who enjoy touching children, and being touched by children? What if I were to acknowledge the emotional and physical pleasure I find in holding a newborn to my chest, in spooning oatmeal into an infant's eager mouth, in the feel of a toddler's hand closing around my finger, in rocking a child in my arms to soothe his tears? Must we cite studies on the disastrous effects of touch deprivation on baby monkeys (Harlow and Harlow, 1969) to justify our touching young children? Must we think of our touching and holding children as acts of altruism? If we can't talk aloud to each other about these pleasures—the erotics of caring for children—all of us who work with and care for young children will be forced to remain in the closet, wondering if we are alone in feeling as we do.

An Age of Sexual Enlightenment?

We contemporary Americans congratulate ourselves on having over-come the repression of sexuality that we believe was typical of earlier generations and for having brought sexuality into the light. But Foucault (1979; 1981) complicates this reassuring story of progress by arguing that when sex was still cloaked in darkness and in many of its manifestations considered a sin, it was in a sense freer than it is now when it has been made into a medical specialization, a subject of academic study, and a juridical preoccupation, before, that is, there were medical, academic, and legal discourses on categories of sexual dysfunction, gender formation, sexual identity, and sexual rights. Enlightened disciplines including psychoanalysis, sexology, and fertility studies created by progressive thinkers in order to bring sex out of the shadows of moral censure are seen by Foucault of having had the paradoxical effect of making sex more visible, more scrutinized, more discursively framed, more open to intrusion, more self-censored, and thus on the whole less pleasurable. As a result, Foucault argues, the body in contemporary times is more disciplined than it was in earlier eras.

We can apply this logic to what has happened to the sex play and bodily interactions of young children. In the early 1990s I researched attitudes towards children's sex play by asking preschool teachers, in focus groups, to discuss a series of vignettes, including one involving kissing:

There's a four-year old girl in my group who runs up to the boys during free play and kisses them. And I don't mean just a peck on the cheek. She kisses them right on the lips. I was hoping the problem would kind of fade away, but now she's got some of the other girls doing the same thing.

As someone who grew up in an era when children's kissing games were considered normal, I was surprised that in discussing this scenario, preschool teachers used the logic and language of medical and psychological symptomatology. The little girls in these stories were seen as having clinical conditions, conditions that could or should be referred to medical specialists. Many associated kissing games with germs, contagion, and sexually transmitted diseases. In nine of the twelve focus groups, germs came up in the discussion. In three groups, the mention of spreading germs through kissing escalated to a discussion of sexually transmitted diseases. The most striking example of such a jump was this sequence of comments made by a group of Honolulu early-childhood-education graduate students in the spring of 1992:

Teacher A: I worry about germs. I'd tell them, "You can kiss on the cheek, but not on the mouth. You have yucky germs in your mouth."

Teacher B: I heard somewhere that actually you have lots more germs on your hands than in your mouth. You're more likely to get sick from shaking hands than from kissing.

Teacher A: We make the children wash their hands several times a day, but it's a constant battle. A lot of them just run in and out of the bathroom and pretend they washed their hands. Or they just stick one hand under the faucet and think their hands are clean.

Teacher B: That's why so many preschool children and teachers are sick. There are germs being spread all over the place because the kids have such bad hygiene. Someone did a study of germs in a preschool classroom using like an infrared device to show how the children spread germs, and germs were literally all over the place. The whole room was red in the picture.

Teacher C: It's scary, all the new germs out there they don't have medicines for. There's even resistance to the old germs that used to be handled by antibiotics. I was reading something the other day about how common herpes is, and that once you get it, it's almost impossible to get rid of it. I mean the kind of herpes you get in your mouth, on your lips.

Teacher D: With this whole Magic Johnson thing, you can't help but think about HIV.

Teacher B: But it's a myth that you can get AIDS by kissing.

Teacher D: Right, I know, but the whole safe sex and AIDS thing, and we have to be really careful. I just mean that somehow this story just brings to mind the whole thing with Magic and AIDS.

Teacher E: And now there's that book that says Wilt Chamberlin had sex with 30,000 different women!

Teacher D: You know how doctors and dentists and nurses have to wear rubber gloves with all their patients. I bet we'll be next. I can just see me putting on gloves to wipe the kids' noses and make their snacks.

Taken one by one, these comments are reasonable and unexceptional. But the conversation taken as whole follows the (il)logic of association, displacement, and substitution characteristic of dreams, hysterical symptoms, and moral panics. The conversation moves from children's kissing, to children's inconsistent hand washing, to children and teachers getting sick, to (oral) herpes, to AIDS, to sexual promiscuity and finally to teachers' needing to wear rubber gloves. Topical jumps and shifts are characteristic of informal human communication. But the associative jumps in this conversation have a logic and directionality characteristic of an anxiety-driven, culturally shared hysteria in which a larger societal panic about adult sexuality and AIDS is projected onto the benign bodily contacts of young children.

This conversation gives us insight into the projective mechanisms that lead teachers to regard as dangerous a kissing game that in other times and contexts would be seen as benign. The conversation leaps from minor worry to apocalyptic disaster, from the common cold to the AIDS epidemic, from a little girl kissing several boys to a man having sex with 30,000 women. This is how moral panics work: by synecdoche (the substitution of parts for whole and wholes for parts) and the erasure of distinctions between dissimilar actors and actions. In this conversation the child's mouth becomes a synecdoche for the sexually vulnerable and dangerous adult body. Critical distinctions are erased between the sexuality of children and adults, as promiscuous kissing by a four-year-old girl is linked to Wilt Chamberlain's improbably prodigious sexual promiscuity. There are substitutions of the mouth for the genitals, of the relatively benign germs of the cold and the sore throat for the deadly viruses of sexually transmitted diseases, of the beginning (kissing as foreplay) and the end (sexual intercourse). In the leap from a little girl to Magic Johnson to Wilt Chamberlain to the gloved preschool teacher we have a collapsing and confusion of perpetrator and victim and of guilt and innocence (guilty victims and innocent vectors) characteristic of the moral panic and projection surrounding AIDS.

We find similar dynamics at work in preschool teachers' reactions to a vignette concerned playing doctor:

> The other day, two girls and a boy where playing "doctor." Actually, they were playing "delivery room." One girl, who was being the patient, lay on her back and said, "It's time for the baby." Then the other girl, who was the nurse, and the boy, who was the doctor, got ready to "deliver" the baby. I was watching from across the room. At first I was thinking this was cute, but then the nurse told the doctor, "Pull down her underpants so we can get the baby out," and that's just what they did. When they pulled her underpants down I could see that she had put a little baby-doll in her underpants and was now holding it between her legs. At that point I came over. The "nurse" told me, "Get away, we're birthing a baby," but I told the "patient" she had to put her underpants back on immediately.

Reactions to this vignette suggest that it is not just children's sexual desire and pleasure but also their sexual knowledge that worries early childhood educators. If the focus-group discussions of the kissing story are classically Freudian in their hysterical conversion of tabooed desires to bodily (somatized) symptoms and in their concern with female immodesty, reactions to the delivery room story are Lacanian in their anxiety about the interplay of knowledge, ignorance, and innocence. In several of the discussions, the conversation turned to the question of how these children knew so much:

- What graphic, vivid language they use!
- Too much maturity for kids of that age.
- Where did they get all this knowledge of where babies come from?
- Kids these days see everything—even films of babies coming out of the birth canal.
- I would question how these children would have such knowledge. I mean actual physical knowledge of the birthing process.
- Maybe one of them was in a delivery room with their parents.
- Maybe they saw a baby book or saw a birth on TV and are acting it out.

- Something about this gives me an uncomfortable feeling. These girls seem to know a bit too much for, how old does it say they are? Four years old?

The core concern here is that excessive knowledge of sex and the body is dangerous. This is knowledge in the old, biblical sense, the kind of knowledge that comes from eating forbidden fruit (or watching someone else do so). These girls who know how to play doctor too expertly are suspicious. Sexual knowledge is dangerous because it suggests a lack of innocence. These girls suffer from lack of a lack. In *Looking Awry: An Introduction to Jacques Lacan through Popular Culture*, Slavoj Zizek discusses the characters in Hitchcock films who are in danger because, by chance, they have come to know things they should not know. Children shouldn't know too much about kissing or the anatomical details of birth (much less of sexual intercourse). This knowing becomes dangerous to others but mostly to the child who knows and who for this reason comes under suspicion of needing treatment.

These examples of preschool teachers citing contemporary medical, social work, and legal discourses about sexuality to back up their concerns about children's sex play support Foucault's thesis that the development of supposedly progressive, enlightened discourses produce new forms of disciplining sex and the body. Children's sex play was freer in the United States of the 1950s than it is now because it was not a focus of widespread anxiety, discussion, or surveillance. Many of the preschool teachers in the focus group discussions contrasted how they feel they must respond to sex play now and the way teachers and parents responded to sex play when they were children, like the preschool teacher in Chicago who reflected nostalgically on her own suburban childhood in the 1950s:

> When I was a kid, my Mom didn't work so I didn't go to nursery school every day. I must have been four or five, and there were tons of kids on my block, and we'd gather in my garage. I remember being the doctor, and making some little boys from next door—they must have been younger than me, maybe three-years-old or so—I remember making them line up and I was the doctor and they were the patients and I'd call out, "Next patient." And when they came over to me I'd pretend to take their temperatures and give them a shot, but really the point of the game was to pull down their pants. Didn't everyone play games like that? My mother was probably in the house, cooking or watching T.V. I'd like kids to have the chance for that kind of sex play. But as a teacher, there is absolutely no way I can look the other way and let kids play doctor in my classroom. Do I sound hypocritical?

We should guard ourselves against idealizing or attempting to recreate the past. I do not believe that children were necessarily happier or family life better in the 1950s, when childcare was less available and middle-class mothers were expected to not work outside the home. But one thing we might attempt to recreate from this era was what one of my respondents described as "the luxury of not having to feel like you have to be watching the children every second." Conservative Americans who would like to see a return to the patriarchal family relations of the 1950s portray postwar mothers as constantly available to their young children, supervising their every move. These critics of institutional childcare argue that a preschool teacher with twelve or more youngsters in her charge cannot give the children the quality of attention a stay-at-home mother can give to her own children. But what if the secret of motherhood in the 1950s was not middle-class mothers' constant attention but their *inattention*? I have memories of playing with my brothers and my friends, and with their sisters and brothers, playing in each other's basements, bedrooms, garages, and in the ravines behind our houses, playing doctor, and having peeing contests, and telling doo-doo jokes, all while our mothers were cooking, doing laundry, running off to the store ("You boys be good—I'll be back soon").

It's not that our mothers were intentionally choosing not to supervise us because they believed in our right to privacy, or because they wanted to make sure we would have opportunities to play doctor and kissing games, or because they were philosophically opposed to panopticism as a parenting technique. The socio-spatial norms governing mothers and children in the suburbs at the time just didn't call for surveillance.

I suspect that in some contemporary American families, in some communities, children still enjoy such unsupervised play. But many American families have concluded that ravines behind their houses and neighbors' basements and garages are not safe places for their children to be without supervision. And the increased use of childcare means that in the 1990s many American children spend the majority of their waking hours, not under the supervision of their mothers, who have the luxury of not scrutinizing their every move, but in childcare and preschool settings with adults who feel compelled to be vigilant, ready at a moment's notice to intervene in disputes or to break up a kissing game.

LOGOCENTRISM

Perhaps no other phrase better exemplifies the core belief of American early childhood education than the preschool teacher's admonition to children: "Use your words." I have no quarrel with the notion that one of the key roles of preschools is to provide ample opportunities for children to become increasingly verbally adept. The problem I have with the phrase "use your words" is with the unstated but implied clause that follows: "use your words *and not your body.*"

For example, consider this vignette (borrowed from the American section of *Preschool in Three Cultures*):

It's playground time at St. Timothy's. Stu and Lisa, playing in the sandbox, begin to fight over a plastic shovel. Gwen, a teaching assistant, quickly appears on the scene. She reaches out and grips the shovel in the middle, her hand between the grasping hands of Stu and Lisa:

Gwen: Lisa! Stu! Stop pulling on the shovel. I'm talking to both of you. Are you listening to me?

Stu: (not letting go of the shovel but looking at Gwen) Yes.

Lisa: (holding onto her end of shovel) I had it first, and then Stu, he grabbed it...

Gwen: One at a time, or I can't understand what you are saying.

Stu: I was using it before, and I was using my hand to dig just for one little minute, and then she took it, and. . .

Lisa: It was just sitting there. He wasn't using it. And then he pulled on my arm real hard like this (pulling hard on her own arm).

Stu: And she hit me, right there (pointing to his chest).

Gwen: Stu, when Lisa picked up the shovel you had been using, what could you have done instead of trying to yank it out of her hand? Could you have told her that you had it first? Do you think that would have worked?

Stu: No! She hit me.

Gwen: She hit you because you grabbed the shovel, right? Lisa, is that why you hit Stu? Were you feeling angry?

Lisa: I had it and he took it.

Gwen: Lisa, when you feel mad, can you think of a way you can let someone know how you are feeling?

The belief that signifiers (words) can adequately represent the signified (feelings) is essentially a modernist belief. But I would suggest that Gwen's approach to dealing with this dispute is more postmodern than modern. In this practice of encouraging young children to replace bodily expressions of strong feelings with a meta-discourse on feeling states, we see an example of a movement from the modernist faith in meaningful communication through the spoken and written word to the post-modern condition in which the word becomes more real and more important than that which is signified. In the postmodern American early childhood educational world, statements about feeling ("I feel angry") replace expressions of feeling ("Give me the truck, you doo-doo head!") which replace feelings (anger? desire?).

As Piaget teaches us, thinking and feeling, especially for young children carry a strong sensory-motor component. To compel young children to express their feelings verbally is therefore, inevitably, to suppress bodily expression of feeling.

The Declining Influence of Psychoanalysis

"Where id was, let ego be," Freud's famous epigram for the goals of psychoanalytic psychotherapy, now takes on the ironic tone of sad prophesy in both American early childhood education and in psychoanalysis, where the ego has replaced the body as the core concern. The history of the decline of the body in American early childhood education can be paired usefully with the decline of psychoanalytic influence in the field.

To chart the rise and fall of psychoanalysis's fortunes in the field of American preschool education, I analyzed the contents of over seventy years of early childhood educational textbooks. My method was simple: I reviewed the table of contents and the index and then the appropriate pages of all of the early childhood educational texts I could find in the Chicago Public Library's main branch as well as at the University of Chicago's libraries. This search led me to fifty-five titles, ranging from 1927 through 1999. I will review this seventy-two year span of history by breaking it into three phases.

Phase one, which runs roughly from 1927 through 1940, is characterized by the explicit citation of psychoanalytic theory. Freud's new ideas are cited as a scientific source of knowledge which nursery school educators should take into account as they grapple with the question of how best to deal with incidents of infantile sexuality. In books from this period it is not uncommon to find direct quotes from *The New Introductory Lectures, Three Contributions to the Theory of Sex* and *A*

General Introduction to Psychoanalysis. The main lesson early childhood educators of this era took from Freud is that repressive responses to young children's fledgling expressions of sexual curiosity are likely to produce negative developmental sequelae. For example, in her 1920 book, *Nursery School Education*, Miss Grace Owens writes:

What numbers of children have their development impeded and their tempers spoiled by their mothers' over-anxiety about furniture and clothes and respectability! We are just beginning to realize, largely through the work of Jung and Freud and other psychoanalysts, how great is the danger of the repression of the instincts and appetites—the dynamic forces of the mind—and how appalling are the disasters that result from it. It has shown beyond all doubt that a powerful impulse or emotion may not cease to exist when it is denied expression. It may be driven into the unconscious and find for itself surreptitious and indirect modes of expression. . . The truth seems to be that the repression of any innate impulse which is sufficiently powerful may be the source of mental and moral inefficiency (p.6).

Later in her book Owens adds: "What the nursery school teacher can do is to prevent unnatural repression of primitive impulses. . . The morality of a civilized community must not be imposed on the child by the wholesale suppression of his natural instincts" (p. 53).

In other publications of this era we find less explicit traces of psychoanalytic reasoning and less liberal stances towards masturbation and other forms of childhood sexuality. But even in the less progressive writings of this between-the-Wars era, masturbation and sex play are not seen as dangerous antecedents of degeneracy, as they were in child rearing manuals of the nineteenth century, nor as signs of abuse, as they would come to be in child development books of the 1990s.

In *Nursery School Education* (1939), by Olive Wheeler and Irene Earl, we find another example of a common sense approach to children's sexual curiosity combined with an indirect reference to the psychoanalytic notion that repression of sexuality in childhood is a primary cause of adult unhappiness:

Active curiosity concerning birth and sex may arise in young children, and, if so, should not be repressed. Questions asked should be dealt with frankly, and without tension or embarrassment—just as other questions are answered at this stage. Most of the difficulties which arise later can be traced back to the irrational attitudes of adults, many of whom attempt to hide in the darkness of a primitive taboo all the matter relating to sex and the creativeness of life" (p. 38).

In the second phase of this history, the post World War II era, citations of Freud and psychoanalysis become more rare in early childhood education textbooks but a generally relaxed and progressive stance towards childhood sexuality continues. For example, Marjorie Green and Elizabeth Woods' write in *A Nursery School Handbook for Teachers and Parents* (1948) "Remember, childish sex play in itself will not harm your child, but wrong attitudes on your part may warp his future attitudes, and seriously impair his social adjustment" (p.109). In her *Nursery School Guide*, Rhoda Kellogg (1949) echoes psychoanalytic reasoning without citing Freud, as she refers to the connection between repression and anxiety and as she links infantile sexual curiosity to intellectuality:

Because children are scolded and punished for wetting, soiling, and masturbating, they come to think that certain parts or areas of the body are "bad," and this becomes a source of anxiety. . . The inability of the adult to deal with the child's sexuality makes the child feel there are some things he must not reveal to anyone. Thus masturbating becomes a clandestine affair, and all sex interest must be repressed as much as possible. Since all learning processes thrive upon the individual's curiosity, the repressive type of sex education may have a very unfavorable influence upon the child's capacity to learn anything (p. 107).

In early childhood educational textbooks of the 1950s and early 1960s, the emphasis in discussions of childhood sexuality begins to shift to the topic of gender formation, as we can see in an excerpt from Katherine Read's *The Nursery School: A Human Relationships Laboratory* (1950):

A girl may not notice sex differences the first time that she uses a toilet beside a boy; but when she does notice a difference, she will usually want to watch boys frequently as they urinate. . . .She may comment and ask questions. If she does, she will be helped by the teacher's casual acceptance of her comments. It may help her to have the teacher verbalize in some way as, "Bill has a penis. He stands up at the toilet. Boys stand up and girls sit down there." Psychiatrists tell us that an important factor in later sex adjustment is the acceptance of one's sex. In this situation it is usually easier for the boys to feel acceptance because they possess a penis. Many times a girl will try to imitate the boy by attempting to stand—with not very satisfactory results! . . . Some girls may need help in feeling that being a girl is desirable. The teacher may remark, "Mothers sit down, too" (p. 101).

Psychoanalysis enjoyed a return as an explicit discourse in early childhood educational textbooks of the 1970s, although this time it was Erik Erikson rather than Freud who was most widely cited. Erikson's *Childhood and Society*, first published in 1950, was reissued in a new, enlarged edition in 1964, which quickly became a staple of child development courses. I view Erikson's prominence in the child development and early childhood education curricula of the 1970s and 1980s as both a plus and minus for psychoanalytic influence in these fields. Textbook authors and readers found Erikson's psychosocial stages more palatable than Freud's schema of psychosexual development. Although Erikson saw himself as applying and amplifying rather than negating Freud's theories, by the time Erikson's formulations made it into early childhood education textbooks the effect was to dilute Freud's emphasis on the centrality of sexuality and to replace a focus on libidinal development with the development of the ego. Although the case studies in *Childhood and Society* are classically Freudian in their depiction of troubled children caught up in confusion over the functions and symbolism of their bodies and genitalia, the primary lesson early childhood educators took from Erikson's work was that the key developmental issues of early childhood are trust, autonomy, and initiative. The shift in early childhood education in the later half of the century from Freud's focus on sex to Erikson's on ego development parallels and anticipates the shift in psychoanalysis from drive to ego theory and from issues of the body to issues of the self.

An example of the turning away from Freud and toward Erikson is Bettye Caldwell and Julius Richmond's 1974 essay in *The Formative Years: Principles of*

Early Childhood Education. After briefly discussing Freud's notion of the oral, anal, and genital stages, Caldwell and Richmond write:

During the "oral period" in infancy, for example, it is thought the child develops feelings about accepting things and the mother's manner of giving them. Erikson (1950) has postulated that from the totality of experiences in this period, the individual develops a basic sense of trust in people—or else a lack of trust which hampers his ensuing development (p. 51).

After presenting similarly Eriksonian takes on the anal and genital stages, the authors conclude:

There is growing recognition among psychoanalytic investigators that the application of knowledge gained from psychoanalysis in preventive efforts must be approached cautiously. The objective of psychoanalytic investigations as stated by Erikson (1950) a decade ago [n.b. actually, twenty-five years ago, at the time their paper was published] remains valid: "Psychoanalysis today is implementing the study of the ego, the core of the individual. It is shifting its emphasis from the concentrated study of the conditions which blunt and distort the individual ego to the study of the ego's roots in social organization" (p. 51).

The psychoanalytic turn toward a focus on attachment, the ego, and object relations had the virtue of making psychoanalysis more palatable to American early childhood educators, but at the cost of a loss of attention to sexuality and the body. The psychoanalytically informed discussions of masturbation and sexual curiosity that could be found in early childhood education textbooks in the between the wars era became much more rare after 1960.

By the mid-1980s, the issue of gender formation aside, discussions of sex had all but disappeared from early childhood education textbooks. But it was to return to the textbooks in the late 1980s in a new visage: the specter of sexual abuse. A review of early childhood education textbooks of the past fifteen years shows that when sexuality is mentioned at all, it is most often in the context of sexual danger. Masturbation and sexual play, no longer presented as natural features of early childhood, are discussed instead as possible indicators of abuse and precursors of sexual danger. From the 1920s through the 1950s, early childhood education textbooks warned of the mental health risks of repressing children's sexuality; in the 1990s the risk teachers are urged to keep in the forefront of their minds is children's sexuality vulnerability.

The current status of discussions of sexuality in contemporary early childhood education textbooks can be summarized quite succinctly: Psychoanalytic perspectives have all but disappeared; "normal" infantile sexuality is rarely discussed; when sex is discussed, it is as a danger.

American psychoanalysis' embrace of the shift from Freud's drive theory to the ego-psychology of Erickson and the attachment theorists, to the self-psychology of the Kohutians has deprived the field of early childhood education of access to the only theory that speaks in a meaningful way about the bodies and desires of young children. With American psychoanalysts no longer talking and writing about infantile sexuality, the sexuality of young children has been left to other specialties, specialties, alas, who hold far more suspicious and fearful attitudes towards children's sex play and bodily explorations.

Brain Research

It's too early to tell what the long-term impact will be of brain research on the field of early childhood education. But early returns are, at the best, mixed. Brain research has been the hot topic at early childhood education conferences and for inservice training for the past few years, but the curricular implications remain unclear. In most brain research presentations for early childhood educators, after delivering a crash course on myelinization and the establishment and disestablishment of neuro-pathways, speakers leave their audience with a sense of urgency that the first five years of life is a critical stage for brain development and with suggestions for what to do on Monday morning that range from playing Mozart to babies, to reading aloud to young children, to purchasing "brain boxes" (boxes filled with activities such as objects of different shapes and colors). I share John Breur's (1997, 1999) concern that the applications of brain research to early childhood education is a "bridge too far," leading to inferences that cannot be supported by the scientific research, to empty pronouncements by preschools whose flyers and websites make such claims as "our preschool curriculum is designed specifically for these years of critical brain development" or "our curriculum is brain-based," and to some unfortunate applications, such as cutting down on playground time and social play in favor of "brain rich" activities teaching pattern recognition, numbers, and phonics. Proponents of brain research would argue these are misapplications. But it's unclear what correct application of this knowledge would be.

My assessment is that the net effect of brain research on the body of preschoolers is negative. When applying brain research concepts to infants and toddlers, proponents tend to emphasize the need for motor activities. But when this research is applied to four and five year-olds, the emphasis tends to be on reading and arithmetic. The sense of urgency pushed by proponents of applying brain research to early childhood education who suggest that children's brains that are not properly supported will miss out at a critical stage on the chance to develop optimally is heard by many preschool directors and teachers as a directive to de-emphasize the life of the body and throw all available resources into the needs of the brain, the favorite organ of the new American millennium.

NO CHILD LEFT BEHIND

The No Child Left Behind initiative of the Bush White House is having a similar, but more insidious effect on American early childhood education. Like brain research, the No Child Left Behind act has the effect of increasing support for the provision of preschools, but only if those preschools emphasize academic over social development. Specifically, No Child Left Behind orders school districts and federally funded preschool programs to focus on using phonics to teach reading:

> The new Early Reading First program will make competitive 6-year awards to Leas (local educational agencies) to support early language, literacy, and pre-reading development of preschool-age children, particularly those from low-income families. Recipients will use instructional strategies and professional development drawn from scientifically based reading research to help young children to attain the fundamental knowledge and skills they will need for optimal reading development in kindergarten and beyond (U.S.D.O.E., 2003).

The effects on the life of the body of this redefinition of the preschool as a site for reading instruction for children from low-income families can be seen at Alhambra Preschool, one of the focal sites for my new study, "Continuity and Change in Preschools of Three Cultures." Alhambra Preschool, located on the campus of a middle school, offers free and reduced-tuition programs to low-income families. Alhambra's school day is fractured, reflecting the fractured, partial nature of public support for early childhood education and care. Department of Economic Security (Welfare) funds, which are intended to allow mothers of young children to get back to work, can be used for childcare, but not for education. Block Grant funds that come through the State Department of Education will pay for half a day of education, but not for childcare. Balancing these restrictive funding streams with the needs of families, Alhambra Preschool has cobbled together a program in which four year old children spend the beginning of the day (7:30–9:30 a.m.) in a childcare room (subsidized by Department of Economic Assistance funds), a 2.5 hour morning or afternoon block in a "Success by Six" preschool classroom (subsidized by Department of Education funds), and then the rest of the day back in the childcare program. This program is enthusiastically supported by grateful parents, who get a full day of childcare and half a day of preschool for their children at a rate they can afford—a rare and precious service in the United States. In my estimation, the director and teachers at Alhambra are doing an admirable job of providing a needed service with barely adequate funds. But the restrictions placed on teachers by the mixed funding streams, combined with the No Child Left Behind act, have some unfortunate effects on the body. The most troubling of these effects is that young children are lined up and marched from one room to another four or more times during the day. Another effect is that children in some of the preschool classrooms go to the playground for recess only twice a week. When I asked why, a teacher explained:

I used to have the kids for four hours a day, which left plenty of time to go to the playground. But with the new system, where I have different groups of kids in morning and afternoon blocks, the kids get only two and a half hours a day with me, which means I have to make some tough choices. That two and half hours go by really fast. Lots of that time is taken up by morning opening, and snack, and getting ready to go home. To get them where they need to be for kindergarten next year I feel I should keep them in the room with me working on their skills instead of sending them out to the playground.

Children at Alhambra get opportunities to play outside on the playground during the childcare portion of the day, which is largely free from the pressure to provide instruction in phonics (which isn't a concern of the Department of Economic Security). But this time spent outside and on the playground under the supervision of poorly trained child minders doesn't fully compensate for the imbalance in the preschool portion of the day caused by pressure to provide disadvantaged children with pre-reading skills, an imbalance which favors the brain over the body and skill acquisition over feelings and more complex thinking.

CONCLUSIONS

The trends I have discussed here—moral panic, the rise of new academic, medical, and legal disciplines of sexuality, the decline of classical psychoanalytic influence, logocentrism, brain research, and phonics instruction—have had the collective effect of making the daily lives of young children and the adults who care for them increasingly disembodied.

By discussing these trends one at a time, I may seem to be implying that they are unconnected vectors that all just happen to be applying pressure in the same direction. Indeed, one could argue that all that these trends share is the unfortunate, unintended side effect of reducing bodily movement and contact in early childhood educational settings. But this is not how I see it. Instead, I suggest that we should view the effect—disembodiment—as the goal rather than as a bi-product. I am suggesting not that there is a conspiracy at work, a concerted plan to attack the body on several fronts, but instead that this disembodiment emerges from the shared logic that transcends and unites the trends I have discussed here. What these six trends have in common is a focus on rationality, control, and risk avoidance. Collectively, they suggest the need for order, policing, discipline, and surveillance. Progressive voices in the field of early childhood education tend to blame the moral panics and the increasingly skill based, pushed-down academic curriculum on religious and political conservative forces—on Christian fundamentalism and the new republican agenda. But, following Foucault, I would suggest that we should read in the decline of the body in early childhood education the workings of forces less parochial than religions and less partisan than political parties. I think it is more useful to view the trends that are contributing to disembodiment in early childhood education settings as symptoms of the prevailing, internally persuasive logic and discourses of our times, logic and discourses that transcend political parties, ideological positions, and religious affiliations.

REFERENCES

Bruer, J. (1997, November). Education and the brain: A bridge too far. *Educational Researcher, 26*(8), 4–16.

Breur, J. (1999). *The myth of the early years.* New York: Free Press.

Caldwell, B., & Richmond, J. (1974). The impact of theories of child development. In S. Coopersmith & R. Feldman (Eds.), *The formative years* (pp. 15-16). Los Angeles: University of California Press.

Erikson, E. (1950/1963). *Childhood and society.* New York: W.W. Norton and Co.

Foucault, M. (1979). *Discipline and punish.* New York: Vintage.

Foucault, M. (1981). *The history of sexuality*: Vol. 1. London: Penguin.

Green, M., & Woods, E. (1948). *A nursery school handbook for teachers and parents.* Sierra Madre, CA: Sierra Madre Community Nursery School Assn.

Harlow, H., & M. Harlow (1969). Effects of various mother-infant relationships on Rhesus Monkey's Behaviors. In B. Foss (Ed.), *Determinants of infant behavior: Vol. 4* (pp. 15- 36). New York: Barnes and Noble.

Johnson, R. (2000). *Hands off!.* New York: Peter Lang.

Kellogg, R. (1949). *Nursery school guide*. Boston: Houghton Mifflin.

Owens, G. (1920). *Nursery school education*. New York: E.P. Dutton.

Read, K. (1950). *The nursery school: A human relationships laboratory*. Philadelphia: W.B. Saunders.

Silin, J. (1997). The pervert in the classroom. In J. Tobin (Ed.), *Making a place for pleasure in early childhood education* (pp. 214- 234). New Haven: Yale University Press.

Tobin, J., Wu, D., & Davidson, D. (1989). *Preschool in three cultures*. New Haven: Yale University Press.

Tobin, J. (1995). The irony of self-expression. *American Journal of Education, 103*, 233–258.

Tobin, J. (1997a). The missing discourse of pleasure and desire in early childhood education. In J. Tobin (Ed.), *Making a place for pleasure in early childhood education* (pp. 1-38). New Haven: Yale University Press.

Tobin, J. (1997b). Playing doctor in two cultures: The United States and Ireland. In J. Tobin (Ed.), *Making a place for pleasure in early childhood education* (pp. 119 -158). New Haven: Yale University Press.

Tobin, J. (2001). The missing discourse of sexuality in contemporary American early childhood education. In J. Winner & J. Andersen (Eds.), *The annual of psychoanalysis volume 23: Sigmund Freud and his impact on the modern world* (pp. 179–200). Hillsdale, NJ: The Analytic Press.

United States Department of Education (2003). No Child Left Behind Act.

Wheeler, O., & Earl, I. (1939). *Nursery school education*. London: University of London Press.

Zizek, S. (1992). *Looking awry*. Cambridge: MIT Press.

LIORA BRESLER

DANCING THE CURRICULUM:
EXPLORING THE BODY AND MOVEMENT IN
ELEMENTARY SCHOOLS

School disciplines, academic or those aspiring to be academic, target the mind and cognition, ignoring the body at best and subduing it at worst. A moving body in school is typically regarded as disruptive.[1] Yet, there is considerable movement even in the most restrictive classes. Under a certain choreography pupils raise their hands, walk to the board, help the teacher distribute materials, sharpen pencils, go to the bathroom. Such instrumental choreography is in marked contrast to the role of the body in the art worlds of dance and drama. There, the body is cultivated towards highly sophisticated movement for *expressive* purposes. The dialectic between these contrasting sets of expectations for the body and movement shapes the school discipline of dance. Based on a multiple-year[2] qualitative study of three elementary (K-5) dance/drama teachers, I examine the learning opportunities for the body in the operational curriculum with a focus on school dance.

School curricula impart deep-rooted cultural values and as such, have tremendous power to shape the consciousness of young children in their formative years. The first set of questions in this case-study centers around the framing and conceptualization of the body in the dance curriculum and its connection to school culture. What are the ways in which students are encouraged to engage in movement and towards what ends? What skills and knowledge are emphasized? Is the body presented as an instrument of public performance, serving the school's social goals and image, or as a tool for students' personal growth and creative expression? How do the different dance/drama teachers negotiate the balance between entertainment and challenge?

In a society whose value systems define cognition and mind as central to learning, the perceived connections of mind/body could potentially either enhance or detract from dance's legitimacy in the school.[3] What are the explicit and implicit messages in the curriculum about body/mind connections? The body/mind connections relate to the inside/outside interaction. Cognition and the senses are typically perceived as taking us into the outside world. Kinesthetics, referred to as a sixth sense (Fitt, 1996),[4] also takes us into the inner world, just as the auditory sense does (cf. Bowman, 1998; Burrows, 1990). "Somatics," first coined by Thomas Hanna in 1976,[5] encompasses mind, body, spirit and environment,[6] "knowing oneself from the inside out" (Fitt, 1996, p. 304) including memory of motion and

127

Liora Bresler (ed.), Knowing Bodies, Moving Minds, 127-151.
©*2004 Kluwer Academic Publishers. Printed in the Netherlands*

position, motor coordination, and integration of sensory information (Fitt, 1996, pp. 276–277). Somatic awareness has emerged as central to contemporary conceptualization of health, fitness and aesthetics (see for example Shusterman, and Markula, in this volume). Given the compelling role of kinesthetics and somatics in conceptualizing the body in contemporary thinking in disciplines outside of education, how and to what extent are somatic notions cultivated in given school dance curricula?

A second set of questions, rooted within education and discourse, addresses the social aspects of body-centered learning. The importance of a community of learners has been acknowledged in the scholarly literature (cf., Lave & Wenger, 1991; Vygotsky, 1979) with important ramifications for practice. Communities of learners are typically addressed in terms of their conceptual and affective aspects, rather than the physical. The role of the body in creating a community through movement is an uncharted territory. The body is personal. At the same time, it has a tremendous capacity to connect with others. The world of dance, like theater and drama, is highly collaborative, where bodily interactions are central to communication and creation. We note the powerful ability of various dance and movement forms, from folk-dances, through bar dances to nationalistic and military marches, to unify and create an intense connection with others, transforming personal experiences into social ones.[7] In contrast, school work is often conceptualized as individual engagement and responsibility. A system that values an independent self does so at the expense of connection among children. Even school play during recess is strongly defined by its "no touch" prohibitions. How are these opposing sets of etiquette negotiated in the dance curriculum? In what ways does the dance curriculum allow and promote meaningful connections among students? How does it draw on the body's power of communication and expression?

DANCE AS A SCHOOL DISCIPLINE

If school arts, as I have argued elsewhere (Bresler, 2002), are a hybrid genre, how does the school discipline of dance negotiate its relationships with the body in a way that is compatible with school's mission and values, as well as with dance?[8] Out-of-school arts genres have offered different options for the role of the body in creating these genres. For example, ballet lessons, (like instrumental and vocal lessons) discipline the body towards high-level performance within well-established, codified traditions (e.g., Anderson, 1992; Kraus, 1969). However, this orientation with its elitist connotations and goals does not fit well with the general school mission and priorities. Through the intensive case study of three dance/drama teachers, I explore various models for the framing and negotiation of the body in midwestern elementary schools. An outsider to dance education, I approach the study as a scholar of curriculum and arts education. The aim of these case studies was to capture the richness, complexity and contextuality of "school dance/drama" in its varied manifestations.

Dancing began to be taught in school for young children in the US during the early 19th century, mostly as a means of "acquiring poise, manners, and social confidence" (Kraus, 1969, p. 124). Dance education programs in various forms spread at the beginning of the 20th century (Kraus, 1969; Hanna, 1999), and became increasingly more visible in the 60s (Kraus, Hilsendager, & Dixon, 1991). The educational climate of the 60's promoted the exploration and creation of new curricula based on child-centered ideologies. School dance education received its conceptual basis and legitimation as an art form, rather than as part of physical education from the new movement of Aesthetic Education developed by CEMREL[9] (cf. Madeja, 1977, 1978). Aesthetic education promoted a broader concept of "arts education," as compared to the individual disciplines of music and visual art with their established traditions. Additionally, the work of Rudolph Laban (Hanna, 1999; Knowles, 1982) and the artist-in-residence project of the late 60s, 70s and early 80s (Kraus, Hilsendager, & Dixon, 1991), proved to be important influences on school dance.

University dance programs and the changes in administrative affiliations they have undergone are important contexts for school dance. The recognition that dance requires a special expertise, grounded in an extensive training in dance, was voiced by Agnes de Mille, a prominent writer, choreographer and dancer, and a strong advocate for the establishment of independent dance programs. De Mille acknowledged in her 1962 book that dance owed an enormous debt to the physical education teacher, but admonishes this "foster parent" to "let it go with grace and take its proper place among the arts" (in Knowles, 1982, p. 10). In 1962, the dance program at UCLA, chaired by Alma Hawkins, became the first autonomous dance department in American education when it moved from Physical Education to Fine Arts (Knowles, 1998). In 1966, Hawkins organized a conference on dance, bringing together a group of artists, scholars and educators for the purpose of exploring the role of dance in education and generating immediate and long-term curriculum (Knowles, 1982, 1998). The conference manifesto called for "An opportunity for every child, male and female, to have a dance experience," and for "A skilled dance teacher in every school at every level" (Knowles, 1998, p. 5).

These visions and tremendous efforts bore fruit, the evidence of which may be seen today in some strong dance education programs in the US (see, for example, Knowles & Sande, 1991; Bresler, 1997). Most existing dance education programs are in secondary schools, and those in elementary schools are often taught in magnet schools. Isolated dance lessons are usually taught by physical education and music teachers and occasionally by classroom teachers. This is also true in other countries (in Norway, see, Espeland, 1997; in Brazil, see Marques, in press; in Australia, see McPherson, 1995). Politically, in the 1990s, dance education established a firm place in the National Standards and State goals. However, dance education never had an agreed-upon curriculum (and hence, no counter-movement either), and of all school subjects, both academic and the arts, dance has the least presence in schooling. If scholars and practitioners of music and visual art education debate contents and pedagogies, and theater educators worry about "How we can steer the field away from focusing on acting and yet keep the active learning thrust of creation and performance?" (Wright, 1994), dance educators plead for a foot in the door of the curriculum. In her chapter "Writing Standards for Dance," Kimball states: "Before voluntary, world-class standards in dance can significantly improve the quality of dance education for all students, dance must first be in the schools. Before we can implement standards for each of the arts or plan unique interdisciplinary projects, dance must exist as a part of the curriculum" (Kimball, 1994, p. 32).

Dance offerings vary across states. A survey in the Chicago Public Schools during 2000–2001 (The Chicago Community Trust, 2002, in Costantino, in press) collected data on school-provided arts education by certified arts specialists and outside programming. The results indicate that the average student received 58 minutes per week of arts education from in-school arts specialists in the four arts disciplines. Within the 58 minutes, music was taught an average of 28 minutes per week, visual art for 27 minutes per week, theater for two minutes per week, and dance for one minute per week.[10] The relative proportion of minutes per week in each of the disciplines in the six regions in the city remained consistent, with music and visual arts receiving the majority of minutes and dance and theater receiving very few, or nothing (Costantino, in press). The statistics illustrate the weak position of these arts areas in the schools vis-à-vis visual art and music.

SETTING

I first encountered elementary school dance in a study conducted for the National Endowment for the Arts (Stake, Bresler, & Mabry, 1991). In the schools we observed, dance was one of the art forms in the school, although less present than other art forms. On the rare occasions that dance was taught, the activities, taught by classroom teachers, involved simple teacher-prescribed choreography (e.g., hopping, jumping), usually for school performances. Another type of dance activity drew on a non-interventionist pedagogy, with free, unstructured movement to music as a way to get children into the school day (Bresler, 1992a). An examination of those instances of dance instruction, revealed teachers' lack of disciplinary knowledge. When designing the present study, I focused on specialists, aiming to capture the kind of knowledge, skills and awareness that they bring to dance instruction. At the same time, I targeted ordinary schools rather than magnet schools.

The complete project focused on all arts disciplines in the program, not just dance/drama. Data sources included: (1) intensive observations of all arts instruction, as well as of after-school clubs, in- and out-of-school arts performances, and meetings of program specialists across arts subjects, (2) semi-structured interviews with teachers (classroom and specialists) and principals, and (3) analysis of materials such as music textbooks, students tests, and program notes. For the first three years of the major data collection, I was aided by a team of eight graduate students[11] who were responsible for parts of the observations in the various arts disciplines.[12]

The arts program, which I followed from its inception in a mid-size Illinois town, came into existence after 11 years without any arts specialists. A couple of years after the study was completed, the program was publicly recognized by a presidential award. Initially created to provide classroom teachers with planning time as part of contract negotiation between the teachers' union and the school board, the program continues to receive support even during major budget cuts. The budget allowed for nine arts specialist to serve 6 elementary schools, which necessitated hiring in only three arts disciplines. Because the body is the central instrument in both dance and drama, the two subjects were grouped together. Having dance/drama specialists in the schools meant that dance in these schools was offered as an integral part of the arts curriculum, rather than as a component of the Physical Education Program.[13] The music and visual art teachers in the schools were certified in their respective areas. Two of the dance/drama teachers we observed– Molly and Mary– had elementary education certification with personal experience in acting and some courses in dance. The third teacher, Jenny (who had also served as program coordinator) had teaching certification in education (physical education with an emphasis on dance) and an MFA in dance. The integrated arts mission was enriched by the strong leadership of the program and frequent communication among the various arts specialists, shaping the operational and formal curriculum.[14]

All six elementary schools in the district, with a total enrollment of about 4400 students, received this program. The schools were racially mixed, with diverse SES. The district consisted of 56.8% white, 32.7% Afro-Americans, and 3% Hispanic, with 40.4% low income rate, and 4.9% limited English proficiency (referring to students eligible for transitional bilingual programs), and 21.8% mobility rate.[15] While we observed dance/drama in all schools, we concentrated our observations in Jefferson and George Washington schools. George Washington School was representative in its ethnic distribution, with 60% white, 30% black, and 2.6% Hispanic, and 4.9% limited English proficiency. Jefferson school housed the school district's elementary multicultural program, with a minority population representing a diverse, multilingual, multicultural, and multinational population. At Jefferson, we twice weekly observed Molly Marks[16] teaching three classes for one academic year; and the following year, we weekly observed Mary Mullen teaching six classes. In George Washington, we weekly observed Jenny Kording teach six classes. When the dance/drama teachers were absent, we observed substitute teachers. Three of the schools in the district have spaces allocated to the arts program, and in the other three there are no dance/drama rooms.

Originally, my questions centered on the more traditional categories of curriculum: the structures of school arts, their operational and formal curricula, the pedagogies and evaluation practices. It was later, in the process of in-depth data analysis that the focus on the body as presented in this chapter emerged.

THE OPERATIONAL CURRICULUM OF DANCE/DRAMA

What is the role of the body in the dance/drama curriculum? Is there a space for mind/body connections? For expressive movement? Is learning presented as a solitary act or as an act-in-community? The following vignettes portray the operational curriculum of dance/drama with a focus on explicit and implicit body-related messages, values and educational goals.

Jenny Kording

9/7, 8:25 a.m., third grade. It is the second week of school, and we are in the computer room, allocated to host the dance/drama lessons. Computer work stations line three walls. On the left side wall Jenny displays two large cut-out paper bodies in motion, one in pink and one in blue. The back wall features large faces of children together, colored for many different ethnic origins, titled the "audience." As we enter, we are greeted with the sounds of "Clair De Lune." Large, clear handwriting on the front blackboard reads, "Collaborate, Cooperate, Communicate." Jenny, at the right corner of the room, is looking into a box of chiffon scarves to be used in a dance later that day. Jenny, in her mid thirties, exudes an intensity and vibrancy. Quick and alert, she moves around, projecting a sense of careful observation and heightened attention to students.

8:30 a.m. A classroom teacher brings a group of 22 third graders and leaves. Jenny asks them to sit in the circle and "take a look at space, how you move through space, how your body interacts with someone else's space. Then we'll talk about it." The children seem focused and concentrated as they look around and adjust the circle so "nobody is scrunched."

For a warm-up activity, Jenny starts with a pattern of "2 pats on knees, 2 claps, snap, snap, one hand at a time." The children say their own name with the left hand "snap," and the person on their right with their right hand "snap." Jenny practices saying the names going around the circle without the motions. As she goes around the circle, most of the kids are not able to follow the rhythm or the names. Jenny: "What does it need? Focus, concentration. You have to use discipline and self-control to keep the rhythm. Bring your own concentration." This time, most of the kids are following the rhythm with their hands.

Jenny invites them to find their own space: "Close your eyes and find all of your space around your body. Find all of the space up and down, to your side. You can change levels if you want to." The children are turning their arms around their bodies, reaching up and down, but staying in one spot. In the walking activity, Jenny encourages children to think about both near and far space, suggesting that they vary their movement ("Can you walk backwards?" "Can you change levels?"). When someone bumps a chair, she reminds them that "Chairs have their space too." When the children start talking louder, she asks them to try to keep their voices down because they need to concentrate on their space.

As they move, Jenny summarizes her observations, ("I see people who are turning around. I see people who are strolling,") and calls for experimentation with other movements ("Can you move in a way that's not forward?"). Asking them to find ways of greeting each other, she summarizes her observations of the various greetings, ("tipping a hat," "doffing a hat," "saluting," "foot wave," "smile," "curtsy, bow," "giving somebody something.") The observation of the communicative aspect of the act involves mindful attention to detail. Jenny asks a girl who pretended to give something as to whether or not she had something specific in mind to give, and whether the person received it well or not. Encouraging them to reflect on what they are doing, as part of *self*-discipline, Jenny inquires, "When you were walking, how did you avoid running into other people?" Some children said that they changed directions, others mentioned that they went around.

9/7, 9:30 a.m., fourth grade. Clearly written on the board we note: Time: Slow/ Quick; Weight: Heavy/ Light; Space: Direct/ Indirect. It's warm-up time, and Jenny directs. "Scream with your arms, shout with your back, giggle with your stomach, laugh with your knees, cry with your fingers." She has them lie down on the floor and gives them 5 counts to get up and 5 counts to lie back down. She asked them to use the "same amount of energy" to make their movements from up to down SMOOTH. They repeat twice. Then she asked them to make it SHARP, counting in a sharp tone –1-2-3-4-5. Using her voice to be both sharp and smooth, she then asks the children to combine the two in slow motion. Now she has them do it in fast motion 1-2-3-4-5 up and down. Next, she draws attention to the qualities of heavy, light, direct, indirect. For "direct," she suggests to "have a purpose" in their movement. For "indirect," she reminded them to "have no purpose," to make it meandering "as if you don't know until you get there." Still counting for the children to lie down and get up in 5 counts, she asks them to use bound movement, then free flowing energy. She urges to "Make it believable, use concentration to do that. Focus."

Having practiced the various qualities, Jenny provides a series of environments for the children's walking, writing each of the environments on the board as she presents it "Walk as if you were walking in a room full of peanut butter." Next they walk as if they are testing ice (some children tip-toeing.) Jenny asks the group, "Is walking on ice different than walking through Peanut Butter?" "Yeah." "Show me." And they do– with movements more pronounced. Next, "Stomp on Rice Krispies, but don't make any sound." The children giggle as they try to make large steps with no sound. Then it is walking on the moon in a moon suit. As they pretend to walk on the moon, Gary and some other children use slow motion, whereas others are not doing anything different from the Rice Krispies stomping. Jenny asks the children to walk through a prickly forest, emphasizing that the children *show* her the different movement experience instead of using words ("It's real easy to take the easy way out and say, "Ow, that hurts!"). She watches the children intently, gives a little appreciative laugh and then calls "FREEZE." Next it's the ocean, "Only I don't want you to swim through it, let the *water move you*."

Next, Jenny suggests, "Hide a delicate object. I don't want to know what it is. Make it very *breakable*, very *expensive*" (stressing the words breakable and expensive with her voice). She continues, "Don't hide it in a real place, like under the chairs or under the computers, hide it in an *imaginary* place, you may not want anyone else to see it." Most people are carrying the "object" in their hands, bending down and putting it in their imaginary space. The last task is to "hit a home run" in "the last game of the world series." Many children seemed to overtly enjoy this one, swinging pretend bats.

At 9:45 a.m., Jenny "freezes" them, then asks them to sit down and talk. Jenny: "Most of the time, I believed the places." She asks the children to tell her what efforts were used when they were walking through peanut butter and why. She then writes up on the board next to peanut butter– BOUND, SLOW, HEAVY. When she asks what they used when they were testing ice, children answered that they felt indirect because "you didn't know where you were going." Next she discusses with them the efforts that they used for stomping on rice krispies, writing: L (Light) F (Free), D (Direct). In addressing why they would use light movements, she elaborates: "Because you couldn't make noise, you started heavy and then pulled the weight out of it."

Jenny questions Gary about his movements on the moon, ("I told you I'd come back to you.") and probes why. Gary answered, "I felt like I couldn't move. I felt indirect because when you're going you didn't know where you were going." As they discuss the "Light," Jenny says, "It would have been different if I said Jupiter." At the end of class, Jenny tells the children that they were doing well: they could identify environments and their movement qualities. She dismisses the class and then comes right back over to her book writing down names of children who impress her as ones who "really got it."

Jenny's questions prompt children to explore their experiences and connect them to kinesthetic vocabulary and new concepts. The vocabulary then is grounded in sensory experiences. Jenny probes if they felt bound or free in the water, ("How many let the *water move you*?"), highlighting the distinction between moved *by* the water and *moving* the water. "If you tried to move water, it was probably bound. If the water moved you, the movement was probably free." When discussing the prickly forest, Jenny clarifies with Joe, "So free for you was more of an *emotional* feeling rather than an *energy* feeling." Children are reflective as they talk about why they did what they did. David, for example, says that he felt indirect because he felt nervous, connecting a movement to an inner state.

Contrary to some common assumptions, analysis and vocabulary go hand in hand with kinesthetic experience and exploration. Jenny's prompting and responsive pedagogy invites the children to expand exploration, to increase observation beyond the surface level. Vocabulary of movement qualities as well as mind states is important in this dance/drama class. The vocabulary is always connected to direct experiences in the analysis of students' creations as well as in the observation of others. Students are expected to show their understanding and learning in words and even more prominently, through the movements and shapes they make. We note exploration of space– up and down and sides, near and far, cultivating somatic sensitivity. Concentration and awareness are inner states of mind that are foundational to the activities– and are framed *within* the individuals.

Students are encouraged to look for the uncommon and subtle. Jenny invites children to watch interesting shapes and movements, to note the differences between walking on ice and walking on the moon, between the feelings of the water moving them as compared to them moving the water. The invitation to create imaginary spaces and move expressively are unusual in American schools. Widening of sensory experiences, and cultivating wonderment, provide the foundation for aesthetic perception and experience.

Communal space is orchestrated through a unison activity with which most classes start, as each child is acknowledged by name and participates in an activity that requires concentration and co-ordination. Other activities are framed as individual open-ended problem solving through movement, with focused awareness on one's body. The reflection and analysis, often involving higher order skills, draws on the input of the group.

Jenny is clearly in charge, using her disciplinary knowledge, and teaching experience to orchestrate activities. She is alert to students' activities and responses. She provides collegial support ("let me support you in not losing control"), and explanation rather than reproach ("chairs, too, have their space"). Her comments nurture the children's sense of ownership, encouraging concentration and self-control, as compared to control imposed from above. (When she senses that students can become disruptive, she tells them: "A lot of work today is self-centered. Other people shouldn't affect you in any way. If I see that you're not focused, I'll ask you to sit out until you can get control. Work on using your space and not letting your space intersect with anyone else's.")

The importance of expressivity is highlighted in the arts education literature as well as the state goals, but is rarely part of the operational curriculum. Jenny's invitation to communicate expressively with body parts ("scream with your arms"; "laugh with your knees") expands from conventional movement to the expressive. One of the ways in which Jenny's class connects mind and body is by cultivating awareness of feelings associated with different mindsets and body states. These explorations are powerfully educational, yet are largely missing in educational settings. Jenny reflects on that precious zone– feeling the feelings, yet not being overwhelming by them:

> "One of the [state] goals says that you're going to explore the expressive qualities of the arts, which means you've got to talk sometime about the feeling that you get, the emotion that happens. And if you're moving in it, you have to feel it, I mean there's that reaction that you have to acknowledge exists. There are days when we work on sad, happy, angry, you know, just kind of the basic surface emotions without putting an incident to them but 'think about how you felt,' 'think about the way your body looked,' 'think about how you reacted,' 'what happened to your stomach, what happens next, where's your body.'

> And there are times when you have children almost break down and cry, and it happens to you too as they're doing it. And then you have to stop them and say, 'always trust me that I will bring you back before it gets too bad.' It doesn't happen very often, it happened maybe three times this year in three different classes that I was doing that emotion feeling kind of study, movement quality thing, and it was just something about the day and about the children that day, they were ready for that lesson, and there wasn't anybody showing off, they were all in their own world, they didn't pay any attention to anybody else, it just gelled and it was very cathartic. Sometimes you need that, but you kind of bring them back before it gets to the place that they're going to completely lose it. You can kind of feel it happening and then that's when you stop them and say ok let's sit down, let's calm down, let's think of a different feeling."

Molly Marks

Molly Marks has taught kindergarten for a year and supervised early childhood practicum students while enrolled in a Master's program. A petite, dark eyed woman in her mid twenties, she wears a variety of hand crafted silver rings and hoop earrings, large sweaters and long skirts or pants with boots. She has a wide smile and greets individual students and teachers warmly. Her relaxed body stance is evident as she sits on the couch and "sinks in." When various kinds of music are played, she often moves her hands, feet, or hips to the beat. During the year we observed her, she was a member of two show casts and also directed a children's show at Jefferson school. She feels that it is very important for her to "practice her art," – in her case, acting. In our conversations, she placed as a primary goal for "children to enjoy themselves," and secondary "teaching skills."

9/8, 10:15 a.m., second grade. Half the class of this multi-lingual, multi-racial, multi-national student group, is involved in ESL classes and returns to the classroom right before dance classes. Sometimes they arrive late and art teachers postpone instruction until they return, but today they are in time.

Molly reviews classroom rules, and has the children practice walking quietly to the carpet. She lists the four tools of acting: concentration, observation, memorization, and imagination. Molly: "Actors have four tools. The first tool is concentration. What does that mean?" As no one answers, she says: "It means thinking." She asks the children to close their eyes and pretend that they have an ice cream cone, their favorite kind. After a few minutes (most kids do have their eyes closed, a few are cheating), Molly tells the kids to open their eyes: "Raise your hand if your ice cream was in a cone." Some children raise their hands. Molly: "Raise your hand if your ice cream was in a dish." Some children raise their hands. "Did your ice cream have ingredients in it like chocolate chips?" One girl says "bubble gum." Other children chat about what ingredients are in their cones. Molly describes her cone as having two scoops of chocolate chip ice cream. It is a hot day so her ice cream is dripping. Molly ends by saying that she would like to hear more stories, but she needs to go on.

Favorite activities during the semester are the concentration game, freeze game, and pantomime. The freeze game comes with several variations. During one version, Molly turns off the lights and the kids lie on the floor with eyes closed. Molly then mentions a body part, and the children are supposed to tense up that body part and then relax it. In another freeze variation, Molly beats on a drum and the children freeze into a shape. Molly reminds the children to use high, low, and mid levels. Later, emotions are added and children are to freeze into happy and sad shapes. Children then move three steps before they freeze. Molly uses questions as rhetorical devices or signals for the children to focus on a different kind of movement in the freeze game ("What would a sad shape look like? Can you do that in low level? Remember the dance in the movie we saw last week, Ostrich, can you incorporate that movement?") Sometimes Molly relates the freeze game to a previous activity (dance video, or a visual arts class), other times it is an independent activity, occasionally functioning as a "rondo," a familiar filler of short time to help establish focus.

During the movement period, Molly sometimes moves among the children and other times, stands by the side and watches. The activity game is fast paced, with brief, telegraphic comments. During the game Molly included a mix of management messages reminding children of the rules and warning individuals of their violations, and evaluative statements acknowledging specific children or group movements: ("no touching, stay in one spot"; "move beautifully and slowly"; "I noticed that someone touched someone, don't do that"; "Marianna, that looks beautiful"; "I really like some of the freezes that I see.") Some children did freeze into the assigned position (for example, rounded shape) while others froze into a straight shape. Teacher commentary emphasized following discipline rules (quiet and staying in their own space), with little feedback on the movements or the concepts.

Pantomime is another favorite activity, part of creative drama– an improvisational, process-oriented form of drama, where participants are guided by a leader to imagine, enact, and reflect upon human experiences, real or imagined. In a class discussion of an animal picture book, children are assigned animal parts to pantomime. Another time Molly describes an outdoor scene and invited children into the scene to pantomime. Children pantomime swimming, fishing, and swatting mosquitoes. In the pretend game, children pretend that an orange marker is a diamond bracelet (or a worm, or a kitten,) handing it around from child to child. In one version of the concentration game, a box of items is displayed, then hidden, and the children, as a group, list the items, and answer questions about the objects.

11/10, third grade. Molly wheels a VCR into the room and announces to the children that they are going to view Dance Black America. As they watch the first dance piece, *Ostrich*, performed by a solo male dancer, Molly observes that "He leads with his foot, then other times he leads with his hands. Symmetrical movement is the same on both sides," pointing out the various movements on the screen.

The video continues with a piece performed by an ensemble. Molly explains that, "they're doing unison dancing, that's when dancers dance the same thing. Are they dancing in unison?" (The kids respond with a "yeah.") She introduces the concept of travel path and traces on the screen how the dancers are moving. Molly's commentary continues throughout the video, relating the techniques and movement in the dance to concepts and elements. The commentary-facilitated children's active viewing and learning with a clear transfer to their own movements. The travel paths provide the basis for the next two weeks' activities. In the next session, the children generated multiple ways to move through the assigned travel paths (drawn on cards) based on her cueing on the dancers' moves in the video. The children were then assigned to small groups, were given a travel path card, and developed a three-part movement sequence involving the whole group. There was a particular richness and intensity to these classes, which expanded the children's repertoire of movements. Evaluation involved questions such as "what were the different ways that Joe moved?" "Can you move 10 different ways?" requiring observations and divergent thinking. The three travel path lessons were tightly related and built upon one another. They involved teacher presentation, group dialogue, individual and group practice, and evaluation. Most children seemed engaged. They listened to and interacted with Molly's video dialogue, and were able to define and demonstrate travel paths.

Mary Mullen

9/7, 8:30 a.m., first grade. It is early September. Mary Mullen, a graceful and elegant woman in her late 20's, stands at the front of the class. She asks the class to push their chairs in and go and find their "personal space." "If you're sitting nicely, you get to be the first people to find your personal space." The desks take up the major portion of the classroom. Several children stand in a small space upfront, another little boy is behind the reading table in a corner of the room, and the rest of the children are standing next to their desks. There is little space for the children to move. 8:34 a.m. "When I say 'go' everybody move their bodies really fast." As the children shake energetically within their space, Mary remarks that she is happy that they remembered to move their bodies and not their mouths. She calls "Freeze!" looking for "really still statues."

Mary: "Now, I would like for you to move in swinging movements." She comments that she sees a lot of the children moving from side-to-side. "Can anyone move a different way?" As they try new movements, she notes that "Tim is moving from the waist and not just his arms. Can anyone move your legs?" She asks for jerky movements, demonstrating jerkiness with her voice and robot-like movements, and explaining that another name for that quality is Staccato.

Moving to the opposite quality, Mary explains: "Another name for this kind of movement is Sustained– very smooth." She reminds the children to move their bodies, not their mouths. Most of the children are swinging their arms slowly in the air. Mary suggests that they stretch their arms out. The effect is striking in its expressivity.

Now, Mary asks the children to show her "exploding movements." While the class is exploding (rather quietly), she walks around the room to observe and supervise. She finishes the Statue Game by telling the children that when she comes over to touch them it means that she thinks they are standing very quietly and they may go sit down at the table. As they sit down, one girl reports that another boy kicked her. Mary turns over a card, using the exact same discipline that the classroom teacher does and tells the little boy: "No violence in dance/drama. That means no kicking or hitting."

Mary reminds the children that jerky movements are called "Staccato" and smooth movements are called "Sustained." She tells the children that they will start acting today. She defines pantomime as acting but without talking and props. "Pantomime is where you pretend." She models pretending and asks for guesses. Jason suggests that she was eating cereal, Greg guessed correctly that she was on the phone. There is no probing of right and wrong interpretations. Mary says that they will have to use their imagination for this coming activity.

These activities are repeated, with variations, across grade levels. In a fifth grade class, Mary provides specific environments for their scenes (bus station; Disneyworld; office; zoo; playground; dentist office); encouraging the children to concentrate on the characters ("you can be an astronaut, chef, or a teacher"). When the first group of volunteers comes up to play their scene, Mary responds with "no fighting." Jeff explains that it was acting– sparring like in a TV show, and Mary cautions him to try to stay away from sparring like a TV show.

10/7, 9:12 a.m., a Kindergarten class. Twelve minutes into class, the kids have worked on the bounce poem, and danced the "Silly Dance Context" where they moved according to the directions in the lyrics. Mary tells the children that they will learn about three levels of space: low, medium, and high. She plays soft, rippling, music in the style of Debussy, asking the children to close their eyes and imagine what the music makes them feel like. Children respond with: "like blind people" (upon probing, Mary figures out that it was because she asked the children to close their eyes); "like the wind was blowing"; "like a fire"; "like sleeping"; "sleeping on a cloud– I fell through"; "staying at Care Bear's House" (to which Mary responds with: "oh my goodness, that's neat, thinking about that"); "running from somebody shooting"; "sleep, somebody's going to break in my house and I ran"; "I was a ghost and I was doing hiya, hiya" (that last one followed with brisk Karate chops movement and a dramatic raising of voice, reproached by the teacher for "acting silly").

With longer stories, children lose their concentration. Mary uses her cymbals for attention, then she plays the music again, and picks children to get up and into their personal space, one at a time. She directs: "Make a shape on the floor, dance in the low level of space," and, to enhance the soft mood of the music, turns the lights out. Many of the children are on the floor in different parts of the room. Robert, a special education child, crawls under the desk. As Frances moves gracefully to the music, Mary acknowledges the beauty of the movement. She is interrupted by the aide telling Mary that they cannot dance in the computer area. Mary asks the children to dance in the higher level, then in the middle level of space. Unexpectedly, the lights are turned on by the aide. The lesson ends with the Silly Dance Contest, to the obvious delight of the children and the aide who joins the dance.

Mary's pedagogy consists of establishing the rules, specifying activities, demonstrating, and monitoring. Acting and moving were mostly constructed as individual activities. Personal space is presented here as a discipline tool, a reminder of boundaries. Interactions with other children consist typically of observations and guessing the content of the pantomime. Qualities like staccato and sustained, and elements of shape and form are related in this, as in all dance/drama classes, to students' learning in music and visual arts. Equally important in this class are the acknowledgement of beauty, and the invitation to move with mindfulness and grace. This was particularly striking when Mary worked with the whole school to create a dance for Martin Luther King's Day. The dance included a middle open-ended section, where children were asked to generate movements of their own, not prescribed by the teacher. The dance involved the public performance of several classes, to the engaged attention of the whole school and guests.

DISCUSSION: THE BODY IN THE CURRICULUM

Criteria for School Dance

It is nearly fifty years since dance emerged as a school discipline of its own, rather than a part of physical education. What lenses and criteria should we apply to school dance? One way to understand school dance is through the examination of the opportunities for moving and being it affords. The famous anthropologist Clifford Geertz wrote that the meaning of art varies according to the kind of being that it promotes and exemplifies (Geertz, 1976).

Another lens, articulated within education, addresses specific skills and sensitivities. The National Dance Association's (NDA) definition (1991, in Kimball, 1994, p. 32) elaborates on the personal and social aspects of the discipline, and the various skills and mindsets involved in dance:

> "Dance is a way of perceiving, a body of knowledge, and a personal and social experience.
> Dance is a way of knowing self, others, and the world around us. Dance education allows

individuals to communicate with others in a way that is different from the written or spoken word, or even from other visual or auditory symbols. Knowing and perceiving in dance occurs on both the conscious and subconscious levels. . .

The act of dancing is not mindless doing, but involves exploration, sensing, concentration, focus, projection, and commitment. There is an active use of memory, translation, interpretation, application, analysis, synthesis and evaluation. Creating dances is a personal engagement in the forming process, finding new movement and/or organization movement in new ways through use of individual resources."

Prominent dance educator, Susan Stinson identifies three key components of dance: rhythmic movement, conscious awareness, and form (Stinson, 2002). The components of form and conscious awareness are directly related to Dewey's notion of the aesthetic as an intensified experience (cf. Dewey, 1934). I draw on these components as a succinct frame for my analysis and interpretation of the operational dance curriculum.

Rhythmic movement, seldom present in other areas of schooling, was practiced by all three teachers. Tambourines and cymbals stimulated children's movements, providing beat and tempo for the activity. Occasionally, recorded, mostly instrumental music, from Renaissance to Debussy and Philip Glass, offered mood and affective stimulus to guide children's movement.[17]

Conscious awareness refers not to what we do, but *how* we do it (Stinson, 2002, p. 158), especially in relation to aesthetic and artistic ways of perceiving and knowing. The *how* draws on the kinesthetic sense, involving the interaction between the outside and the inner perception of movement. The inside/outside interaction is often neglected in education. Cognition is regarded as taking us into the outside world. Stinson points out that the kinesthetic sense, combined with the visual, and the auditory, can also take us into the inner world. Internal sensing has great significance not only for how we *perform* dance but also for how we *perceive* it. The kinesthetic sense "allows us to go inside the dance, to feel ourselves as participants in it, not just as onlookers" (Stinson, 1995, p. 43). It can transfer to daily life, where we feel "the weighty sadness of a friend, the tense anxiety of students before an exam" (ibid).

Concentration and focus are essential to making these connections. All three teachers emphasized concentration, but it was mostly Jenny who connected concentration to the bodily awareness of inside and outside interactions. For example, Jenny framed the Freeze activity as an opportunity to "listen to the inside," whereas Molly, Mary and the substitute teachers seemed to use Freeze as a way of quieting down and control.

Form, the third component of dance, has to do with creating an activity with a beginning, middle and end. Though aesthetic form is less attended to in schooling, functional form is prevalent. All teachers attended to form as they planned their teaching, using the beginning of class as warm up time, and bringing the class to closure. Equally important are sequence and transition, the connection between one activity and the next. Jenny's teaching appeared seamless with one activity flowing to the next. Her fast paced practice of counting gave the activities a certain rhythm and heightened focused. Molly and Mary's activities seemed more separate from each other, with frequent breaks for classroom management. Form was applied to dance when Mary asked children to create shapes composed of symmetrical, then asymmetrical, then back to symmetrical, resulting in an ABA. Jenny often addressed explicitly the importance of form in dance, asking students to create a beginning, middle, and end in their dance.

The tri-partite stages of dance consisting of exploring-forming-performing (Stinson, 2002) distinguishes between dance as an art form and dance as entertainment or fitness/physical education. Exploration is a necessary precondition to genuine creativity and is an essential aspect of an art form. Mary and Jenny provided a space for exploring movement, had the children develop and practice their movements to form a dance, then created a more formal space for a "performance." The presence of an audience (even an informal one), that observes intently with an aesthetic frame of mind, heightens the performers' experience. The distinct stages of practice and performance framed dance as a premeditated, complex art form rather than an improvisatory activity. These three distinct but connected stages allowed children to go beyond the prescribed, towards an expressive mode of presentation (Eisner, 1982).

Dance education aims to emphasize children's engagement, creativity and skills (Stinson, 2002). What promotes engagement and creativity? Children seemed most engaged when given challenges and guidance for exploration. Challenging tasks ranged from the specific to the broad. Specific directions included moving quickly and lightly, as in walking on rice krispies, or connecting to other children with elbow, shoulder, finger, and back, body parts that are rarely used to touch others. Broader challenges included requiring the interpretation of a piece of music through movement. These tasks provided a space where children could be creative. Invitations to experiment with movement expanded not only the children's movement skills, but also their problem solving and higher order cognitive skills. The open-ended assignments of "make a sad face," or "make any shape," produced more stereotypically responses.

What are the ways in which children are encouraged to engage in movement? Here, the dance curriculum did not target specific dance skills, did not require additional practice or particular talent for dance. Drawing on the genre of creative dance/movement, school dance uses natural movement (rather than a particular dance style) presented. Through the combination of movements with vocabulary as a form of kinesthetic literacy through which they can perceive and express, qualities of movement are central. How are these movements chosen? Activities borrowed from creative drama included freeze and pantomime, with focus on narrative. Setting for pantomime movements centered around familiar environments from daily life or from the media (baseball; school; outdoor; ice-skating; outer-space and spaceship). Another source for influence was Laban movements and concepts including space, direction and level, and the different qualities of energy and effort. These concepts formed the basis for vocabulary, cultivating sensory awareness. Molly and Mary prioritized movements associated with "fun" (e.g., eating ice cream; playing baseball), highlighting action and doing, Jenny chose movements that aimed to teach something new. Aiming to expand children's repertoire of movement, she prompted children to move "out of the box," emphasizing sensorial awareness and "aesthesizing" the familiar. Stinson (1990) points out that sensory awareness "can help give depth, richness, and texture" to children's understanding of themselves and the world. Children can "come to realize that they can make shapes; just as leaves and clouds have shapes; they can move with stretch and lightness, just as the mind can move with these qualities" (p. 36).

The balance between entertainment and challenge/expansion is one faced by any artist, conductor, or performer who wishes to communicate as well as expand their audience. The right balance between the familiar versus the new and more demanding involves the education of perception. Here, perception is critical in developing concepts and analytic skills, through observation of others as well as the inner experience of movement. The teaching of perception and categorization was guided by the vocabulary of formal elements, akin to Broudy's scanning (Broudy, 1972). Perception is part of state goals and national standards. However, because its cultivation requires depth and therefore time, it is often narrowed in the operational academic curriculum. The dance/drama curriculum reflected the same tension between surface versus experiential perception. When the goal became a "correct" answer ("is this a unison?"), perception stayed at the stage of recognition. At other times, it was developed through imagination towards an expanded mindful perception that connected inner and outer experiences. It was that expansion and mindfulness that made the dance/drama curriculum at its best different from the prescribed movement that we encountered in the school dance of classroom teachers (Bresler, 1991).

The general emphasis of process over product was evident in the culminating event of the Integrated Arts program– *informances* rather than the traditional school performances at the community mall. Weaved through the presentation of a demo-lesson, informances served to inform the audience (mostly parents and family members) about the arts curriculum and its aims. Another channel of communication with families was through the occasional "Arts-Share" that the dance/drama and visual art teachers conducted in individual schools for parents and children. These were unique situations where parents participated as learners, engaged in creating, reflecting and sharing.

Goals and Orientations

Framing movement as an art form implies different goals from fitness and entertainment. Dance as an art form includes established traditions and body of knowledge. Occasionally, the curriculum incorporated these traditions, but it was mostly constructed around "child dance." The spectacular entered the curriculum in the highly skilled, exquisitely inspiring "Black America" dance video presented in Molly's class, or in children's own composition, and performance for Martin Luther King's Day in Mary's class. On these occasions, children were being inducted into dance as audience, sometimes as amateur performers. When the teachers referred to great artists (e.g., the work of Merce Cunningham, or Black America) it was not in the context of dance history session. Rather, it involved observation and analysis of the movements, connecting them with students' class activities. The role of child-centered inquiry versus a discipline-based knowledge of dance education, is a long standing curriculum issue at the heart of contents, pedagogy and evaluation. The dialectic between these orientations reflects the different emphasis and values of the progressive versus traditional curriculum movements. A discipline-based notion of knowledge lends itself to prescriptive curricula such as, "what every child should know" (Hirsch, 1987) or the accountability measures of "No Child Left Behind" (2003). These prescriptions and standards assume a solid, agreed-upon body of knowledge and skills to be transmitted and mastered by all. In contrast, progressive orientations highlight inquiry, creativity and personal meaning. Knowledge is acquired by learners' active exploration and interpretation, and is demonstrated through public demonstration/exhibition, rather than norm-based test scores (see, for example, in Sizer, 1996).

The transmission-centered versus child-centered orientations are manifested in contrasting curricula and pedagogies in all school subjects– from science and math, to language arts and the fine arts. In music education, these two orientations are reflected in the pedagogies developed by Kodaly, Suzuki, and Gordon versus composition-based approaches, like Comprehensive Musicianship (e.g., Choksy et. al, 2001), and those developed by Paynter (1970); Schafer (1975); Wiggins (2000); and Espeland (1997). In the areas of arts appreciation, these conflicting orientations manifest themselves in the traditional approach to art history emphasizing the transmission of facts and information, as compared to dialogical approaches such as Visual Teaching Strategies (Housen, Arenas, & Yenawene, 1994). A variation on the discipline-based orientation, especially relevant to the popular and folk forms of the arts, is transmission of craft traditions. In school art, this orientation is reflected in the wide practice of "child craft" with its uniform holiday and season products, as contrasted with the more individual "child art" experiences that aim to promote creativity and expression through open-ended pedagogies (e.g., Bresler, 1992b).

Inquiry and creativity require a process of exploration. Allocating space to explore facilitates discoveries and insights. Children made connections between inner and outer experiences, or perceived discrepancies (reflected, for example, in Luke's comment to Jenny: "I *felt* right when I was doing it, but it did not *look* right."). The disciplined mind and body states of concentration, and observation, enable inquiry and creation. Popular thinking sometimes assumes that exploration that draws on the inner self is antithetical to following directions, imposed from outside. However, Jenny's emphasis on inner control clearly integrated both. The false distinction between inner control versus control imposed from the outside echoes child-centered inquiry versus discipline-centered teaching, a dichotomy deconstructed by Dewey (1938). Disciplinary knowledge, as Dewey has pointed out, is not antithetical to inquiry but complements and deepens it. Jenny's dance/drama lessons provide instances and opportunities for explorations of expressive movement, but draw on discipline-based vocabulary from the Laban movements and somatic sensitivities, requiring self-discipline for focused engagement. Thus, vocabulary and concepts from the discipline of dance serve to direct, ground, and expand exploration and personal experiences, where concepts and movements are connected in new ways.

Accountability. What counts as evidence of learning? Defined standards may enhance mastery of some aspect, assuring that some skills are covered by all. Prescribed standards may also confine and limit open-endedness, creativity and exploration– not only for students, but for teachers as well. Exploration is essential to learning but is hard to evaluate and by definition can lead to different outcomes. Exploration may also be difficult for children who are accustomed to being rewarded for the correct response. In these classrooms, evaluation was closer to informal responses to the arts than to the traditional school assessment. Teachers' comments of "interesting," and the occasional "beautiful," typically in expressive tone communicated differently from the vague "nice work" frequently used in other classes. These comments marked a different value in a school setting that typically does not celebrate the interesting or the beautiful. Jenny said to me that she used "beautiful" sparingly in order not to embarrass the child in front of his peers, but enough to acknowledge that she was impressed. In her feedback to the group, Jenny praised thinking (a frequent comment was: "You're thinking today. I like it when you think!"). In contrast, other dance/drama teachers' feedback typically focused on following directions, being quiet, staying in place. With no mirrors in the room, the visual aspects of form and grace were not emphasized. The use of scarves enhanced the visual effects in the modern and post-modern styles.

Jenny used various types of evaluation emphasizing self-evaluation. For example, in a questionnaire, ranking from 1 (no, never), through 3 (sometimes), to 5 (yes), children had to self-evaluate various aspects of their dance (e.g., did the work show at least one movement quality?) Jenny used students' dance journals for written self-evaluation and critiquing dances. She also used quick, informal self-evaluation at the end of class, when children were standing at the door, asking them to respond to statements (such as: "I could copy shapes exactly"; "I knew when to freeze, when to move"); using thumbs up for "yes," thumbs down for "no," one up and one down for "sometimes." Here, evaluation enhanced the students' ownership and reflection on what was learned, rather than provide accountability.

INTERACTIONS IN MOVEMENT: POSSIBILITIES AND HINDRANCES

The interaction of inside and outside worlds extends to self and others– learning with and from others, as compared to learning besides others. Cooperation, collaboration, and communication were key concepts in the dance/drama curriculum. Orchestrating a space for interactions in small groups, or large group work, shaped learning and body experiences.

School expectation of students' collaboration are different from those of the dance/drama worlds. Schooling typically minimizes those elements of social learning which are at the heart of dance/drama in out of school contexts, including spontaneous feedback and applause from others. Dance/drama classes were at an intersection– in-between the two worlds. In general, dance classes were more interactive than other classes, (both academic and arts disciplines). Dance/drama lessons started with "circle time" with children coordinating rhythm and movement. They incorporated students' observations of each other's shapes and movements and included collaboration on a creation of dance or pantomime, building on peers' ideas. Mary and Jenny's small groups followed a chamber group model where children interacted with each other's work. Group work in dance and in pantomime ranged from couples to groups of seven, where children entered the scene to become part of the action with others, (i.e., becoming part of a living machine). Kinesthetic interactions (e.g., "Put your elbow on your partner's knee"; "Put your head on your partner's back") encouraged children to explore different body positions. Broadening their repertoires of movements provided children with more tools for creating their own dances.

Most of the dance/drama activities were individual, a solo within a crowd. Teachers often restrained interactions between children, possibly as a way to achieve control, frequently reminding children that if they talked or touched each other they would be timed out. In a group pantomime, for example, Molly instructed the children several times they should enter the scene and do something related to the theme but *not* involving another child.

Individual boundaries facilitate and reinforce discipline. Collaborative open-ended activities, where children are invited to generate ideas and movements, create richness. However, if not orchestrated well, they can result in chaos. Indeed, when the children were allowed to work together and negotiate a scene the noise level increased. Clearly, it was a productive noise, a product of the cooperation involved in problem solving or planning scenes. However, children's talk was quick to be interpreted as disruptive, with little interest for its contextual meaning and relationship to learning.

INSTITUTIONAL CONTEXT

Arts Specialists as Subculture: A Room of Their Own

The institutional contexts in which dance practices are embedded, and the structures and values of their institutions, shaped the practice of dance/drama. Arts specialists represent a distinctive subculture within schools, where theirs is frequently the only subject that is not taught by classroom teachers. Hence, their position is a marginalized one, as "the other" teacher. The ambivalent institutional view of dance/drama is reflected in the allocation of space. As I have observed elsewhere (Bresler, 1998, 2002) one's own room is a highly significant possession in school terms, symbolizing professionalism, autonomy, and self-control. In their room teachers have control over use of materials and rules for comportment, autonomy that is lacking in most other arenas of teacher life. Dance is modest in its requirement. Unlike ballet, cheer leading, physical education, it requires no special outfits and equipment. Unlike the visual arts, it needs no materials. The dance/drama teachers observed used simple instruments like cymbals or tambourine, and occasionally, recorded music. But the seemingly simple requirement of having space to move was not easy to find. In the three schools where rooms were allocated to dance/drama, they were not built for these activities (for example, no floor for dancing, no mirrors so students can look at themselves and evaluate their position). It is indicative of the status of the arts within schools that half of the schools in the district had no rooms for the arts, in contrast to regular teachers' classrooms, as well as to libraries, gyms, offices for social workers and counselors.[18]

Classrooms typically feature a tightly bounded individual space. Desks accommodate predictable patterns of eye contact between students and a teacher at a center stage. However, in dance classes, children's confinement behind their desk hinders their viewing of other children's movements. Sitting on *top* of the desk (as compared to sitting behind the desk), facilitates a view of the community, but is considered by classroom teachers as breaking the rule. Jenny:

> "I had one fifth grade teacher who was appalled that I let those children sit on the tops of their desks. Well, it was the only way we could get them in that room to see what was going on: If we put them into chairs they wouldn't be able to see anything or comment on it. When they were in their chairs, they were still in their straight rows and her rigid structure. She was very authoritarian, 'do it my way or you don't do it at all' and if I could break that by letting them sit on their desks, then there will be more room to take risks. It was a kind of atmosphere that classroom was with those children in those desks in those rows and it worked for her, that was the way she did things but when I walked into that room, they were willing to take the kind of risk they needed [for the activity] and by allowing them a little more informality, by letting them sit on the desks, then we kind of tumbled down one barrier and got down to the next place. But it made her furious and eventually it got to be not worth the fights. Some of the teachers were just real possessive, 'these are my children and they're all going to behave the way I want them to behave.'"

Most classroom teachers expected a continuity of management rules through the dance/drama lessons. Each classroom had its own rules and within a classroom there were individual contracts with different children. The individual choreographies that classroom teachers created with twenty some children were unmanageable to a specialist with many hundred of children each week. Jenny:

> "It's almost impossible to keep track of 50 behavior contracts in your head. Teachers always say, well you know you have a note this child is on a behavior contract, yeah right, I have 50 children with behavior contracts at this school and maybe 50 at my other school, so if his contract says he's not suppose to be going like this on his desk I probably am going to let that slide because this is not interfering with anybody."

The constraints of space, and the related dynamics with classroom teachers added technical and emotional pressures for dance/drama specialists. When dance/drama was taught in homerooms, classroom teachers and even aides monitored dance/drama teaching, sometimes interfering with the instruction in what they felt was their "territories." When dance/drama had a space of their own, classroom teachers were sometimes late to pick up their students from dance/drama lessons. An extra couple of minutes needed to bring the dance/drama lesson to a closure, required negotiations with the classroom teachers. Thus, the ability to negotiate positively with classroom teachers and to create allies among different faculty members was central for specialists.

The aim of expanding repertoire of shapes and movements sometimes required the pushing of classroom rules. When Jenny asked a first/second grade group to make a Picasso shape, (referring to the visual art class they had the previous day,) Maya asked if she could use a chair. Jenny looked slightly nervous as Maya climbed a chair and stood on in with one foot. Standing by Maya's side, and giving her a hand, Jenny's tone expressed ambivalence: "That's beautiful but be careful."

In dance/drama, safety, as well as management and control, shaped the choice of space. Molly, for example, viewed the classroom space as inadequate and mentioned to the students on several occasions, "If I had a gym, you move could move faster. We have to move slowly because of the room." She was aware that the gym was available for some of the afternoon classes, but told us that when she had brought children to the gym, they had gone "wild" and it was hard to control them. She felt that it was better to confine them to the familiar space of the classroom.

TOWARDS AN EMBODIED PEDAGOGY: WHO SHOULD TEACH DANCE

Dance/drama teachers' expressive voices, dynamic facial expressions and whole body movements, created a heightened sense of communication, providing an expanded invitation for students to engage and create. As we contextualize the dance/drama teachers' curriculum within their professional background, enculturation and visions, teacher preparation is key to the understanding of their practice. Expertise in the subject matter of dance is key. The perceptions and repertoire of movement activities of teachers not trained as dancers is limited. They are less likely to be aware of the cognitive and expressive possibilities embodied in movement. Furthermore, those with little dance experience are less likely to be touched or inspired by it. On the issue of what it takes to teach dance, Patricia Knowles (1998) quotes well-known choreographer Jean Erdman:

> The artist-teacher, to be inspiring, need not always be a professional performer or professional choreographer, for teaching is a creative art with its own kind of ecstasy. But, the artist-teacher must have had a life-transforming experience in dance in some way– an experience that subsumes all information and knowledge about the art, welding it into an organic self-generating creative activity. This is the indispensable requisite if teaching in the school curricula is to contribute to the development of the art itself.

All three dance/drama teachers attended to some extent to beauty through heightened perception of remarkable performances. Viewing professional dancers on video served as a role model for the students. However, teachers' lack of dance background was a hindrance in their cultivating their students' kinesthetic knowledge and perception.

It may not be surprising that Jenny who has an MFA in dance and an extensive experience as a choreographer, communicated the qualities of creativity and intensity in relation to dance. In her teaching, dance often became a way of knowing self, others, and the world. Jenny aimed to expand communication among children towards the expressive, turning her students away from using the conventional and stereotypical, by guiding them into complex perception, problem solving, and creation. This learning process was not a spontaneous one, but required careful cultivation, as well as concentration, focus, exploration, and mindfulness. Jenny's skills drew on her expertise in dance as well as in teaching. As she suggested in our member checking conversation, it also drew on having children of her own and believing that children were capable and deserving of respect.

CODA: THE VALUE OF SCHOOL DANCE

The discussion about the place of dance in public education relates to the larger question of educational mission and goals. In a submissive school choreography we note children holding themselves with head bowed, shoulders up, shuffling steps. A different choreography expands, lengthens, opens up. The physical, the cognitive, and the expressive are intertwined. Dance/drama afford fields for bodily action that exercise and expand cognitive and affective capacities. Clearly, dance/drama can extend the kinesthetic, cognitive, and affective possibilities for students, but it does not guarantee it. Through their choice of movement experiences, teachers teach the child not only how to express ideas and feeling but also *what* to express, expanding or confining students' ranges of bodily states, emotions and cognition. At its best, school dance provided a space where children could engage in thinking and communicating in movement, introducing somatic and kinesthetic experiences that are not a part of current schooling, not even part of movement in athletics which is more fitness and achievement-oriented. Indeed, the genre of creative dance which school dance draws upon can, at its best, be regarded as a form of self-actualization– physical, emotional, and intellectual. It can open students up to awareness of the outside world, from shapes and movements to the inner worlds of energies and qualities of experience, combining ways of doing with ways of *being*.

NOTES

[1]Michel Foucault (1979) describes the rise of institutions including military academies, schools, factories and prisons in the late eighteen and nineteen centuries that discipline and silence the body. The body in school settings has also been addressed by Jan Nespor (1997).

[2]Two years of extensive data collection and several more years of analyzing and further data collection, including member checking.

[3]The connections of body and mind has been addressed through history, from Greek philosophers (Kraus, 1969), through Decartes (Danto, 1999), and Spinoza (Damasio, 2003). In this volume Peters presents an overview of the mind/body connection in the past century, and Markula addresses contemporary theories of the importance of body/mind relationship to physical and mental health.

[4]Kinesthetics has been recognized as an important form of intelligence along with mathematical, verbal, spatial, musical, and social intelligences (Gardner, 1983).

[5]Described as the "art and science of inner-relational processes between awareness, biological function, and environment [with] all three factors [being] understood as a synergistic whole" (Hanna, in Fitt, 1996, p. 303).

[6]Fitt writes: "The central objective of most somatic approaches is the encouragement of easeful, mindful, efficiency of motion, which simultaneously promotes health, balance, and achievement of one's potential. Another aspect of all somatic approaches is tapping into the inherent wisdom of the body. Learning to listen to that wisdom is one of the values of all somatics...It is thought that somatics with its multidimensional emphasis on mind, body, spirit, and environment, most accurately represents this domain, which includes Alexander Technique, Rolfing, Feldenkrais, Ideokinesis, Pilates-based work, Cohne's Mind-Body Centering, Laban Movement Analysis, Bartinieff Movement Fundamentals, and others."

[7]The interaction between participants and audience presents yet another kind of relationship, central to the performing arts. The relationship between the performer and the audience is experienced by all performers and shapes all live performances, including that of teaching. While the audience are separated from the performers in space, (a distance that is considered to contribute to aesthetic appreciation, see, for example, Beardsley, 1983; Smith, 1994), the relationship can be powerful, adding to that essential intensity of live performance.

001

[8]Dance education has in fact two parent-disciplines: dance and physical education (Kraus, 1969; Knowles, 1998). Interestingly, in library classiciation, dance is not a separate item but is divided between theatre and amusement (Sparshott, 1995). The current interest and legitimation of dance as part of the curriculum as an art form is relatively recent.

[9]CEMREL stands for Central Midwest Regional Educational Laboratory, a private non-profit corporation supported in part as an educational laboratory by funds from the national Institute of Education.

[10]The meaning of these one or two minutes was not elaborated.

[11]Typically participating in the project for 1–2 years.

[12]For a description of the second and third year of the project, see Davidson, this volume.

[13]Dance is typically taught as part of physical education. In Knowles and Sande's (1991) survey, dance was included in 68% schools in the US as a component of the Physical Education Program, and in 44% as a part of other curricular disciplines such as history, geography, or social studies. This district chose not to have physical education program.

[14]All specialists traveled to two schools each and typically taught nine classes per day. The entire fine arts team met once a month to discuss organizational issues and the discipline teams met to plan curriculum. Initially, the curriculum focused on themes and interdisciplinary teams met to plan curriculum in all art forms. It later changed to focus on *elements* of art (as defined by this particular program), where the specialists in each art form interpreted the implementation of the elements. Elements across the art disciplines areas included line, shape, color, and tone. Elements specific to dance included body, space, time, weight, energy, form, design, and mood. Elements in Drama included: plot, character, theme, sequence, language, form, design, and mood.

[15]Based on the number of times students enrol in or leave a school during the school year.

[16]All names are pseudonyms.

[17]"Describing music through movement" is advocated in Dalcroze, Boardman's Generative Approach, and Orff. However, in most music classes, classical music is "for immobile listening," and the occasional dancing is typically folk or ethnic.

[18] Magnet schools as observed by and Knowles and Sande's (1991) and Bresler (1997), had special dance facilities.

REFERENCES

Anderson, J. (1992). *Ballet and modern dance*. Princeton, New Jersey: Princeton Book Company.

Beardsley, M. (1983). Aesthetic definition of art. In H. Curtler (Ed.), *What is art education?* (pp. 15–29). New York: Haven Publishing.

Bowman, W. (1998). *Philosophical perspectives on music*. New York: Oxford University Press.

Bresler, L. (1991). Armstrong elementary school, Chicago, Illinois. In R. Stake, L. Bresler & L. Mabry (Eds.), *Custom & cherishing: The arts in elementary schools* (pp. 95–136). CRME, Urbana, IL: University of Illinois.

Bresler, L. (1992a). Dance education in elementary schools. *Design for Arts in Education, 93*(5), 13–20.

Bresler, L. (1992b). Visual art in primary grades: A portrait and analysis. *Early Childhood Research Quarterly, 7,* 397–414.

Bresler, L. (1997). *General issues across sites: The role of the arts in unifying high school curriculum*. The College Board/Getty Center for the Arts.

Bresler, L. (1998). The genre of school music and its shaping by meso, micro and macro contexts. *Research Studies in Music Education, 11,* 2–18.

Bresler, L. (2002). School art as hybrid genre: Institutional contexts for art curriculum. In L. Bresler & C. Thompson (Eds.), *The arts in children's lives: Context, culture, and curriculum* (pp. 169–183). Dordrecht: Kluwer.

Broudy, H. (1972). *Enlightened cherishing: An essay on aesthetic education*. Urbana, IL: University of Illinois Press.

Burrows, D. (1990). *Sound, speech, and music*. Amherst, MA: University of Massachusetts Press.

Choksy, L., Abramson, R. M., Gillespie, A., Woods, D., & York, F. (2001). *Teaching music in the twenty–first century* (2nd ed.). Toronto: Prentice Hall.

Costantino, T. E. (in press). The impact of philanthropy on arts education policy. *Arts Education Policy Review, 105*(1).

Damasio, A. (2003). *Looking for Spinoza: Joy, sorrow, and the feeling brain*. New York: Harcourt.

Danto, A. (1999). *The body/body problems.* Berkeley: University of California Press.

Dewey, J. (1934). *Art as experience.* New York: Capricorn Books.

Dewey, J. (1938). *Experience and education.* New York: MacMillian

Eisner, E. (1982). *Cognition and curriculum: A basis for deciding what to teach.* New York: Longman.

Espeland, M. (1997). Once upon a time there was a minister: An unfinished story about reform in Norwegian arts education. *Arts Education Policy Review, 99*(1), 11–16.

Fitt, S. (1996). *Dance kinesiology* (2nd ed.). New York: Schirmer.

Foucault, M. (1979). *Discipline and punish: The birth of the prison.* New York: Vintage Books.

Gardner, H. (1983). *Frames of mind: The theory of multiple intelligences.* New York: Basic Books.

Geertz, C. (1976). Art as a cultural system. *MLN, 91,* 1473–1499.

Hanna, J. L. (1999). *Partnering dance and education: Intelligent moves for changing times.* Champaign, IL: Human Kinetics.

Hirsch, E. D. (1987). *Cultural literacy.* New York: Random House.

Housen, A., Arenas, A., & Yenawine, P. (1994). *Visual thinking curriculum.* New York: Museum of Modern Art. Distributed through Department of Education (MoMA) and Development through Art, Inc.

Kimball, M. M. (1994). Writing standards for dance. In *"The vision for arts education in the 21ˢᵗ century: The ideas and ideals behind the development of the National Standards for education in the arts"* (pp. 32–35). Reston, VA: Music Educators National Conference.

Knowles, P. (1982). *The emerging role of dance in American education: 1807–1982.* Paper presented at the VII International Conference on Sport and Dance, University of Queensland, Bisbane, Australia.

Knowles, P. (1998). *Connecting to the legacy of the past.* NASD President's Report, Tuscon, Arizona.

Knowles, P., & Sande, R. (1991). *Dance education in American public schools (case studies).* Urbana, IL: Council of Research in Music Education.

Kraus, R. (1969). *History of the dance in art and education.* Engelwood Cliffs, New Jersey: Prentice-Hall.

Kraus, S., Hilsendager, S., & Dixon, B. (1991). *History of the dance in art and education.* Engelwood Cliffs, New Jersey: Prentice-Hall.

Lave, J., & Wenger, E. (1991). *Situated learning: Legitimate peripheral participation.* New York: Cambridge University Press.

Madeja, S. (1977). *Arts and aesthetics: An agenda for the future.* St. Louis, Missouri: CEMREL.

Madeja, S. (1978). *The arts, cognition, and basic skills.* St. Louis, Missouri: CEMREL.

Marques, I. (in press). *Contribution of school art curricula to quality education in Latin America and the Caribbean.* Paris: UNESCO.

McPherson, G. (1995). Integrating the arts into the general curriculum: An Australian perspective. *Arts Education Policy Review, 97*(1), 25–31.

Nespor, J. (1997). *Tangled up in school: Politics, space, bodies, and signs in the educational process.* Mahwah, New Jersey: Lawrence Erlbaum.

Paynter, J. (1982). *Sound and silence: Classroom projects in creative music.* London: Cambridge U.P.

Schafer, M. (1975). *Rhinoceroes in the classroom.* Wien: Universal Edition.

Sizer, T. (1996). *Horace's hope: What works for the American high school.* Boston: Houghton Mifflin.

Smith, R. (1994). *General knowledge and arts education.* Urbana, IL: University of Illinois Press.

Sparshott, F. (1995). *A measured pace: Toward a philosophical understanding of the arts of dance.* Toronto: University of Toronto Press.

Stake, R., Bresler, L., & Mabry, L. (1991). *Custom and cherishing: Arts education in the United States.* CRME, Urbana, IL: University of Illinois.

Stinson, S. W. (1990). Dance and the developing child. In W. J. Stinson (Ed.), *Moving and learning for the whole child* (pp. 139–150). Reston, VA: American Alliance for Health, Physical Education, Recreation & Dance.

Stinson, S. (1995). Body of knowledge. *Educational Theory, 45*(1), 43–54.

Stinson, S. (2002). What we teach is who we are: The stories of our lives. In L. Bresler & C. Thompson (Eds.), *The arts in children's lives: Context, culture, and curriculum* (pp. 169–183). Dordrecht: Kluwer.

United States Department of Education (2003). No Child Left Behind Act.

Vygotsky, L. S. (1979). *Thought and language* (A. Kozulin, Trans. & Ed.). Cambridge, MA: Cambridge University.

Wiggins, J. (2000). *Teaching for musical understanding.* Boston: McGraw Hill.

Wright, L. (1994). Writing standards for Theater. In *"The vision for arts education in the 21st century: The ideas and ideals behind the development of the National Standards for Education in the Arts"* (pp. 36–39). Reston, VA: Music Educators National Conference.

ACKNOWLEDGEMENT

This study would have been impossible without the generosity and help of the teachers who welcomed us into their classroom and gave their time, as well as insights. Many thanks to Deb Ceglowski and Nancy Hertzog for their tremendous data collection. I am deeply indebted to Eve Harwood, Pat Knowles, and Sue Stinson for reading a preliminary draft and their insightful comments, and to Alma Gottlieb, Beth Ann Miller, Joan Russell, Saville Kushner, Kyung-hwa Lee, and Daniel Walsh for a careful reading of this manuscript and their excellent suggestions. Thanks to Yu-Ting Chen for her first-rate secretarial help.

SUSAN W. STINSON

MY BODY/MYSELF: LESSONS FROM DANCE EDUCATION[1]

"The body" is currently a hot topic among those who claim residence in cultural foundations of education. In this home where I have lived for many years, words, ideas, theories about "the body" are produced, usually without revealing anything about the bodies of those who produced them. Following scholarly tradition, much thinking about the role of "the body" in culture and classroom is delivered in abstract, disembodied language. As Julie Sandler writes,

> For all that many poststructuralists call for a re-insertion of the body into texts, they seem to forget about this body here with the eyes burning from staring at the computer screen and the back aching from hunching over the keyboard. (1997, p. 221)

My other professional home, in which I have lived even longer, is dance education. In contrast to educational theory, most dance experiences, whether on stage or in a studio, require that the body be revealed. Dancers are usually keenly aware of every bulge and sag, every twinge and tension, expending extraordinary time training, shaping, preserving, often obsessing about, their own bodies.

In recent years, we have seen the appearance of a good bit of critical theoretical work written about the dancer's body (Albright, 1997; Desmond, 2001; Foster, 1995, 1996; Fischer-Hornung & Goeller, 2001; Friedler & Glazer, 1997; Fraleigh, 1996; Green, 1999, 2001; Ramsey, 1995; Shapiro, 1999; Thomas, 1993). So many authors, including myself (Stinson 1995, 1998), have made the point that the low status of dance reflects its connection with women and the body, that I feel no need to go into these issues again here. Instead, I have tried in this essay to look both personally and reflectively at what I know from living as I do, with one foot grounded firmly in dance education while the other remains connected with curriculum theory.

From my life in dance education, I bring my lived body, subject of my embodied experiences. I write this essay from the perspective of a personal body, especially my own, not that abstracted virtual body which is the subject of so much post-modern discourse. I thus must acknowledge that, when I look in a mirror, I do not see the kind of a body that the general public assumes belongs to a dancer—young, svelte, perfectly toned. I look at my body with the judgmental eye that dancers—and most women—have, when it comes to their own bodies, and see far more signs of aging than just graying hair. Inside my body, I receive multiple and ongoing signals that I can no longer move as I did when I was a young adult; this has been made worse by my spending the past nine years not in a studio, but sitting in an administrator's chair. My aging body nevertheless stores memories of past

153

Liora Bresler (ed.), Knowing Bodies, Moving Minds, 153-167.
©*2004 Kluwer Academic Publishers. Printed in the Netherlands*

experiences, including memories of lessons learned and taught. It is three of these lessons that I will describe in this essay.

From my lived experience in cultural foundations of education, I bring another way of perceiving the world, one that often feels like I am looking not "up close and personal," but from a distance. It is from this distance that I can question the taken-for-granted, especially that within my own thinking, and ask larger questions like, "In whose interest?" and "What's worth knowing?" The critical reflections woven into this essay most reflect this way of being.

In the choreography that follows, I have tried to create a duet between these parts of myself, a dance between personal knowledge and critical social theory. In doing so, I have tried to engage in the "dual dialectic" called for by James B. Macdonald, who wrote, "Values, I believe, are articulated in the lives of people by the dual dialectic of reflecting upon the consequences of an action and sounding the depths of our inner selves" (1995, p. 79). Through remembering cherished moments and asking myself difficult questions about them, I hope to be living this call.

Feeling from the inside to understand self and others

In trying to become aware of the values I embody as a dance educator, I have been considering what I teach first and what I keep returning to, when I teach K–12 students or coach my university students who will become dance educators. This first lesson has to do with inner sensory awareness, which is studied by those in the field of somatics. The term *somatics* is attributed to Thomas Hanna, who described it as a way of perceiving oneself from the "inside out, where one is aware of feelings, movements and intentions, rather than looking objectively from the outside in" (1988, p.20). The increasing popularity of a somatic approach in teaching dance is indicated by the 2002 issue of the *Journal of Dance Education* (Greene, 2002), which was devoted entirely to it.

Long before I knew the word *somatics*, I began teaching even the youngest students to "feel from the inside," initially because I recognized that this kind of consciousness of even everyday movement transforms it into dance movement. With three year olds, we begin simply—I ask them to quiver their hands for a long enough time that, when they "freeze" (stopping the movement with hands in mid-air), they can still feel the tingling inside their fingers. I tell them that this is their dance magic that lives inside their muscles, and they need to use it to dance. By third grade or so, when students love the power of knowing a big word that their parents don't know, I teach them about the *kinesthetic* sense, which allows them to know what their body is doing even when their eyes are closed.

This internal sensing has great significance not only for how one learns and performs dance but also for how we perceive the art. Without it, we certainly can see movement and patterns on stage, and hear any accompanying music, but internal sensing allows us to feel the dance and our response to it. We become participants, not just onlookers, as we breathe along with the dancers on stage, feeling the stretch that continues past the fingertips, feeling the body landing silently from a jump. Those who have never experienced a dance performance from this perspective have missed half of it.

This same sensing serves us in places other than a dance theatre. We also use it to connect with the Olympic athlete on the television screen—straining to beat the clock, bursting with exhilaration in victory, slumping in defeat. It allows us to share the weighty sadness of a friend, the tense anxiety of the unprepared student before an exam. Philosopher Kenneth Shapiro (1985) calls this kind of participation *kinesthetic empathy*. Martin Buber uses the phrase, "feeling from the other side" (1955, p. 96), which he describes as feeling within our own bodies the kind of touch we give to others, whether that is a loving caress or a painful blow.

Donald Blumenfeld-Jones, who writes about bodily-kinesthetic intelligence from the lens of a dancer as well as that of a critical theorist, has drawn some conclusions similar to my own, in defining dancing as paying attention to one's own motion. He cites Merce Cunningham (1977) in speaking of an "appetite for movement" experienced by some dancers:

> It does not mean the need to display oneself but rather the need to be moving and to feel the movement and to think movement. It does not mean that one always has to be moving but rather that one feels another's motion almost as if one were also moving. (in press)

So it is clear that I am not the only dancer who has learned from my life in dance to feel from the inside and to use this inner sensing to know others and myself. I think that the other two important lessons from dance which I will share are probably grounded in this one. I cannot move on to consider them, however, without stopping to problematize my privileging of inner awareness. To begin with, sensing myself from the inside is only the beginning to knowing myself. How many times has fatigue or thirst made me think I must be hungry; how many times have I interpreted boredom as fatigue? What I feel on a body level may require critical thinking in order to interpret accurately.

Internal sensing is even more limited as a way of knowing someone else: How do I know that feelings I attribute to another are the same as those I am feeling? The senses that allow us to feel from the inside, like our other senses, provide only a private experience, and validation of private experiences is problematic. Assuming that everyone perceives an experience the same way I do is the ultimate in arrogance. While I can use my kinesthetic empathy to try to feel what someone else is feeling, there is no guarantee that it will be the same. Of course, we can *ask* others to describe what they are feeling, but words have different meanings to different individuals, and words cannot directly and completely represent our lived experiences. As Michael Polanyi (1966) has reminded us, we know more than we can tell.

Going beyond personal interaction to social concerns, one must admit that it can't be very helpful for those living in chronic poverty to become more aware of their hunger, or for those who have no choice other than hard physical labor to become more aware of their weariness and strain. I wonder if well developed internal sensing becomes a value only after basic human needs are met. How useful is it for those without sufficient food, without clean water, without the comfortable bed or easy chair or even a bit of shade from the sun, much less the climate-controlled environment in which I can rest on hot summer days? How self-indulgent is it to say that people need to be aware of what they are feeling on the inside when their basic needs can't be met? How can we bear to focus on our own bodies and ourselves when others are suffering?

As a woman who has filled and continues to fill a great many roles involving service and care-giving, I know all too well the dangers of focusing only on others and not caring for myself as well; the work of Carol Gilligan (1982) came at a time I needed to consider how to include myself as one to be cared for. Yet it is all too easy for this discovery of what I feel on the inside to become naval gazing self-centeredness. I remember a friend from some years ago, who entered a mid-life crisis to which he responded by taking one body-based class after another to develop more awareness of what he was feeling. Although it made sense at the time, especially to those of us who advocate being in touch with one's own feelings, he eventually became so focused on himself that the needs of others seemed completely unimportant. Similarly, as Martha Eddy reminds us, "Dance-making from a somatic source often gets lost in personal experience and only grows to the level of personal ritual" (2000, p. 147).

How important it is that we start with ourselves, but not end there. How important it is that we let the kinesthetic sense take us beyond our own sensations into the world, to recognize our connectedness with others—and that we go beyond sensing the pain we feel (our own or that of others) to acting upon it. I admire educators like my colleague Jill Green, who are making the connection between the inner somatic sense and social consciousness (Green 1993, 1996a, 1996b, 1996c, 2002).

Yet when I sound the depths of my inner self, as Macdonald (1995) called me to do, I still question my efficacy as a dance educator, teacher educator, and scholar to make a difference in a world that, as Maxine Greene so eloquently describes it, "includes homelessness, hunger, pollution, crime, censorship, arms build-ups, and threats of war, even as it includes the amassing of fortunes, consumer goods of unprecedented appeal, world travel opportunities, and the flickering faces of the 'rich and famous' on all sides (Greene, 1988, p. 12). I have long been attracted to Greene's belief that arts education should not be "linked entirely to the life of the senses or the emotions, or…subsumed under rubrics like 'literacy' (1988, p. 13), but should emphasize moving people "to critical awareness, to a sense of moral agency, and to a conscious engagement with the world" (1978, p. 162). In my deepest questioning, however, I wonder whether this stance is just a way to justify work that I love and avoid guilt for what I am not doing. Nell Noddings' work (1984, 1992) has been meaningful in speaking to my still-unresolved dilemma of negotiating the distance between what I can do and what needs to be done in the world.

"Being your own teacher"

The second most important lesson of the body that I teach in dance has to do with "being your own teacher." I first came upon this phrase while teaching many years ago in a Quaker school, but I have come to connect it closely to self control (telling oneself what not to do) as well as self direction (telling oneself what to do); this kind of self-management (or lack of it) seems to me to be intimately connected with my body. I often feel out of date when I fume over a culture that seems to constantly advocate immediate sensory gratification, regardless of the consequences, when prime time television teaches young people that sexual attraction must be acted upon before the hour's end. The morality of "If it feels good, do it" began during my adolescence in the 1960's, but its consequences have become more dangerous today. Another example of the emphasis on immediate gratification comes in the commercials. Consumerism—buying regardless of whether we need something—has even become a patriotic duty for Americans. I sought to teach my own children to recognize their own power not just to become aware of their own bodily desires, but also to make conscious choices after considering the options and the consequences; this is a lesson I think all children should learn.

Much of the language that I use in teaching dance derives from this value. I direct children to "choose a spot on the floor" rather than to "spread out," to "choose a shape" rather than to "make any shape you want," seeking to enhance their consciousness of their choices. "Telling yourself" when to begin, change, or stop any movement, and then developing the skill and discipline to follow through on such inner direction, connects inner sensory awareness with conscious thought.

Such a connection seems just as important in other settings. As I continue to age, I find myself saying more often, "I can push myself to do this, but should I?" At any age, telling oneself to keep going past one's comfort level requires courage and stamina—and also critical reflection if pushing onward is to be an act of extending one's boundaries rather than ending a career or even a life.

Being in control of oneself becomes especially important for students in an activity that involves movement. When children are not nicely seated in desks that serve as containers, the possibility for chaos becomes distinctly more likely. I flash back to that third grade class I taught some years ago, as part of a series of demonstration classes I was doing before I became an administrator. I can't remember whether the children came straight to me after racing on the playground, but they were exceptionally "wild" in the first two of three dance lessons I taught. They seemed to perceive that entrance into the spacious gym came with a license to run around, accompanied by screaming when the urge came upon them. I decided that, more than anything else, they needed to learn how to control their own energy. When they came into the gym for the third lesson, I had them sit against a wall, and spoke seriously to them about the recent massive hurricane which had been so much in the news, reminding us that energy can be very destructive when it is out of control. I then told them some version of the following:

> We all need energy to *make* things, but our energy, too, can be destructive when it is out of control. If we don't know how to control our own energy, someone else does it for us. As children, you might get punished by a parent or sent to the principal's office. When people get to be grown-ups and don't know how to control themselves, they can get sent to jail. So in this class I will teach you how to control your own energy; this way, you can be your own teacher and tell yourself what to do.

They each then went to a designated spot on the floor, where I directed them to lie down and feel their heart beating. Then they were to stand up, lie down, stand up, over and over again, until they could feel their heart beating really fast—and then stay lying down. I explained that, by making their muscles soft and breathing more deeply and slowly, they could actually help slow down the speed of their heart.

When they felt their heart beat slowly again, I asked them to let me know by sitting up, without disturbing others. Fascinated by the experiment and the power they realized (or perhaps afraid of jail in the future—I had never used this kind of language with children and felt very odd about it), they seemed to take this lesson seriously. We then continued the class, which, I warned them, would include some activities that could get dangerous if they were not in control of themselves. The rest of the lesson involved a theme of a storm: They began in soft curved shapes travelling through space (image of clouds), which eventually got tighter and tighter until they burst into sharp pointed shapes (lightning image) and eventually "thunder jumps" (jumping high and then lowering themselves all the way down until lying on the floor). They made hard rain sounds pounding the floor, gradually getting softer and softer before stopping the sound and transforming themselves into curved shapes or pointed ones (responding to their chosen image of a rainbow or stars). There were multiple opportunities in the class to use different kinds of energy and to tell themselves what to do and when to do it, and the children were successful at it.

When their classroom teacher returned to claim her students, I told her that she would not need to tell the children to walk quietly down the hall, because they could be their own teachers and tell themselves. My own teacher education students watched this transformation in awe, and I felt quite self-satisfied when I told them that this lesson was probably more important than anything else students learn in dance.

I still think that it is essential for all of us to be able to self-manage our own energy and our own actions. When I reflect critically on my teaching of this class, however, and the messages of self-control and "being your own teacher" which I continue to teach, I can't help but find them potentially problematic. It is seductive to get children to do what we want them to do while thinking that it is their own idea. Neither the classroom teacher nor I would have been so pleased if a child had told herself to run down the hall yelling and screaming. No, I wanted the children to make choices within carefully presented options, and to tell themselves to do what they knew their teachers wanted. My manipulation was pretty effective. The children learned, performed well (using their energy constructively to create a dance about a storm), and seemed to emerge feeling proud of themselves and the dance they made. I wanted to empower them—but did I really? Or was I just using more seductive means to produce docility? I am mindful of the words of Valerie Walkerdine (1992), who has noted that this is the seduction of progressive education, a movement that established the schoolroom

> as a laboratory, where development could be watched, monitored and set along the right path. There was therefore no need for...discipline of the overt kind....The classroom became the facilitating space for each individual, under the watchful and total gaze of the teacher, who was held responsible for the development of each individual....[In such a classroom] the children are only allowed happy sentiments and happy words...There is a denial of pain, oppression...There is also a denial of power, as though the helpful teacher didn't wield any. (pp. 17–20)

Although far removed from progressive education, the goal of traditional dance pedagogy often seems to be the creation of docile bodies, mostly those of young women (Stinson, 1998; Green, 1999). And highly trained dancers seem to represent the epitome of bodily control, making their bodies do all sorts of things that are not "natural." Too often, dancers have learned to separate body and mind, viewing their bodies as machines or instruments to be controlled by their will. Dancers are admired for their physical feats, and often for their self-control when it comes to diet, maintaining a weight that allows their bodies to be regarded as beautiful objects in a society that places high value on slenderness in women. Yet too many dancers maintain their weight through decidedly unhealthy means, including smoking as well as weight reduction strategies that may be clinically classified as eating disorders. Such disorders are closely connected to issues of control (Bordo, 1993; Woodman, 1982), and they are more prominent in women, who may perceive that the amount of food they eat is the only aspect of their lives they can control. There are certainly other issues of control run amok among dancers; literature reporting related health problems among dancers (Brady, 1982; Buckroyd, 2000; Gordon, 1983; Green, 1999, 2002-2003; Innes, 1988; Kirkland, 1986; Vincent, 1979) is sufficiently prevalent to make anyone realize that dancers do not have all issues of control figured out.

While individuals suffering from eating disorders deny themselves pleasure in food, and exercise excessively to maintain a particular body shape and size, I struggle with other issues related to control and pleasure. I am aware of how rarely I allow myself to choose pleasure over a never-ending to-do list (only some of which I find pleasurable).

One of the experiences that I do find pleasurable is physical work such as gardening or hiking, and on occasion I give myself permission to indulge. Perhaps for the same reason that I chose dance in my earlier days, I appreciate the pleasure of working hard, really using my muscles. How delightful it is to get hot and sweaty and tired, followed by a shower. Yet I cannot ignore the connection of my pleasure to social class and economic privilege. I have the luxury of choosing to garden because I do not have to raise my only source of food, and I have hot and cold running water available to me for showering off the dirt afterwards. Physical work was looked down upon for generations, as something the upper class should avoid, until its health benefits became known. Today, working out at a gym and recreational running are seen as more acceptable than physical work that is connected with earning an income.

Although many people work out purely for health reasons, it is likely the pleasure of such activity that keeps them going. And yet I know that such pleasure is not universal. In my current research (in progress) on young people's experiences of dance as "work," I am fascinated to realize that not all appreciate challenge (whether physical or not). Certainly one of the most important outcomes of research for me is discovering that everyone does not perceive a situation the same way I do. Yet we know too little about why perceiving that a task is hard makes it more desirable to some and less desirable to others, even though such perception has critical influence on learning, especially if we wish, as I do, for children to be self-directed in their learning.

Finally, teaching students to become their own teachers is not very useful if they will not be allowed to make their own decisions about their art or their lives. Oppression comes from outside as well as inside the self, and we must address both if we are to live in the kind of world in which freedom of expression exists for everyone. Paolo Freire (1983) and other critical pedagogues have helped us see the connection between inner and outer transformation. David Purpel, another of many theorists who see this kind of connection as essential, writes that

> the essence of education can be seen as critical, in that its purpose is to help us see, hear, and experience the world more clearly, more completely, and with more understanding...Another vital aspect of the educational process is the development of creativity and imagination, which enable us not only to understand but to build, make, create, and re-create our world." (1989, pp. 26–27)

With a similar view, Maxine Greene even titled her 1995 book *Releasing the Imagination: Essays on Education, the Arts, and Social Change*. It is my hope; too, that arts education will nourish this kind of imagination, resulting in not only art making but also world-making.

Bodily knowledge and meaning

The third lesson which I most value is more complex, and has to do with the body as a source for meaning making. Put more simply, I have found that my body is, in a sense, a microcosm of the world, and thus a laboratory for understanding its meaning. I concur with Kenneth Shapiro (1985), who writes that the body is "the ground of metaphor" (p. 155). Certainly it does not take long to recall a multitude of bodily-based metaphors: sticky fingers, tight ass, tight lipped, belly up, hang tight, loosen up, and so many more that give us vivid ways to express what we mean. I think of all the concepts that are grounded in body level experience, yet are often used metaphorically to describe what has nothing to do with the body—empty/full, stretched/relaxed, heavy/light, weak/strong, wide/narrow, high/low, sharp/smooth, inner/outer, holding on/holding back, balanced/falling, and more. Even beyond these obvious examples, I agree that

> the primary vehicle of experience's meaningfulness is not language or any structure that is intelligible as language. Rather, it is my body as I live it, my body as it is called to action and as it is actively situated. The ringing telephone interrupts my present activity and grips my heart well before I posit that it is that long awaited call. In a conversation I have a sense of what I want to say before I have the words. What I intend to say I find lodged bodily in me. The implicit meanings of situations and, as well, my own intended meanings are felt; they are present bodily. (Shapiro,1985, p. 40)

Despite the common perception that knowledge resides above the neck, I find that my entire body is the repository for all that I know. My memories of my educational experience, like my memories of everything else, reside in my body. I remember not pictures in my mind, but sensations—even how hot my cheeks felt that day in the third grade when my teacher, whom I adored, humiliated me in front of the class. I have felt affirmed in my memories by the words of Madeline Grumet (1988), who wrote about

> body knowledge, like the knowledge that drives the car, plays the piano, navigates around the apartment without having to sketch a floor plan and chart a route in order to get from the bedroom to the bathroom. Maurice Merleau-Ponty called it the knowledge of the body-subject, reminding us that it is through our bodies that we live in the world. (p. 3)

Unless/until I know something on this level of body knowledge—in my bones, so to speak—the knowledge is not my own, but is rather like those facts one memorizes which seem to fall out of the brain the day after an exam. Further, the knowledge that comes this way is not just about my physical body or even dance, but also about the questions that I face as a person, an educator, and a researcher. My somatic self—the self that lives experience—is necessary in my struggle to find forms which represent that experience, whether those forms are presented on stage or in a scholarly journal.

I am certainly not the only scholar who has recognized the significance of somatics in research (Stinson, 1995). Jill Green (1996a, 1996b), as a somatics practitioner, also calls for such bodily awareness as a researcher. Deidre Sklar (2000) has written powerfully about the significance of this awareness in dance ethnography. Helen Thomas (2000) makes a similar point, when she calls attention to the importance of researchers'

> bringing reflexive self-awareness as experiencing, moving and dancing, culture-bearers into the research arena. The consequences of not reflecting on our taken-for granted routine bodily practices can limit or inhibit our comprehension of the bodily activities of 'others', and this once again emphasises [sic] the need to enter the embodied field with some self-knowledge. (pp. 429–430)

One particularly vivid memory of my own thinking body comes from the time when I was working on my dissertation (Stinson, 1984). I was struggling with a very abstract topic: the relationship between the ethical and the aesthetic dimensions of human existence as they relate to dance education. All of my attempts to figure out a theoretical framework felt disconnected from the concerns that had initially propelled me into the study. One day, still searching for my elusive framework, I went for one of those long walks that were a necessary part of my thinking process. When I returned, I lay down to rest and instantly became conscious of how differently I perceived the world and myself when I was standing compared to when I was lying down. Within moments I knew my framework, which was based upon a metaphor of verticality (the impulse toward achievement and mastery—being on *top*) and horizontality (the impulse toward relationship and community—being *with*). I noticed how lying horizontal felt passive and/or vulnerable while the return to vertical made me feel strong and powerful; these feelings offered important insights as to why we value achievement so much more than community. Once I had identified this dual reality in my own body, I found it in the work of others: in Eric Fromm (1941), who spoke of freedom and security; David Bakan (1966), agency and communion; and Arthur Koestler (1978), self-assertion and integration. While I had read each of these authors previously, I had to find my framework in my own body before I could recognize the connection between the concepts they had identified and the issues with which I was grappling.

Another time I remember, I chose swimming for a break in between writing sessions. But one memorable day as I swam, I became aware of the excess tension in my neck. Rather than releasing my neck to allow the water to hold up my head, I was holding on as though afraid it would sink down into the water. This awareness pointed me toward awareness of other situations in which we use unnecessary control—over our own bodies or others—and I again attended within my body to try to understand why. Climbing out of the water, I realized how much we hold on in making the transition from horizontality (the dependence of infancy) to verticality (which allowed us real mobility and independence). Embedded in our musculature, generally beyond the reach of rational thought, are this impulse toward control and the fear of letting go. I realized that, as long as holding on or letting go are perceived as the only alternatives, holding on seems far preferable, because excess tension seems less dangerous than falling down or "falling apart." Only through bodywork in dance have I found another alternative—releasing into the direction of internal body relationships that facilitate movement that is both safe and free. For example, I become aware of holding in my shoulders, a frequent accompaniment to stress and anxiety in my life. I try to "let go" of the tension, but it quickly reappears. Another choice, found through what is known as "Alexander work" (Jones, 1997), is to release my shoulders out to the side, which immediately gives my neck a sense of lightness and freedom. Considering this choice within my own body helps me consider alternatives to holding on or letting go as choices for classroom management. Releasing into relationship based on mutual trust and respect would take committed work on the part of a teacher and a classroom of children, just as it has taken work for me to learn to release into lines of movement within my own body, but it could be just as productive.

Again, this is an insight that could not have arisen without attention to embodied knowledge. These incidents, and many others, have convinced me that we can think only with what we know "in our bones," and that attending to the sensory, followed by reflection, is a valuable source of such knowledge.

Extending even further the idea of the importance of the body in thinking, Maxine Sheets-Johnstone (1990) claims that the lived body is the basis for the evolution of human thought, and she finds a bodily basis for the origins of counting and language, as well as art-making. She cites extensive paleolithic evidence, concluding, "the thesis that thinking is modelled on the body is actually supported by the same evidence that supports hominid evolution"(p. 5). When she writes about the role of the body in this process, however, she is referring to

> the *tactile kinesthetic* body...the sentiently felt body, the body that knows the world through touch and movement. It is not the body that simply *behaves* in certain observed or observable ways, but the body that resonates in the first- person, lived-through sense of any behavior. It is the experienced and experiencing body. The thesis that thinking is modeled on the body thus links thinking to spatial and sentient-kinetic life. (p. 5)

Despite the number of dance-based theorists who agree with me, I must critically examine my own thinking about my body as a source of knowledge and meaning. In doing so, I am immediately struck by what is too often a large gap between my ability to understand a situation, even on a somatic level, and my ability to do anything about it. An example experienced by aging dancers is the knowledge of how to do a movement one can no longer accomplish. On a more universal level, most of us are aware of times that our feelings about a situation are getting in the way of how we want to be, but we find ourselves unable to change them. One painful example that I recall was when my anger about something in the past got in the way of a relationship, one that I desired to be warm and caring. Knowing the source of the problem did not give me the ability to rid myself of the anger. So my thoughts about using bodily-based reflection to transform the complicated web of relationships in a classroom are offered with humility. When I go into a school classroom, even though I believe in the principle of release rather than control, fear of chaos often keeps me bound within practices I know will help prevent it. I respect that some dance educators have gone further than I have in living their beliefs about liberatory relationships with children they teach (Anttila, 2003).

Beyond the dilemma of translating consciousness into action, I have more difficulty in critiquing my call to recognize the role of the body in knowing and meaning making, because I cannot imagine thinking without using my whole self. How many times as I was writing this essay (and every other one), I must get up and move, relishing every bodily need that gives me an excuse to leave the computer, not only to relieve the knot growing beneath my shoulder blade, but to allow my confused thoughts to shake down into my feet, where I may walk in them and figure out where they are going. I cannot claim to know how widespread the experience of bodily-based thought may be—only that I do not know how to think otherwise. I know from conversations with others, and from reviews of my previous work, that all scholars do not perceive their own thought process as I do mine. This is a good reminder of the danger in knowledge that derives from the body, if we assume that what we have found is more than personal knowledge. Because our bodily experiences are constructed within a cultural context, there are no universal truths which derive from them.

CONCLUSIONS

So I have learned these lessons about my body in dance: how to "feel from the inside" and "feel from the other side," how to be my own teacher, and how to pay attention to my body as a source of knowledge and meaning. While I advocate teaching them to others, I recognize that they are not a panacea for all the ills facing humankind or all the goals of education. These and all other lessons should be accompanied by the kind of reflection that I have attempted to do in this essay, inspired by the critical social theorists who call us to attend to more than our own lived experience.

Despite these disclaimers, in sharing these lessons and suggesting that they are worth teaching others, I immediately feel the same sort of embarrassment most people feel about the naked body. This embarrassment goes beyond my recognition of the limitations that I have already addressed and the realization that others will find still more within each of my proposed lessons.

First of all, there is something so mundane and ordinary about these lessons, nothing I needed a doctoral degree to discover. Someone else has already written *All I Really Need to Know I Learned in Kindergarten* (Fulghum, 1989), with much more wit than I possess. And others with much more credibility than I have suggested some version of these same lessons.

For example, ever since Dewey and other progressive educators, the idea that students learn best by doing (1938) has been popular in theory if not always in practice. Even in the 19th century, Dewey wrote words which point toward the lessons I have suggested:

> I believe that the active side precedes the passive in the development of the child nature...that the muscular development precedes the sensory; that movements come before conscious sensations; I believe that consciousness is essentially motor or impulsive...I believe that the neglect of this principle is the cause of a large part of the waste of time and strength in school work....I believe that ideas (intellectual and rational processes) also result from action... (1998, p. 233)

Dewey continued to develop his ideas throughout his life, and it is no surprise that there is still a John Dewey Society within the American Educational Research Association, a testament to their value.

More recently, Howard Gardner (1983, 1999) has suggested that the bodily kinesthetic is one form of intelligence, and a number of schools have attempted to base the curriculum on multiple intelligences as described by Gardner (Armstrong, 1994; Campbell, 1999). It is not surprising that elementary classroom teachers have enthusiastically sought ideas for active learning for their active young students, based simply upon their recognition that many of their students prefer moving to sitting still. For some time, I have felt concern that many dance education advocates have seemed to uncritically claim bodily-kinesthetic intelligence as the Holy Grail for the field without having a clear sense of what Gardner means by the term. Donald Blumenfeld-Jones (in press) goes even further in his critique of Gardner's conception of bodily-kinesthetic intelligence and its implications for education in a context of democracy, with particular concern for Gardner's emphasis on examples of "genius."

Another source of embarrassment arises because of the historical and current context of dance in education. The origins of dance at the K-12 level as well as higher education are in physical education. For many years, and still in many schools today, dance has been viewed as simply another form of physical activity, much like soccer or basketball except that it uses music instead of a ball. In more recent years, I have been one of those dance educators seeking to build a closer relationship to the other arts, which has involved distancing the discipline from physical education. This has become especially significant at a time when the primary goal of gym class has become physical fitness rather than educating the body.

At the same time that dance has been moving away from physical education and toward a closer tie with the other arts, arts education has been moving toward a more cognitive emphasis (Clark, Day & Greer, 1987; Hutchens & Pankrantz, 2000), with a corresponding de-emphasis on the body, and a focus on apprehending art rather than creating it. Certainly, there are many important lessons to learn in dance education in addition to ones I have presented here, and there is more to dance than the body.

But when I affirm that dance education is about not only the body, what I really mean is that it is about not only the physical dimension of the self. And yet, as I have been describing throughout this essay, neither is the body. As the ground for lived experience, for knowing myself, others, and the world we share, my body is involved in thinking and feeling as well as doing. I agree with Donald Blumenfeld-Jones, who writes,

Whether we desire it or not, students live bodily in school...Such lived experiences may be productive of an 'understanding' or educative outcome, but only if we can become aware of our educated bodies. Aesthetic experience, because it focuses on the senses, is particularly well-positioned to aid us in coming to this experience...an experience which joins intellect and body. (1997, p. 2)

I believe that all of the lessons we teach in dance education—about creating, performing, and responding to the art—can be taught from the perspective of the lived body. Sherry Shapiro (1999), who advocates a "Critical Pedagogy of the Body...where the body/subject as a lived medium becomes part of the curriculum" (p.142), gives one example when she describes how she creates choreography in collaboration with her students, helping them use personal memory to create movement while transforming their consciousness of who they are as women.

I would even go so far as to suggest that it is time to claim education of the lived body as appropriate terrain for not just dance education, but all of arts education. The arts begin in education of the senses: Seeing, hearing, and feeling from the inside are essential if one is to be an artist or appreciate the arts. To be an artist is to be one's own teacher. To be an artist is to create forms, grounded in lived experience, which express knowledge and meaning—forms that will touch others. That is why I believe that these lessons are ones that we must teach young people who will be the artists, arts educators, and audiences/arts supporters of the future, who will be creating the art we live *with* and the world we live *in*.

NOTE

[1]Small portions of this chapter were adapted from Stinson, 1995.

REFERENCES

Albright, A.C. (1997). *Choreographing difference: The body and identity in contemporary dance.* Hanover, NH: University Press of New England [for Wesleyan University Press].

Anttila, E. (2003). *A dream journey to the unknown: Searching for dialogue in dance education.* Unpublished doctoral dissertation, Theatre Academy, Helsinki, Finland.

Armstrong, T. (1994). *Multiple intelligences in the classroom.* Alexandria, VA: Association for Supervision and Curriculum Development.

Bakan, D. (1966). *The duality of human existence.* Boston: Beacon .

Blumenfeld-Jones, D. S. (in press). Bodily-kinesthetic intelligence and the democratic ideal. In J. Kinchloe & A. Johnson (Eds.), *Revisiting Gardner.* New York: Peter Lang.

Blumenfeld-Jones, D. S. (1997). Aesthetic experience, hermeneutics, and curriculum. *Philosophy of Education.* Retrieved September 8, 2003, from http://www.ed.uiuc.edu/EPS/PES-yearbook/97_docs/blumenfeld-jones.html.

Bordo, S. (1993). *Unbearable weight: Feminism, Western culture, and the body.* Berkeley: University of California Press.

Brady, J. (1982). *The unmaking of a dancer: An unconventional life.* New York: Harper & Row.

Buber, M. (1955). *Between man and man* (M. Friedman, Trans.). New York: Harper.

Buckroyd, J. (2000). *The student dancer: Emotional aspects of the teaching and learning of dance.* London: Dance Books.

Campbell, L. (1999). *Teaching and learning through multiple intelligences* (2nd ed.). Boston: Allyn & Bacon.

Clark, G. A., Day, M. D., & Greer, W. D. (1987). Discipline-based art education: Becoming students of art. *Journal of Aesthetic Education, 21*(2), 130–193.

Cunningham, M. (Choreographer), & Brockway, M. (Director). (1977). Event for television [Television series episode]. In *Dance in America.* Retrieved September 8, 2003, from http://www.merce.org:80/filmvideo_danceforcamera.html.

Desmond, J. C. (Ed.). (2001). *Dancing desire: Choreographing sexualities on and off the stage*. Madison: University of Wisconsin Press.

Dewey, J. (1938). *Experience and education*. New York: Macmillan.

Dewey, J. (1998). My pedagogic creed. In L. A. Hickman & T. M. Alexander (Eds.), *The essential Dewey, volume 1: Pragmatism, education, democracy* (pp. 229–235). Bloomington: Indiana University Press.

Eddy, M. H. (2000). Access to somatic theory and applications: Socio-political concerns. *Dancing in the millennium: An international conference*. Proceedings of a joint conference of Congress on Research in Dance, Dance Critics Association, National Dance Association, and Society of Dance History Scholars, 144–148.

Fischer-Horning, D., & Goeller, A.D. (2001). *Embodying liberation: The black body in American dance*. Piscataway, NJ: Transaction Publishers.

Foster, S. L. (Ed.). (1995). *Choreographing history*. Bloomington: University of Indiana Press.

Foster, S. L. (Ed.). (1996). *Corporealities: Dancing, knowledge, culture, and power*. London: Routledge.

Fraleigh, S. H. (1996). *Dance and the lived body*. Pittsburgh: University of Pittsburgh Press.

Freire, P. (1983). *Pedagogy of the oppressed* (M. B. Ramos, Trans.). New York: Continuum.

Friedler, S. E., & Glazer, S. B. (Eds.). (1997). *Dancing female: Lives and issues of women in contemporary dance*. Amsterdam: Harwood.

Fromm, E. (1941). *Escape from freedom*. New York: Rinehart.

Fulghum, R. (1989). *All I really need to know I learned in kindergarten: Uncommon thoughts on common things*. New York: Villard Books.

Gardner, H. (1983). *Frames of mind: The theory of multiple intelligences*. New York: Basic Books.

Gardner, H. (1999). *Intelligence reframed: Multiple intelligences for the 21st century*. New York: Basic Books.

Gilligan, C. (1982). *In a different voice: Psychological theory and women's development*. Cambridge, MA: Harvard University Press.

Gordon, S. (1983). *Off-balance: The real world of ballet*. New York: Pantheon.

Greene, M. (1978). *Landscapes of learning*. New York: Teachers College Press.

Greene, M. (1988). *The dialectic of freedom*. New York: Teachers College Press.

Green, J. (1993). Fostering creativity through movement and body awareness practices: A postpositivist investigation into the relationship between somatics and the creative process (Doctoral dissertation, The Ohio State University, 1993). *Dissertation Abstracts International, 54(11)*, 3910A.

Greene, M. (1995). *Releasing the imagination: Essays on education, the arts, and social change*. San Francisco: Jossey-Bass.

Green, J. (1996a). Moving through and against multiple paradigms: Postpositivist research in somatics and creativity - Part II. *Journal of Interdisciplinary Research in Physical Education, 1(2)*, 73–86.

Green, J. (1996b). Moving through and against multiple paradigms: Postpositivist research in somatics and creativity - Part I. *Journal of Interdisciplinary Research in Physical Education, 1(1)*, 43–54.

Green, J. (1996c). Choreographing a postmodern turn: *The creative process and somatics. Impulse, 4(4)*, 267–275.

Green, J. (1999). Somatic authority and the myth of the ideal body in dance education. *Dance Research Journal, 31(2)*, 80–100.

Green, J. (2001). Socially constructed bodies in American dance classrooms. *Research in Dance Education, 2(2)*, 155–173.

Green, J. (Ed.). (2002a). Somatics in dance education (special issue). *Journal of Dance Education, 2 (4)*.

Green, J. (2002b). The body as content and methodology in dance education. *Journal of Dance Education, 2(4)*, 114–118.

Green, J. (2002-2003). Foucault and the training of docile bodies in dance education. *Arts & Learning Research Journal, 19(1)*, 99-125.

Grumet, M. R. (1988). *Bitter milk: Women and teaching*. Amherst: University of Massachusetts Press.

Hanna, T. (1998). *Somatics: Reawakening the mind's control of movement, flexibility, and health*. Reading, MA: Addison Wesley.

Heshius, L. (1994). Freeing ourselves from objectivity: Managing subjectivity or turning toward a participatory mode of consciousness? *Educational Researcher, 23*, 15–22.

Hutchens, J., & Pankrantz, D. B. (2000). Change in arts education: Transforming education through the arts challenge (TETAC). *Arts Education Policy Review, 101(4)*, 5–10.

Innes, S. (1988, Winter). The teaching of ballet. *Writings on Dance, 3*, 37–47.

Jones, F. P. (1997). *Freedom to change: The development and science of the Alexander technique* (3rd ed.). London: Mouritz.

Kirkland, G., & Lawrence, G. (1986). *Dancing on my grave*. New York: Doubleday.

Koestler, A. (1978). *Janus: A summing up*. New York: Random House.

Macdonald, J. B. (1995). A transcendental developmental ideology of education. In B. J. Bradley (Ed.), *Theory as a prayerful act: The collected essays of James B. Macdonald* (pp. 69–98). NY: Peter Lang.

Noddings, N. (1984). *Caring, a feminine approach to ethics and moral education*. Berkeley: University of California Press.

Noddings, N. (1992). *The challenge to care in schools: An alternative approach to education*. NY: Teachers College Press.

Polanyi, M. (1966). *The tacit dimension*. Garden City, NY: Doubleday.

Purpel, D. E. (1989). *The moral and spiritual crisis in education: A curriculum for justice and compassion in education*. Granby, MA: Bergin & Garvey.

Ramsay, B. (1995). *The male dancer: Bodies, spectacle, sexualities*. London: Routledge.

Sandler, J. (1997). Standing in awe, sitting in judgment. In S. E. Friedler & S. B. Glazer (Eds.), *Dancing female* (pp. 197–205). Amsterdam: Harwood.

Shapiro, K. J. (1985). *Bodily reflective modes: A phenomenological method for psychology*. Durham, NC: Duke University Press.

Shapiro, S. B. (1999). *Pedagogy and the politics of the body: A critical praxis*. New York: Garland.

Sklar, D. (2000). Reprise: On dance and ethnography. *Dance Research Journal, 32*(1), 70–77.

Sheets-Johnstone, M. (1990). *The roots of thinking*. Philadelphia: Temple University Press.

Stinson, S. W. (1984). *Reflections and visions: A hermeneutic study of dangers and possibilities in dance education*. Unpublished doctoral dissertation, University of North Carolina, Greensboro.

Stinson, S. W. (1995, Winter). Body of knowledge. *Educational Theory, 45*(1), 43–54.

Stinson, S. W. (1998). Seeking a feminist pedagogy for children's dance. In S. Shapiro (Ed.), *Dance, power, and difference: Critical and feminist perspectives in dance education* (pp. 23–47). Champaign, IL: Human Kinetics.

Thomas, H. (2000). (Dance) ethnography strikes back. *Dancing in the Millennium: An International Conference*. Proceedings of a joint conference of Congress on Research in Dance, Dance Critics Association, National Dance Association, and Society of Dance History Scholars, 426–430.

Thomas, H. (Ed.) (1993). *Dance, gender, and culture*. New York: St. Martin's.

Vincent, L. M. (1979). *Competing with the sylph: Dancers and the pursuit of the ideal body form*. Kansas City: Andrews & McMeel.

Walkerdine, V. (1992). Progressive pedagogy and political struggle. In C. Luke & J. Gore (Eds.), *Feminisms and critical pedagogy* (pp. 15–24). New York: Routledge.

Woodman, M. (1982). *Addiction to perfection: The still unravished bride*. Toronto: Inner City Books.

JANICE ROSS

THE INSTRUCTABLE BODY: STUDENT BODIES
FROM CLASSROOMS TO PRISONS

INTRODUCTION

In this classroom there are no desks, no chairs, no pencil sharpeners, no papers, no books, no computers. The floor is smooth, unpolished wood. The walls are lined with mirrors, and attached to these walls, at waist height, are wooden poles that circle the perimeter of the room. In this room students position themselves as far away from each other as possible. Looking in the mirror to survey oneself is not only encouraged, but also required. Shoes are forbidden and bare feet are the rule. Occasionally, fragile, specially designed pink satin or very soft leather slippers, footwear that can be worn only in this room and never outside, is permitted. The clothing worn in this room must make visible the musculature of the body. Long, loose hair is fastened back to reveal the face and neck. Eating, drinking and gum chewing are prohibited. Sitting down is interdict, unless one is specifically told to do so. The bodies in this space are to be primed and alert, freed temporarily of appetites and bodily needs and prepped to explode into physical action.

If this sounds like the antithesis of most classrooms, it is, but only because the focus here is the student as body rather than the student as mind. The room that has just been described is a dance studio. This is a classroom where, unlike the traditional public school classroom, the transformation of student bodies is the end as well as the means. More moving than talking happens in this room. Communication is by sight, by touch and rhythmic sound. The task is to collectively transform the individual bodies of the students through drill, repetition and coaching into a different regard for the body. The body-of-knowledge becomes the body-of-means and the body-in-view.

The body has been the hidden student in America's classrooms. It has been absorbing lessons we weren't even aware were being taught. Responding in ways direct and obvious and hidden and recondite, it has shown itself as a product of academia, a product few were aware was being produced. In its own way, the body is as instructable as the mind. It can be just as resistant to certain lessons, and as readily absorbent of untaught ones. Understanding how the body learns is a critical first step in making these inadvertent lessons of America's classrooms conscious and deliberate.[1]

One classroom where the body *has* been the explicit focus of instruction is the dance studio. Centuries of training have perfected a language, a method and a kinesthetic response system for shaping and remaking the musculature, posture, expressiveness and speed-in-action of our physical selves. If this is a ballet class

169

Liora Bresler (ed.), Knowing Bodies, Moving Minds, 169-181.
©*2004 Kluwer Academic Publishers. Printed in the Netherlands*

then feet are trained into a tapering curve, spines and necks are elongated, centers of gravity are raised, or lowered, knees are taught to be pliant, heads to snap in circular paths as the body rotates while the feet take tiny traveling steps forward through space. The body is taught to become airborne here and to move with a speed and precision of placement unattainable without years of training. It is instructive to see what might be learned about the instructable body from this room of transformation of the dance studio.

It is an argument of this essay that the body is "mindful" and that mindfulness of the body is exemplified in the performing arts but also promotable in every school classroom. I will be arguing in this essay for the application of contextual somatic and philosophical analysis to the consideration of student learning, and particularly to the education of the student body in the classroom. This article explores and contrasts the nature of learning when the body is the explicit focus of instruction as well as the indirect medium of teaching targeted at "the mind." The specific nature of somatic learning has rarely been analyzed as a constitutive factor in educational or scholarly dance research.

What lessons might there be in this body-based dance classroom for the classrooms of America's schools in general? This essay explores some of the practical and theoretical bases of educating the body in dance contrasted with conceptions of the body in the academic classroom. Using one specific locale in which the body has been addressed and the mind has answered—a dance in the prisons program for incarcerated teens, issues of corporeality will be highlighted. The parallel and contrasting ways in which bodies of students are cultivated, disciplined, instructed and rendered knowledgeable in dance and in academia will be articulated. In the dance studio the bodies of students are what is seen—they display what the mind has grasped. In contrast in the classroom they are invisible, or at best translucent, signifiers of the real target, the student mind.

DISCOVERING THE BODY IN THE CLASSROOM

Learning to see the student body in our classrooms requires making a significant shift in our conception of knowledge, academic habits, traditions and vocabularies. In *The archeology of knowledge* Michel Foucault enumerates four of the leading elements around which our concepts of knowledge have traditionally been formed. The first one he names is "knowledge is that of which one can speak in a discursive practice and which is specified by that fact."[2] His three subsequent elements of knowledge focus equally on the discursive – specifically speech, statements and discourse—as the verbal artifacts of cognitive growth:

> Knowledge is also the space in which the subject may take up a position and speak to the objects with which he deals in his discourse. Knowledge is also the field of co-ordination and subordination of statements in which concepts appear and are defined, applied and transformed. Lastly, knowledge is defined by the possibilities of use and appropriation offered by discourse.[3]

In each of these definitions knowledge is linked to the literary or the oral. It is the *talking* or writing body, not the physical, body that is positioned as the medium transmitting information and relaying understanding. The tradition is that to know something is to be able to put it into words. My contention however, is that the parameters of language are not the parameters of knowing. Foucault continues: "There are bodies of knowledge that are independent of the sciences, *but there is no knowledge without a particular discursive practice* and any discursive practice may be defined by the knowledge that it forms." (Emphasis added.) Discursive practice in Foucault's conception is a way of presenting, in a public form, concepts apart from the subject perceiving them. It is "a space of exteriority," a means for making external an interior process and rendering public the private part of the network of communication of understanding.

Throughout most of the last two centuries education has tended to closet the body in this way, suggesting that knowledge acquisition and cognition are essentially non-corporeal, or at best fleetingly corporeal, tasks. When the material presence of the student has been addressed it has generally been as an accessory to a crime, like the restless body of a hyperactive student, or the listless posture of a sleeping, bored or exhausted student. Each of these bodies is seen as a physical manifestation of something more crucial, a mind that has tuned out (G. K. Hall, 1902; Cavallo, 1982). The history of the body in education has thus been paradoxical because as the body has been targeted as a means for indirectly controlling and changing the student intellectually and morally, institutionally it has been ignored except when it is seen as a pathway for an academic end.

NINETEENTH CENTURY CONCEPTIONS OF THE BODY AND EDUCATION

One of the more revealing documents concerning early conceptions the body in American education from the late nineteenth-and early twentieth-century eras is a treatise on education written by Granville Stanley Hall. An American psychologist who trained in Germany, Hall was among the earliest Americans pursuing the latest German study in psychology. He returned to the United States determined to use psychology toward a practical end.[4] For Hall and a number of his colleagues, education loomed as a particularly fertile field for this exploration, and as a result the "child-study movement" was launched in the 1880s.[5] Initially, Hall began applying experimental methods to the study of the mind at Clark University, where he established a psychological laboratory that trained students in experimental techniques and sent them out to observe children, recording their data on questionnaires.

Approaching his study with religious zeal, Hall declared that his efforts would "give education what it had long lacked—a truly scientific basis and help to give teachers a really professional status."[6] Hall's educational interests were extremely broad reaching. He saw many opportunities for social betterment through education, particularly through the right kind of bodily activity in sports and the performing arts. One of Hall's earliest formal publications to address the issue of physical activity in education was a 1902 essay he wrote on "Christianity and Physical Culture." It appeared in the September issue of *Pedagogical seminary*, which he edited, and its tone is messianic in linking social salvation to the male's toned muscles. The theme of this article is summed up in Hall's closing statement: "But there is one language and one only, of complete manhood, and that is willed action, and it is to make our lives speak in this language and thus to make them historic that we train, what psychology now sees to be the chief power in man, the will, the only organs of which are muscles."[7]

Hall's use of the metaphor of language for bodily expression echoes Foucault's equation of discourse and knowledge. It's a habit of speech that, when spoken about as the "language of movement," also implies a hierarchy with corporeal expression as a *lesser* physical way of doing what speech and words do better.

The historian Dominick Cavallo in *Muscles and morals*, his history of late 19th century playgrounds, also notes how strong educational links were made between muscular activity and moral development.[8] Skill in the right kinds of physical activities for young men was seen as a path toward moral development. Similarly historian William McNeill has researched how the regimented and repetitive rhythmic action of the marching body can function as a way to control the mind and render it open to command. "Men risked their lives on foreign soil because of muscular bonding through drill," he writes.[9]

This linking of "the will," or moral choice, with disciplined muscles also has important repercussions for the body in education. Specifically, linking a physically vital and a swift and strong body with moral rectitude helped position higher education's initial valuing of dance. "There is a sense in which all good conduct and morality may be defined as right muscle habits," Hall had proclaimed. "Rational muscle culture, therefore, for its moral effects...[is] for the young, the very best possible means of resisting evil and establishing righteousness.... We are soldiers of Christ, strengthening our muscles not against a foreign foe, but against sin within and without us."[10]

EMBODYING THE MIND

In these previous examples the body is used as a conduit to the soul and the moral mind, but it is rarely addressed as important in its own right. Similarly, in the typical classroom the focus is the invisible mind. It is the real object of instruction. The visible body is ignored, or at most ordered to be still, in order for the teacher to address the "active" mind. The mind becomes visible through the body, through speech, of course, but also through silent actions. Yet ironically the metaphors used to describe a well functioning mind are all words of the physical body – "vital," "active," "vibrant," "alive."

The goal of education is the construction of a body of knowledge and it is interesting to question what that body looks like. The body informed by knowledge, the instructed body, is obedient, disciplined, quiet and still. The body of knowledge that fills it is invisible. Education is not the only arena in which Western culture has informally used, yet formally ignored the body. It is only in the last few years, as notions of embodied knowledge have proliferated, that the arts' regard for the body is being reexamined. It is now becoming apparent that the cost of ignoring the body in the classroom has been high. So much of what students do in their out of school hours focuses on liberating their bodies through full and free physical activity, sports, play or sensory experiments.

The performance theorist Peggy Phelan has observed, "the body does not experience the world in the same way consciousness does. The gap between these two ways of processing experiences punctuates the formation of the unconscious."[11] Yet traditional education rarely admits this kind of sophisticated or nuanced view of the body's interface with consciousness. In Phelan's analysis she extends Foucault's more narrow focus on the linguistic, claiming an equally important temporal physical dimension as well. "The body is always a disciplined entity. One part is temporal linguistic the other is temporal physical," she writes.[12] This idea of the schism between physical and mental experience punctuating the formation of the unconscious reflects how internally linked and complex somatic and cognitive experiences are. Thus the instructed body shapes us on the most profound level of all – the subconscious. Yet even in the highest levels of practice, in the performing arts studio, myths persist about the discursive and somatic and the possibility of separating and dividing them.

STAGES OF LEARNING: THE BODY IN THE CLASSROOM

The performing arts, and especially dance, contain some of the best models we have for the body as the explicit focus of instruction and education. Yet a very different kind of information exchange happens in these classrooms. This is an arena where stages of learning are evidenced in physical as well as verbal behavioral changes, and teachers and students communicate deeply and efficiently by physically "performing" understanding, or, confusion. In these contexts the body of the dancer is transformed into what dance scholar Susan Foster has called "a body of ideas." Foster speaks of the dancing body as formulating a "dancing bodily consciousness." Thus one progresses in dance training when there is a momentary matching of one's knowledge and awareness of the body with a developing physical capacity.

The body in the dance studio is molded, shaped, and re-created through training that begins with the demonstrative body of the teacher and ends with the newly compliant body of the student. New perspectives on embodied knowledge are illuminated by this exploration into how dancers labor to meet the standards for the ideal body, contrasts with how students in traditional academic disciplines deal with corresponding challenges of bodily incapacity and resistance on the path toward consolidating knowledge. Progress through the educational system brings with it increasingly less time and permission for the physical participation of the body. The student body's presence in the classroom from Kindergarten to 12th grade gets quieter and quieter until it is effectively mute. In most classrooms bodily movement happens when sanctioned by the teacher. She is generally the one who stands and performs "thinking" and its expression by writing on the chalkboard, talking and moving around the room.

> This pattern of the teacher as the doer and the student as the observer gets inverted in the dance studio where the teacher sets in motion and then observes the room filled with dancing students. Often the learning can be active and the instruction more passive in the dance studio. In part this is because it is exhausting to dance full out (with actions at the scale of a full performance) and teach, correct and observe at the same time, but also because showing too much can hinder rather

than inspire. Our relationships with our bodies are complex and nowhere more so than in the dance studio.

Dance scholar Susan Foster has created a framework to describe the multiple perceptions of the bodily self that are addressed in professional dance training by describing what she sees as the two initial bodies dance training creates; one, the perceived and tangible and the other, the aesthetically ideal. [13] "The dancer's perceived body derives primarily from sensory information that is visual, aural, haptic, olfactory, and perhaps most important, kinesthetic."[14] The other body, the aesthetically ideal, exists in the discrepancy between what the dancer wants to do and what she can do. Foster explains that in the dance studio both bodies are constructed in tandem; "(E)ach influences the development of the other. Both result from the process of taking dance classes, as well as watching dance and talking about it."[15]

Finally there is a third body, "the demonstrative body," this is the body that displays itself most readily in the body of the teacher as she didactically emphasizes actions necessary to improve dancing. Daily life in dance class is about laboring to incorporate the demonstrative body into one's own image in the mirror and perhaps thus, fleetingly, to have the ideal fold momentarily into the tangible in performance.

Dancers alternate between, or sometimes fuse together, images from all these bodies as they objectify, monitor, scan, regard, attend to, and keep track of bodily motion throughout the day. The metaphors learned during instruction serve as both markers and interpreters of developing bodily consciousness. They also integrate the training of the body with aesthetic, social, and moral beliefs about dance. The repertoire of metaphors learned in class functions not only to define the dancer's body but also to establish the epistemological foundation for performing dance.[16]

The impact of language on the body can be a direct and brutal as a physical blow. Language, as Foster suggests, doesn't just describe, it constructs somatic realities. Dozens of young women dancers testified that a cutting remark from a dance teacher about not being thin enough has often tipped them into anorexia. Alternatively, dancers who have been criticized for having a short neck or too thick calves on their legs, attributes that cannot be changed, can also develop warped images of their body to conform to these insults.[17]

"The daily practical participation of a body in a discipline makes it a body of ideas," Foster notes. "Each discipline refers to the body using selected metaphors and tropes and these tropes may then be worded or enacted as physical actions that show the body how to behave."[18] These sites of the remaking of the body are where essential aspects of culture, and its desired knowledge about self and others, are demonstrated and perpetuated, refined and, finally, embodied.[19] We have long known this about the discursive aspects of schooling, it is time we understood it about the somatic as well. Using the "discipline and punishment" conceptions of bodily control articulated by Michel Foucault, these practices of bodily transformation and redefinition in both academic and artistic institutions can be examined as part of the fabric of culture itself.

DELINEATING THE INSTRUCTABLE BODY

The dance studio offers a particularly vivid medium for observing the parallels between how the body and mind of the student as well as the teacher are all constructions, stages on the path toward "assembling oneself." There is labor and diligence in this assembly, beginning with the task of the student perceiving what the correct action or position is and then disciplining and fashioning one's body into a medium capable of doing that action. "God creates. I assemble," George Balanchine said once of his profession as a choreographer. He was describing the work of communicating a movement vision to a room full of dancers and highlighting the labor in the task of orchestrating bodily movement into deliberately planned dance art. "Delineating rhythmic structures and regulating the flow of effort from one part of the body to another."[20] This actually might be seen as one definition of dance. Balanchine's statement also reveals his awareness that he is assembling not just steps in choreography but also the bodies deliberately sculpted to perform those steps.

In the public school classroom similarly, it is not only knowledge that is imparted to students, but the methods of getting and accepting that knowledge. In the process the instructable body is also delineated. Through the classroom's etiquette and procedures, rows, seating hierarchies, protocols about speaking and moving and organization of space student bodies are taught to maintain what Foster calls "the disciplinary lineaments of culture."[21] There are always several different bodies in play in sites of learning, but their presence in the academic classroom is generally recondite. Transposing Foster's multiple body model of the dancer in the studio into the classroom by rewriting it slightly, offers a rich lens for understanding the construction and the consequence of some of these bodies. In schools the mind of the student is what is customarily seen as the focus of education, but of course the physical manifestation of that mind comes through the student's body. The teacher is the demonstrative body, and the student is the tangible body.

THE BODY BEHIND BARS

Prisons, like schools, are institutions that have certain conceptions of the body and explicit and implicit disciplinary procedures to produce what each sees as the ideal body. Looking at how the body is shaped in prison gives us another way to exemplify the relationship between institutional constraints and bodily conceptions. The very act of putting someone in jail, or juvenile hall, represents a clear delimiting of physical mobility and an imposing of physical control over an individual's body. It is almost as if having lost social control over that individual's ethical mind, the state seeks to regain it through corporeal control. Similarly admitting someone into a university carries with it another set of restraints on gendered and bodily behavior. Prisons then are also institutions designed to control activity and access. Access to the social world outside the individual and also, indirectly, to the imaginative and affective world within. In education the goal is generally to broaden not constrain access to these conceptual sites. As Foucault has noted in his *Discipline and punish*, in the chapter titled "Docile Bodies," there can be competing tensions between these institutional goals and their implementation on an individual, social, private and coercive bodily level.

While jurists or philosophers were seeking a primal model for the construction or reconstruction of the social body, the soldiers and with them the technicians of discipline were elaborating procedures for the individual and collective coercion of bodies.[22]

When we create curricula for our schools rarely is a somatic curriculum drafted as well, but an implicit one is always being implemented in the classroom.[23]

Dance is generally imagined to be a humanizing rite and one of the realities of prison is that it is customarily a site of dehumanizing practices. Israeli-born jazz dance teacher Ehud Krauss works with incarcerated teens in the San Jose and San Mateo juvenile halls by using hip hop styling as a way of rewriting these incarcerated teens body coding away from gang semiotics and toward a more neutral, or at least malleable, somatic social presence. On average, minor juvenile offenders are kept for ten days to two weeks in these two Northern California Juvenile Halls where Kraus teaches several classes a week, so the population continually changes. However, for the male convicted felons, (90% of the juvenile hall population studied) two or three years in juvenile hall is more the average until they turn 18 and are moved to adult jail where they finish out sentences that can stretch for years or decades. Since 1995 Krauss has taught two 45-minute jazz dance classes a week with 12 incarcerated 13-to-17 year-old males and 48 females of the ages 13–17, in these juvenile hall facilities. Occasionally an offender as young as nine or ten is incarcerated, although this is rare. There is a sad irony here—usually the better the dancer the more classes he has taken in "juvie," but also the longer he has been in juvenile hall and thus the more serious his crime. While one generally doesn't elect to be in prison, participation in these dance classes represents a little oasis of choice. Someone can be coercively locked up but it's hard to force someone to dance. Recognizing this basic point. If one chooses not to dance one can stay in his cell.

The dance classes, primarily jazz technique with some street dance and hip-hop styling, are offered twice a week for 45 weeks a year. The ethnic make-up of the teens in these classes are generally 65% Latino, 15% African American, 10 % Pacific Islander, 5% Asian, 5% White. Many of these teens were not English proficient although the verbal instructions the students are given in class are spoken only in English.

The physical restrictions on the youths in Juvie are extreme; whenever they walk down the halls they must be accompanied by a guard and they are required to always hold their hands locked behind their backs with hands grasping elbows, if a visitor approaches they must stand still on a line painted on the floor until the visitor passes. Bathrooms are open spaces with sinks and showers exposed and partial walls screening the toilets. Running is prohibited, and walking outside the inmate's "unit" is forbidden unless accompanied by a probation officer or guard. The guards and probation officers are stationed at a central desk and closed circuit cameras are in evidence throughout the building. Clothing is jail-issued T-shirts, elastic waist shorts or pants (no belts), socks and tennis shoes.

The student body that is constructed in these prison dance classes begins by peeling back physical identities – first it works back from the comparatively docile prison façade through a layered presentation of self created for the streets to a reconceived individual identity of the "rehabilitated" inmate. In prison dance the body showcases the opposite of the spectacle of deviance that is rewarded outside – here it is the spectacle of social *obedience*, compliance and following the rules that wins points from the staff. Any educational discussion of the uses of dance in prison also have to engage with cultural discourses that posit the body as a surface onto which both the subsets and controlling mainstream society inscribe their political and social ideologies and onto which the student inmates carve their resistance.[24]

The first level of instruction in these classes begins before a single step is made. The simple presence of Krauss is a critical starting point for the success of each dance project. Krauss, a former Olympic Volleyball player, is a strong, independent, charismatic individual, and he responds to the inmates first as student dancers, a redefinition that is crucial for them.

As the teacher leading the Juvenile Hall classes Krauss, seems at once to be teaching dance, and at the same time defining himself through dance as an impressive and formidable presence by virtue of how he moves and conducts himself physically. So dance, and the specific genre of jazz with its emphasis on coolness, subtle control and smooth moves, becomes both the medium and content of the exchange between Krauss and his incarcerated students.

Krauss's jazz dance curriculum is contemporized with some hip-hop, funk and street dance moves. In addition the music he uses to accompany his classes are the current CDs the youths listen to, but with lyrics the prison approves of as "clean." The result is a structured movement experience that may at first feel more like a party than school; particularly compared to the other remedial math, English and history classes the students in Juvenile Hall must take. However, rather than trivializing dance, this similarity to personal leisure activities actually accomplishes the reverse. It offers a model of how feeling good about oneself, how taking small social risks and pushing for mastery of one's physical self, can give a sense of accomplishment with serious and important benefits and this capacity for growth, or regression, is possible in every arena in which one makes behavioral choices. The larger lesson here is that dance is one of many forums in which we operate that offers the possibility for physical learning that ripples through to the mind. For example, in dance certain aspects of one's physical identity and presence are rendered malleable in a way that parallels the conscious manipulation of self-presentation concerning so may adolescents and especially gang members. Learning how to perform using the body as art medium introduces the idea that one can exercise an equal freedom in choosing how to be off stage.

As in sports, there are demands, structures and expectations in this dance class, yet most of them are expressed and responded to on a purely physical level that invites personal expression rather than obedience to a set of regulations and overseers. Doing what you see is different than doing what you are told. For example, a typical command in a jazz class might be: "Do this fast crossing side step and end at this spot on the final beat, facing the audience triumphantly in this direction." That the genre of dance being taught was jazz was useful in the capacity for personal expression this dance class opens up. The nature of Krauss's presence as a dance instructor is built in significant measure on the qualities of improvisation, choice and discovery of a path that jazz dance invites. Krauss embodies coolness and power as a male dancer in a manner that is clearly very attractive to the youths he teaches. A physically big and powerful man, (he works out at the gym daily), Krauss demonstrates a rich paradox of physical skills and social ways of—being a dancer, being male, being caring—when he teaches dance.

When one learns dance phrases and patterns, they are almost always learned by the student closely observing the teacher's body moving before him. Unlike most other art forms, learning dance technique demands heightened perceptual acuity toward one's immediately perceived body and other's bodies as well. Physical demonstration of authority, strength, power, flexibility, grace and smoothness are attributes of a good dancer that are seductive for many of these male youths, particularly when they are demonstrated on a six-foot-tall, muscular male. This is when the "I can do that" and the "I want to look like that" drive takes over.

> Students are absorbing the content knowledge of specific dance phrases and movements within the jazz, hip-hop style, but they are also learning how fluid and consciously shaped physical identities can be. In turn there are emotional and psychological shifts in one's sense of self that continued engagement with physical actions, postures and manners can impart to the practitioner. It is the nature of dance that with a ready instrument students can build on whatever life skills they already have in their body that makes it, and them, unique.

Comments from several of the juvenile hall dance students confirmed this as a part of learning in dance class. Marie T. and Fran E., fifteen and sixteen-year-old females in the Girls Unit at Juvenile Hall, credit the dance classes with giving them confidence, helping them overcome their shyness and releasing stress. "My confidence is the biggest surprise I've felt from these dance classes," Marie T. says. "The teacher taught us how not to give up if we miss a step. I think this will help me keep my self control so I'll get off probation this time when I'm finally out." Fran E. concurs about the positive socializing influence of these dance classes. "There are people in here I don't like, but when I'm dancing with them I forget about it. If you keep in mind how things went with them dancing then the differences don't seem so important." As a first lesson in embodied truths, this idea that compassion for another human outweighs personal dislikes is an important place to begin with these teens.

Learning through the body for these teens allowed them to discover, test and then embrace fundamental somatic truths. The links between emotions and body posture and shape is one – that between recalcitrant muscles and new strength and control is another. The physical reward of wresting with both of these usually carries with it an emotional bonus, as Fran and Marie suggest.

CONCLUSIONS: THE BODY AS AN ACHIEVEMENT

In recent years there has been increased acknowledgement of "mind as an achievement," in education but seldom does one hear about the ways in which "body is an achievement" as well.[25] The inseparability of body and mind can often be proclaimed, but the deep similarity of the stages of learning in each has been explored very little. Dance and the performing arts have always addressed the mind as well as the body of the dance student. Yet they do so with the reverse of the standard classroom teachers' bias. Here it is the recalcitrant mind that gets chided while the body is regarded as infinitely malleable and swiftly responsive, if only the student would focus her attention.

Classroom rhetoric however, can sometimes suggest, falsely, that discipline and control over the body are the exclusive keys to success in the performing arts. Here the mind can be looked to as an impediment. "Don't think. Do!" is a common directive in the dance studio as if intuition and understanding by-passed the mind and went straight into the tissues and tendons. In the academic classroom the body is rarely conceptualized as more than a bundle of recalcitrant muscles and surging hormones. These implicit assumptions about body/mind hierarchies and dichotomies, affect classroom learning.[26]

What new perspectives might dance studies offer for the relationship between the perceived and tangible body the dancer grapples with daily and the perceived, tangible and demonstrative mind each learner similarly struggles to reconcile and master? The experience of knowing more than one can say is familiar to everyone, yet so too is the less often acknowledged truth that our bodies can demonstrate an understanding or confusion that anticipates and at times outstrips our capacity to verbalize. In both the dance classroom and the regular education classroom this deep understanding is exemplified by a heightened awareness of sensory knowledge and by the capacity to amplify and improvise. For the dancer these stages happen physically, yet they also have parallel stages in cognitive development the educational researcher can recognize because in each stage matters of cognition and awareness are intimately intertwined.

This kind of new heightened regard of the body in education is particularly important now because we are in a period of defining ultimate truths as residing in the body. Foucault observed that since the Greeks the highest truth was believed to reside in what was said. Truth moved from the ritualized act, "potent and just," to settle on what was enunciated instead. Now the will to truth is being linked with physicality. As the body is seen as the repository of certain immutable truths about who we are and where we come from, the body is being newly theorized as a site of special wisdom.

The educational implications of having the targeted object of change in our classrooms shift from what was once just the soul, to the body and soul, or more accurately the multiple bodies and soul of each student, are myriad. Education has long been accustomed to conceptualizing the mind as complicated. It is time that student bodies in the classroom were regarded with a similar appreciation for their rich complexity, flexible potentialities and signification of understanding.

Although knowing emerges in many forms, and is not restricted to language, it is being diminished in schools where there are growing constraints and increasingly non-physical conceptions of the student body that can limit opportunities to learn. No institution, a school or a prison, should neglect this aspect of awareness that is reachable only through focused engagement with the aesthetic and physical life of the student – a practice that dance exemplifies.

Note: Special thanks for Elliot Eisner for suggestions on an earlier draft of this essay.

NOTES

[1] I am indebted to Elliot Eisner and his pioneering concept of the "null" curriculum to designate the content or subject areas that are absent in school curricula and the intellectual process that schools neglect. Eisner, E. (1985). *The educational imagination on the design and evaluation of school programs* (2nd ed., pp. 97–98). New York: Macmillan Publishing Company.

[2] Foucault, M. (1972). *The archeology of knowledge and the discourse on language.* New York, Pantheon Books, 183.

[3] Foucault, M. (1972). *The archeology of knowledge and the discourse on language.* New York, Pantheon Books, 183.

[4] Robarts, J. R. (1968, Winter). The century of hope: The quest for a science of education in the nineteenth century. *History of Education Quarterly, VIII*(4), 431–447.

[5] Ibid., p. 440.

[6] Ibid., p. 441.

[7] Granville Stanley Hall (1902). Christianity and Physical Culture. *The Pedagogical Seminary, IX* (8), 378.

[8] Cavallo, D. (1981). *Muscles and morals: Organized playgrounds and urban reform 1880–1920.* Philadelphia: University of Pennsylvania Press.

[9] McNeill, W. H. (1995). *Keeping together in time: Dance and drill in human history.* Cambridge: Harvard University Press, 132.

[10] Ibid.

[11] Phelan, P. (1996). Dance and the history of hysteria. In S. L. Foster (Ed.), *Corporealities: Dancing knowledge, culture and power* (pp. 90–105). London: Routledg. 91.

[12] Phelan, P. (1996). Dance and the history of hysteria. In S. L. Foster (Ed.), *Corporealities: Dancing knowledge, culture and power* (pp. 90–105). London: Routledg. 94.

[13] Foster, S. L. (1997). Dancing bodies. In J. D. Durham (Ed.), *Meaning in motion: New cultural studies of dance* (pp. 235-257). Durham, NC: Duke University Press. 236.

[14] Foster, S. L. (1997). Dancing bodies. In J. D. Durham (Ed.), *Meaning in motion: New cultural studies of dance* (pp. 235-257). Durham, NC: Duke University Press. 237.

[15] Foster, S. L. (1997). Dancing bodies. In J. D. Durham (Ed.), *Meaning in motion: New cultural studies of dance* (pp. 235-257). Durham, NC: Duke University Press. 237.

[16] Foster, S. L. (1997). Dancing bodies. In J. D. Durham (Ed.), *Meaning in motion: New cultural studies of dance* (pp. 235-257). Durham, NC: Duke University Press. 241.

[17] "Dying To Be Thin," video portraits of women with anorexia.

[18] Foucault, M. (1978). *The history of sexuality: An introduction.* New York: Random House.

[19] Giroux, H. A. (Ed.). (1997). *Education and cultural studies toward a performative practice.* New York: Routledge.

[20] Foster, S. L. (1997). Dancing bodies. In J. D. Durham (Ed.), *Meaning in motion: New cultural studies of dance* (pp. 235-257). Durham, NC: Duke University Press. 239.

[21] Foster, S. L. (1997). Dancing bodies. In J. D. Durham (Ed.), *Meaning in motion: New cultural studies of dance* (pp. 235-257). Durham, NC: Duke University Press. 241.

[22] Foucault, M. (1977). *Discipline and punish: The birth of the prison.* New York: Random House. 169.

[23] Elliot Eisner had identified the terms implicit and explicit curricula to denote the unintended and intended curricula that are in effect in every classroom. Eisner, E. (1985). *The educational imagination on the design and evaluation of school programs.* New York: Macmillan Publishing Company.

[24] Foster, S. L. (1997). Dancing bodies. In J. D. Durham (Ed.), *Meaning in motion: New cultural studies of dance* (pp. 235-257). Durham, NC: Duke University Press.

[25] I am indebted to Elliot Eisner for this concept of the mind as an achievement.

[26] Dewey, J. (1934). *Art as experience.* New York: Capricorn Books.

REFERENCES

Albright, A., C. (1997). *Choreographing difference: The body and identity in contemporary dance.* Hanover, NH: Wesleyan University Press.

Banes, S. (1998). *Dancing women: Female bodies on stage.* London: Routledge.

Cavallo, D. (1981). *Muscles and morals: Organized playgrounds and urban reform 1880–1920.* Philadelphia: University of Pennsylvania Press.

Cooper Albright, A. (1997). *Choreographing difference: The body and identity in contemporary dance.* Hanover, NH: Wesleyan University Press

Desmond, J. (1998). Embodying difference: Issues in dance and cultural studies. In A. Carter (Ed.), *The Routledge dance studies reader* (pp. 154 -162). London: Routledge.

Dewey, J. (1934). *Art as experience.* New York: Capricorn Books.

Eisner, E. (1991). *The enlightened eye.* New York: Macmillan Publishing Company.

Eisner, E. W., & Peshkin, A. (Eds.). (1990). *Qualitative inquiry in education: The continuing debate.* New York: Teacher College Press.

Eisner, E. (1985). *The educational imagination on the design and evaluation of school programs.* New York: Macmillan Publishing Company.

Foucault, M. (1972). *The archeology of knowledge and the discourse on language.* New York: Pantheon Books.

Foucault, M. (1977). *Discipline and punish: The birth of the prison.* New York: Random House.

Foucault, M. (1978). *The history of sexuality: An introduction.* New York: Random House.

Foster, S. L. (1997). Dancing bodies. In J. D. Durham (Ed.), *Meaning in motion: New cultural studies of dance* (pp. 235-257). Durham, NC: Duke University Press.

Gallop, J. (1995). *Pedagogy: The question of impersonation.* Bloomington: Indiana University Press.

Giroux, H. A. (Ed.). (1997). *Education and cultural studies toward a performative practice.* New York: Rutledge.

Hall, G. S. (1902). Christianity and physical culture. *The Pedagogical Seminary, IX*(8), 374–379.

McNeill, W. H. (1995). *Keeping together in time: Dance and drill in human history.* Cambridge: Harvard University Press.

NOVA. *Dying to be thin.* Video portraits of women with anorexia.

Phelan, P. (2001). *Art and feminism.* London: Phaidon Press Limited.

Robarts, J. R. (1968, Winter). The century of hope: The quest for a science of education in the nineteenth century. *History of Education Quarterly, VIII*(4), 431–447.

Turner, B. S. (1984). *The body & society: Explorations in social theory.* Oxford: Basil Blackwell.

KIMBERLY POWELL

THE APPRENTICESHIP OF EMBODIED KNOWLEDGE IN A *TAIKO* DRUMMING ENSEMBLE

We believe that taiko for us is not just the drum; but it's the connection between the drum and the player. So at a certain point if we concentrate too much on technicality and we lose that feeling or that spirit behind the playing, then it becomes just the drum. They become separated. The player is just using the drum rather than creating the relationship with it.

(Wisa, San Jose Taiko performer)

All educational experiences involve the body; but these experiences vary according to our learning environments. The above statement, made by a performer engaged in the Japanese-based art of *taiko*, a form of ensemble drumming and choreographed movement, depicts a particular quality of experience that entwines agency, cultural tools, and perceptual activity. The performer's use of words such as connection, feeling, and relationship – as well as her ability to reflect on aspects of learning that are most critical to the success of the ensemble – are indicative of a learning environment that integrates the feeling body with mindful feeling.

If the work of this book is to develop a paradigm of embodied knowledge for educational theory and practice, then the work of this chapter is to contribute to conceptions of embodied knowledge by exploring an educational setting that challenges commonly held notions of the role of the body in learning. By describing the teaching and learning processes involved in the apprenticeship of *taiko* drummers, I interpret the ways in which knowledge is embodied through participation in socially and culturally prescribed systems of meaning, and how such participation serves to organize sensory experience into knowledge of art, self, and self in relation to learning. Because of the explicit focus on the processes of learning, I treat the concept of embodiment in this chapter as it pertains to the phenomenological tradition of "being-in-the-world" and to scholarly traditions concerned with the interaction of sensory engagement, cognition, and environment (e.g., Basso, 1996; Csordas, 1994; Dryfus, 1982; other Feld, 1990; Feld & Basso, 1996; Lakoff & Johnson, 1999; Merleau-Ponty, 1962; Plath, 1998; Sudnow, 1978), rather than to semiotic or post-structuralist traditions of representation. At the end of this chapter, I consider the educational implications of *taiko* for a more general theory of curriculum and pedagogy.

Liora Bresler (ed.), Knowing Bodies, Moving Minds, 183-195.
©2004 Kluwer Academic Publishers. Printed in the Netherlands

San Jose Taiko

Taiko refers to the contemporary art of Japanese drumming (sometimes referred to as *kumi-daiko*, or harmony drum) as well as to the actual drums used in the art form. *Taiko* is a growing artistic and political movement in North America, with currently over one hundred fifty *taiko* ensembles. San Jose Taiko, founded in 1973, stands as one of the oldest and perhaps most influential *taiko* groups of North America. The co-founders of San Jose Taiko, Roy and PJ Hirabayashi (Roy is Managing Director, PJ is Creative Director), have developed their approach to *taiko* into a forum for social action, community development, cultural preservation, and Asian American identity, characteristics that mark many North American taiko ensembles (Hayase, 1985; Hirabayashi, 1988; Uyechi, 1995). Over the years, the organizations' primary goals have been to develop a professional performance ensemble as well as community-based classes that focus on the artistic learning and practice of drumming. Today, San Jose Taiko is a fully established non-profit organization with offices and studio space located in San Jose, California, conducting public workshops, schools visits, and other public outreach initiatives.

The professional adult performance ensemble is arguably the most significant aspect of San Jose Taiko. In the year 2000, the ensemble consisted of 14 performers, with a larger Japanese Americans, a smaller number of other Asian Americans (Chinese and Filipino, most notably), and a few non-Asian, white Americans. Over the recent years, San Jose Taiko has established a two-year apprenticeship[1] they call the Audition Process (often referred to as AP) influenced by their work with the professional Japanese *taiko* group, Kodo. The Audition program is a sequenced, two-year program in which new potential members are evaluated at regular phases during the first year, and, for those who are accepted, integrated into the professional ensemble the second year.[2]

During the apprenticeship, we engaged in multiple activities, notably cardio-strength training (e.g., calisthenics and running), caring and maintaining instruments, volunteering at San Jose Taiko's performances, and engaging in the cultural expectations of the *dojo* (place of learning) such as bowing at the door of the studio, removing one's shoes, and bowing to each other, and cleaning the rehearsal space.[3] We also participated in seminars to discuss such issues as the role of *taiko* in the Japanese American community. Most notably, however, San Jose Taiko has developed a framework for teaching, learning and ongoing evaluation of apprentices and performers based on four principles: attitude, which involves respect for one's self, other players, and the instruments themselves, and a discipline of both mind and body; *kata* (form), structured movements based on martial arts stances, traditional Japanese drumming and other choreographed movements; musical technique, and *ki* (energy), an Eastern concept of spiritual unity of mind and body, an essential principle of martial arts and a basic element of *kata* (San Jose Taiko, 2001). Through these four principles – attitude, *kata*, musical technique and *ki* – San Jose Taiko hopes to attain what they call the "ultimate expression of *taiko*, when the art becomes a part of our personality, a way of being and life expression" (2001, p. 2). As a means for organizing this chapter and presenting key concepts for general educational practice, I focus on three of these principles – *kata*, musical technique and *ki*, each of which are explicit parts of the apprenticeship training. In the following sections, I describe the teaching and learning practices involved in *kata*, musical technique, and *ki*.

Poles, Rectangles, and Lines

Unlike many western drumming practices, the visual impact of *taiko* is as important as its aural impact. *Kata* is a visual form of movement that is inseparable from the playing of *taiko*, dating back to an aesthetic convention originating in a form of Japanese court music that accompanied certain dances. San Jose Taiko uses a coordinated set of movements that include a strong, low stance, a stance found in many martial arts, which helps to center the body and optimize the arm and other movements that go along with drumming. *Kata*, San Jose Taiko states, is a means through which members can achieve "oneness" with the *taiko*. In this way, *kata* links the body with the drum, creating the whole instrument, defined as the relationship of the body to the drum. San Jose Taiko uses a coordinated set of movements that include a strong, low stance, helping to center the body and optimize the arms and other movements that go along with drumming. A typical stance used by San Jose Taiko is associated with a style of drumming called *sukeroku* style, named for its Japanese region of origin. In this style, most of the drums are positioned diagonally on stands instead of perpendicular to the floor. The body is positioned in relation to that slanted angle: the legs are set wide apart (generally with the left foot in front), knees slightly bent, toes angled away from each other, and the tailbone dropped slightly, so that one's *hara* is more stable. The arms begin their position diagonally, so that the left arm typically crosses the body to form a diagonal line with the right arm, which is extended diagonally upward. Each song has a choreographed set of moves that are learned along with the rhythms, producing a uniform flow of movements that help create a visual style marking not only a unique song but also a particular ensemble's style.

On the very first day of the apprenticeship, we experienced particular ways of thinking about the body in relation to learning *kata*. After an hour of synchronized stretches, calisthenics and cardiovascular exercise led by PJ and Yumi, an experienced long-time member of the performance ensemble, we are ready to begin our work with *kata*. "With *taiko*," PJ begins, "your body is an expression of who you are. Pay attention from this day forward. Be cognizant of your actions. Challenge yourself to open up; be expansive." Demonstrating her next phrase by holding her body upright, she continued: "Hold your chest up as if you have a mirror. Hold that mirror open. Be aware of the positive, of how you hold your head, focus your eyes, breathe, how you walk." As she talks, she places her hands on her upper chest, raising it and opening her ribcage. Others in the class check their posture and imitate her stance. She continues with her description, coaching us with her words as we follow her actions:

> Be aware of how you see yourself using imagery. Imagine there's a pole going into your head and through the floor, this infinite pole going upwards and downwards. Now, there is another pole: your center of energy, your ki [in Japanese], your qi [in Chinese], just below your naval, and this pole passes through your body in front of you and behind you. You have this axis to register how you hold your body: your hara. Measure yourself. Monitor yourself. Evaluate.

As she talks, she demonstrates these poles by sliding her hands out in front of her, as if she were feeling an imaginary pole. Sometimes, she makes fists and places them in front and behind her body as if to suggest a little pole. "The *hara* has infinite expanding lines. Be aware of the infinite dimensions of your body. Become aware of under your armpit, behind your knee.... If we do this, maybe we can learn how to relax." While engaged in this exercise, I felt a sensory shift in the way I perceive the boundaries of my body in relation to space. I am aware of a different sense of my body, the way that it occupies positive space against negative space. Much in the way that artists talk about positive and negative space in paintings, this pole imagery challenges my perception of body and space and expands my sense of sense of self and balance.

Several times throughout our apprenticeship training, descriptions evoking awareness of space beyond the physical body were used. Beginners and long-standing members are continually taught to be aware of their body in space and time, and to pay attention to sensations (such as pain) that can teach a learner about the limits and possibilities of movement. "Show me exactly what it feels like not standing on top of the floor. Feel the energy flow through the soles of your feet. Open the crown of the head…. Think of the body as an open, empty vessel. Let it all concentrate right here, the *hara*." At this point, PJ adds the next element, one that she calls her "gazut" element, a word that evokes the feeling of dropping the pelvis. "Inhale and drop," she tells them. "This is your relaxed state." I watch as everyone visibly drops their torsos and tailbones closer down to the floor, so that our thighs are almost parallel to the floor, and our feet are still spread wider than the width of our shoulders. With this "gazut" in place, PJ introduces another image: the rectangle. For the many rehearsals to follow this class, the rectangle will remain a central image and concept that PJ and others use to teach *taiko*.

> This is your rectangle, from your shoulders to your hips. (With pointed index fingers, PJ draws a rectangle in front of and close to her body, marked by the parameters of her own shoulders and hips.) Take that rectangle, and move it to your left. (She frames the imaginary rectangle in front of her with her hands and twisting from the torso "pushes" this image to her left.) Take all that energy and push it to the other side of the room. Feel the resistance in the palms of your hands. (She demonstrates resistance by moving her hands, arms, and torso slowly to the right, keeping them in the same plane.) This is all about becoming aware of dimensions of space. Your center's not just here," (pointing to her lower abdomen), it's here (drawing a circle around her waist with her hands)… This is awakening parts of our body that we will have to build to make our bodies strong.

The imagery that PJ and others provided served as a metaphor for physical approximation of movement. Eventually, as these movements became a habitual part of our experience of *taiko*, we became more fluid with *kata*, internalizing the meaning of each movement and performing them with less conscious effort, as well as learning to embody these movements with our own personal styles. Developing a sense of space around the body, so that one gains a sense of the body traveling *through* space, was a focal point in the apprenticeship that required a significant perceptual shift in our thinking past the physical boundaries of the body. This was a process of learning how to inhabit the space around us with our bodies, building the foundations for becoming aware of spatial dimensions and shifting the perception of self from bounded entity to a self positioned within multiple spatial and temporal zones.

The next step in learning to play *taiko* is taken only after apprentices have been immersed in slow, repetitive movements, guided by personal and group feedback about the body in relation to planes and space. This step involves learning to use the body in relation to the instruments: learning to hold the *bachi* (drumsticks), the placement of the body in relation to the drum, and how to incorporate *kata* with strikes to the drum. Learning to coordinate the *bachi*, the body, and the drum is a central preoccupation of San Jose Taiko both of the San Jose Taiko performing group and in their apprenticeship program. Each week during the three hour AP class, significant time – sometimes up to an hour – was spent repeatedly working on holding the *bachi*, moving the body, and striking the drum. In this way, we learned to assign meaning to specific movements involved in the overall visual aesthetic of *taiko* through the processes of repetition, imitation of our teachers' movements, and slowing down movements so that we could feel exactly where our bodies needed to be at any given point in a movement.

During our AP class, the teaching staff, consisting of professional ensemble members, introduced the *bachi* in a significant way. "In Buddhism, the *bachi* is considered the sacred link between the spirit world and the earth, connecting the body to the sky," PJ explained in our first class. The wood body of the drum, the animal hide comprising the drumhead, and the large metal tacks that fix the hide to the drum are all "elements that comprise the spirit of *taiko*. It has its own spirit, and we bring out that spirit, with our attitude and technique. It's not just an instrument. You, *too,* are the instrument. We, *together* (gesturing in a circular motion between the drum and herself), are *taiko*."

An example from our first encounter illustrates the types of teaching and learning strategies that are used in service of creating this type of holistic and relational experience with the *taiko*. When first teaching us to hold and use the *bachi*, San Jose Taiko engages us in what they call "air *bachi*" (referring to the popular notion of "air guitar"), so that we rehearsed the motions without striking an actual drum. "For San Jose Taiko style, the wind-up with the *bachi* is like seeing sound," PJ explains. Visual imagery is then used by PJ to emphasize this seeing of sound. We work on shaking the "sticky rice" – another image provided by PJ, off the end of our *bachi* with wrist snaps, practicing this movement for a few minutes. Added to this is a new image to help us envision lines: "Imagine, if you've seen Chinese Ribbon Dance, I want to see those ribbons go up in the air and unfurl." We air *bachi* one hand at a time. I imagined colorful long ribbons trailing from my *bachi*, as I snap my wrist upward and then extend my arm diagonally across my body down to an imaginary drum. When it came time to coordinate the *bachi* and *kata* with the drum, PJ reminded us to use the imagery of the *hara* to "focus into the center of the drum," in which drum and body centers are aligned on the same plane. As she watched us practice, she also reminded us of imagery that helped extend the lines of the body and the feel of the movement, such as the Chinese ribbons. "See the ribbon go up from the tip of the *bachi* and as you release and snap you'll get that furl."

In her sentiment about the role of the *bachi*, PJ has begun to shift our thinking about ourselves in relation to the cultural tools of *taiko*. She also expands the definition of *taiko* from its literal translation, which means drum, to a conceptualization of *taiko* as an artistic practice that embodies a particular relationship between self and art. The techniques of metaphor, imagery and repetition help us to develop a perception of blurred boundaries between instrument, person, and space, shifting the view of the self as bounded entity to an expanded and relational view of the self, in which person, instrument are bound as a single entity within a spiritual and aesthetic framework of meaning.

"Time to Dongo!"

Learning to coordinate the *bachi*, *kata*, and drum was a central preoccupation of the apprenticeship. While *kata* is an essential element in learning to drum, significant class time was also spent on mastering technical aspects of rhythm without concern for *kata*: mastering which hand plays which beat, understanding rhythmic concepts such as triplet meter versus duple meter, and acquiring competency and efficiency with drum hits at varying rates of speed and dynamics (volume). If *kata* training focuses on the use of the body as an aesthetic form of taiko, wherein the movements often carry artistic as well as cultural significance, then drill training focuses on the use of the body for technical purposes. While there are many aspects of the musical technique required of *taiko*, the pedagogical strategies are similar. I focus on the practice of drilling in order to highlight these strategies as well as the qualities of embodied knowledge required that mark *taiko*.

Time is nearly always set aside for drilling. Sometimes these drills lasted for an hour, with very few breaks. Roy, the managing director, had such a reputation for extended drilling that experienced members referred to these moments as "Roy Drills," accompanied by a slight wince or warning to those of us less knowledgeable about the practice. For a period of time, during which apprentices and experienced members practiced alongside each other, Thursday night practice was dubbed "tech night," an agreed upon format in which the group would challenge themselves by practicing techniques both known and unknown to them.

An example of one such drill practice illustrates the teaching and learning activities common to most of these "tech" rehearsals. On a rehearsal night dubbed "Time to Dongo," Franco, a member of San Jose Taiko and primarily responsible for "tech nights," introduced the entire week's practice as "Dongo week." Dongo refers to a rhythm common across all *taiko* groups, a swing rhythm in which the rhythm follows the speech meter of "long, short-long, short-long:" Dón, goDón, goDón. During this practice, Franco sits in front of the group, demonstrating on the floor by beating the floor with his *bachi*. The ensemble, working alongside the apprentices, gather in a semicircle with a variety of drums: *josukete* (medium-sized drums made from wine barrels), *shimes* (small frame drums with rope-tied hides), *sumos* (small barrel drums), and *okedo* (in this case, a medium barrel drum in which the hide is held in place by rope). Members either play these different types of drums together during such drills or alternate so that only those on one type of drum would play at a time.

The group starts with a drill of eight beats (or counts), first with the right hand, then the left, developing an alternating hand ("sticking") pattern. This sticking is then truncated so that each hand plays four beats, then two beats, and then eighth note rhythm (a rhythm played twice as fast as the previous counts). They practice at a very fast pace, according to the electronic metronome settings that Franco has set: first at 115 beats per minute, a moderate march-like tempo; then after five minutes, he sets it at 130 beats, a very fast marching tempo in which one foot barely has time to hit the ground before the other foot lifts off. As they practice, some players stop and shake out their wrists from fatigue, others stumble over the beats, and others close their eyes, focusing intently on controlling the *bachi* during the faster rhythms.

In this drill, Franco is building technical accuracy for the aesthetic form of the Dongo rhythm. In the next part of this rehearsal, they practice triplets (a type of rhythm in which a beat is broken down into three equal parts), with Franco beating the pattern, 1-2-3 on the floor, alternating hands, in which each beat is played with equal stress. This is a very different rhythm from those that they have been practicing, and is a rhythm that has consistently given both apprentices and performers difficulty. To evoke the feeling he is looking for, Franco and others offer advice that emphasizes and heightens awareness of the kinesthesia involved in this rhythm:

Franco: For this part of the drill, to keep it from being kind of boring, really feel the flow of your strokes. So it's not such a forced – (*he plays with hits that look stiff and forced*) but more of a – (*he plays with a bit more flow, lift, and grace*), kind of feel the pulse of it more internally that way. Try to get up to speed a little more. It's really important when we go really fast, because it has a tendency to go straight (*He demonstrates by playing the beats as if each has equal value*).

PJ: I have another thing that's kind of helpful. You can use almost any kind of conventional syllables. I use *Po-ke-to*, [the Japanese word for] pocket, and give each syllable equal weight: *po-ke-to, po-ke-to, po-ke-to*.

Franco: eventually, it gets to a tempo where you can't say the words and you have to relax.

A critical aspect of the way in which In San Jose Taiko teaches drilling concerns the importance of connecting these isolated exercises to a larger context. Franco and others would scaffold these drills, layering rhythmic exercises to build towards an understanding of how the parts undergird a whole pattern. For example, after practicing triplet rhythms, Franco asks them to take out the unaccented beat, and has them play the same pattern with out the second beat, essentially just the accented beats from the previous drill. This rhythm is the essence of Dongo.

Drilling exercises were used to learn and perfect rhythm patterns so that attention could then be focused on ensemble issues such as coordinating rhythms that comprised a song, *kata*, dynamics, and musical interpretation. For example, the next step in the rehearsal depicted above, and in many others I observed, was to integrate the practiced rhythms into a larger context such as a song. The above drills were incorporated into the practice of two songs, "*Fuurin Kazan*" and "*Oedo.Bayashi*." The pedagogical emphasis on embedding the smallest technical details of musical learning within a larger frame serves to reconnect the learner with the purpose of drilling: scaffolding for further artistic development and experience.

Beginning players as well as long-time members of San Jose Taiko spoke of the qualities involved in muscle memory. Joey, a first year apprentice, explained that, for her, understanding drumming meant understanding the mechanics involved, in order to move from what she called "forced movement" into something more natural:

> [For example], which way your hand is rotated. How your fingers are wrapped around the *bachi*, how tight, how loose. *When* you're touching the *bachi* after you strike. So being conscious of almost every movement—kind of like in golf. Every part of swinging a club you have to make sure you do something the correct way. And the samething [is true] with the *bachi*. When you strike the drum you have to make sure that everything is... you know, like your palm is facing the correct way.

Joey's response underscores the development of kinesthetic awareness, a consciousness of specific qualities of movement, the sensing of weight and of the ways in which muscles, tendons, and joints coordinate to achieve a particular motion. Others, including myself, became aware of a "felt" knowledge, a rightness in our movements that would be manifested through accuracy of strikes, the pitch of the drum, dynamics of sound, and other forms of auditory, visual, and kinesthetic feedback. Stewart, a member of San Jose Taiko for about four years at the time of this study, reflected on his own beginning experiences of learning *taiko* and the critical role of repetition:

> I mean even the "simple rolls" was something that was completely foreign to me…. And so a lot of it is practicing. Practicing in front of a mirror, practicing with the guidance of people who give you feedback. And just doing it over and over and over again until you say, "okay, get in your stance." And you can just get in your stance and your arm will be in the right position, your shoulder will be down, and you're dropping your *hara*, and you're standing up straight, and you're not raising your shoulders, and your weight is distributed properly, and your sticks are holding their correct lines…. It's something that you have to learn, that you have to train your muscles, and get the different [appropriate set of factors] involved so that you … don't have to think about it.

Both PJ and Roy are conscious of the concept of muscle memory as a critical factor in the ensemble's success and stress this in their training of apprentices. In fact, in the course reader that they distribute to their apprentices during the first year of the Audition Process is an article called "Why practice makes perfect" (cited in Jaret, 1987), which summarizes neurophysiological research into the concept of ballistic movement. According to the theory, actions are akin to firing a gun in which the bullet will only go where it is aimed. Such movements only last long enough for the muscles to move in the right direction, and are therefore not guided by sensory feedback. These concepts have thus worked their way into the pedagogical practices with the ensemble. Roy explains that this article encapsulates their belief in the method of repetition, slowing down movements, and chunking patterns of movement for the purpose of muscle memory, "so that you don't have to think 'doro suku' (a common pattern played as a base rhythm) when you play," Roy says. "For me, taking it slow and building on it works best. Start basic. Don't be afraid to slow things down.

Perhaps surprisingly, drilling and other types of repetitive practices often yielded a highly aesthetic quality of experience. Several of the more experienced members described this quality as a connection with something larger than themselves, becoming a vessel or conduit for the music, the feeling of being out-of-body, or of spiritual unity with instruments, sounds, and others; such descriptions of artistic performance have been depicted elsewhere (e.g., Berliner, 1994; Blum, 1986; Csikzentmihalyi, 1991; Steinhardt, 1998). Mary, a former, long-time member, discussed the way in which muscle memory led to the pleasurable experience of "playing with abandon." Ironically, it appears that repetitive, well-practiced movement, which involves conscious attention to body mechanics on a micro level, is a necessary precondition for achieving the more desirable out-of-body, aesthetic experience of forgetting such mechanics altogether: "For if practice is a special kind of memorizing based on repetition and refinement, performance becomes a special kind of forgetting," writes Peter Jaret (1987, p. 91) in his article on ballistic memory. "That's the moment when the musician leaps from mere technician to artist….". Thus, the more one drills and repeats, the more those movements are encoded into the body, freeing the performer to consider other technical or aesthetic matters.

Embodiment of musical technique, then, shifts between qualities of visceral attention– in which the muscles ache, the hands trip over themselves, and the mind responds to ballistic and somatic activity – to qualities of aesthetic experience in which the body forgets and the mind releases. Repetition, chunking discrete elements into larger patterns, and slowing down movements to attend to detail are critical steps in the in the same way that the teaching and learning experiences of *kata* develop an expanded sense of self, the embodied experience of musical technique can ultimately create a feeling of self without physical borders.

"A So-Re!"

If *kata* and musical technique concern the ways in which movement connects the body to the drum, then *ki* (pronounced "kee," known more commonly in American society as chi, the Chinese spelling of the same principle) concerns the way in which energy is used to connect the player with *taiko* and with other players. Defined by the ensemble as "the spiritual unity of the mind and body" San Jose Taiko feels that *ki* is the "ultimate challenge that each member of SJT must meet." (San Jose Taiko, 2001). *Ki* is an essential principle of martial arts; and, for San Jose Taiko, it is an essential part of *taiko* playing. Along with *kata*, musical technique, and attitude, *ki* comprises the fourth principle upon which San Jose Taiko bases its philosophy, and members are evaluated formally on this dimension as well as the others. Through *ki*, oneness with the *taiko*, with other members, and even with the audience can be achieved through sound and energy – what SJT calls a "physical communication." In many ways, *ki* is the key to successful ensemble playing.

While *ki* might express the spirit of *taiko*, it is the most elusive to teach and learn because of its basis in the Eastern concept of spiritual energy and unity. But two aspects of *ki* are explicitly taught, learned, and evaluated for successful membership in San Jose Taiko. *Kata*, discussed above, is one way, a visual form of creating and maintaining *ki*. A second form is known as *kiai* (pronounced kee-eye), or shouted syllables, an aural form of creating and maintaining *ki*. In some cases, *kiai* are actually part of a song. For example, the syllable *tsu*, which is sometimes used to mark non-hits to the drum, can be composed into a song itself, so that the *tsu* becomes part of the sound pattern. For example, in a dance called *"Ei ja Naika!*," members would dance to a drum beat and yell in unison *"a so-re!"* at certain points in the song. At other times, *kiais* were invoked individually, often in relation to helping others maintain their energy and stamina, or to help a fellow soloist find her way back to the downbeat and structure of a song.

The ways in which *kiai* is taught and learned are similar to the ways in which *kata* and drumming are taught: repetition, mimicry, and imagery. Because *kiai* involves producing sound, the focus of teaching and learning is on quality of sound as it is produced and felt in the body. One exercise, developed by PJ and another long-time performing and staff member, Yumi, involved "passing" sound back and forth between people. Sounds that were explicitly taught in this manner included "Yoh" and it's response, "Hoh." We were instructed to "try to see if you can really feel each other come out and come together." The desired sound is one that is unencumbered, produced with support from the diaphragm and an open, relaxed throat. Metaphoric language was used extensively throughout our training in *kiai* to describe the internal functions required of the bodily production of sound

> Remember the inner tube *(PJ circles her waist as a gesture)*. Let's push with your hands and send it along this way. Now, [act as if] your life depended on pushing that wall to me.... You can feel your *hara* really push. Really feel that resistance pushing from here *(points to her hara)*. Keep [the sound] in your body. You're not removed from anything. I'm going to really be pushing the concept of hara a lot more. It's a really difficult concept to grasp. You know it because you can feel it in your body.

In my observations and participation, finding the right moments in which to *kiai* was a critical aspect of understanding the elusive nature of *ki*. While as apprentices we were explicitly taught how to *kiai*, we were never explicitly taught *when* to *kiai*. During each practice, we were encouraged to *kiai* while hitting the drums, accenting the silent moments with syllables like "*Hip!*" or "*sup!*" or "*Yoh!*" Some members developed signature *kiais*, like Stewart, who would often call out during our apprenticeship rehearsals, "*Yah-Sah!*" Upon hearing this for the first time, Marian, a first year apprentice, asked him what it meant. "I don't know," replied Stewart, smiling. Tyler, another player with the ensemble, discussed how he would kiai if he heard a soloist drifting from the established beat; in that case, the *kiai* was used as a vocal signal to other players. Often, when we rehearsed with more experienced players, we would take our lead from them as to when and where to *kiai* during a particular song. In this way, we learned that *kiai* served an aesthetic and unifying purpose: accenting drum sounds, orchestrating rhythms and patterns, and adding to the overall texture of the song, ultimately serving to create a soundscape punctuated by shouted syllables.

One of the significant qualities of learning *taiko* is the way in which learners have to coordinate instruments, other people, and the spaces in and around the drums, a quality that underlies the concept of *ki*. Learning to play *taiko* in many ways requires an individual to think beyond the immediate physical self, to integrate these various environmental features into one's playing. To play *taiko* requires an expanded, or relational, sense of self, a self that is always conscious of instruments, people and spaces. Significantly, the embodiment of *ki* involves a knowledge of the overall texture of a piece and how one's voice or drumming will contribute to the *gestalt*, the overarching aesthetic of the song. Recall, for example, PJ's statement: "It's not just an instrument. You, *too*, are the instrument." *Ki* calls for a blending of elements, a spiritual unity between player and drum, and between players themselves, bringing to the forefront a conception of artistic practice that differs radically from many of the Western artistic practices that have embedded themselves into the texture of arts education. *Ki* is an element of practice that causes the player to think and act with intention, to understand not only the "what" and "how" of playing but also to imbue his or her learning with purpose and connectivity. To embody *ki* is to embody an understanding of the holistic relationship that exists among discrete elements and sites of activity and how the self figures into that relationship. *Ki* is, in many ways, the ultimate expression of a player's agency.

The Ki, Kata, and Technique of Educational Theory and Practice

Concepts such as *ki*, *kata*, and technique have been discussed as key philosophical principles of San Jose Taiko, and I have used them as an organizational framework for the chapter in order to discuss the teaching and learning activities involved in *taiko* drumming. These various qualities of embodiment are orchestrated by local and broader sociocultural meanings, beliefs and values that are embedded in the purposes of learning *taiko*. If this chapter focused on a cultural analysis of *taiko*, my conclusion would dwell on theoretical issues of cultural representation and identity as mediated through the embodiment of cultural practice; indeed, these issues have been addressed elsewhere (Powell, 2003; see also Fromartz, 1998; Nakasone, 2002). Instead, I offer an analysis of these cultural and social practices as general concepts for educational practice. When treated as educational concepts, *ki*, *kata*, and technique offer ways in which to think about a paradigm of embodied knowledge for effective school practices. What is the *ki*, *kata* and technique of schooling? What qualities of embodiment are orchestrated by local and broader sociocultural meanings, beliefs, and values of American schools? And, finally, how might a study of *taiko* as a teaching and learning environment inform our vision of pedagogical and curricular practices that encourage the types of learning experiences we desire for our students?

One of the most significant issues raised by the embodied experience of taiko concerns the self in relation to learning, a quality that involves connection between person, instrument, and other players by developing a relational identity with learning. The philosophical underpinnings of San Jose Taiko's curriculum involves *ki*, the spirit or energy behind *taiko* that fosters a sense of unity with the mind and body, with drum and person, and between people. Learning to play *taiko* successfully requires an individual to think beyond the immediate self, to configure an identity through practice in which the self is relational and expanded, always conscious of the relationship between the self, instruments, people, and spaces. To navigate and calibrate the spaces between drums and people, wherein one develops a sense of the body traveling through space in relation to people and objects, is a crucial form of embodied knowledge and a central preoccupation of teaching and learning in San Jose Taiko. *Ki* as a philosophical principle helps to orchestrate this experience of the body with *intention,* a sense of agency in which the drummer is aware of how his or her embodied knowledge fits into a larger framework of meaning.

Kata and musical technique offer ways in which *ki* is orchestrated and supported. *Kata* is instrumental in creating a relationship between the body and the drum. "If we just focus on technicality," states Wisa, the performing member cited in the opening quote of this chapter, "the player is just using the drum rather than creating a relationship with it." Her statement offers an indirect critique of the estranged learning (McDermott & Lave, 2002) that schools often orchestrate for students. As such, *kata* functions as a connective tissue between cultural tools and the self by providing a series of intentional movements that orchestrate and bring out certain qualities of experience. Additionally, kata is an aesthetic form, in which every movement has a graceful quality and purpose. There is always a connection between where one has been and where one is going.

When examining the *kata* of schooling, a very different vision of the body's role in learning presents itself. The embodied experience of traditional schooling is often, as educational philosopher John Dewey might suggest, an anaesthetic experience, devoid of any heightened sensory experience or perception. In school, our bodies are still, serving primarily a utilitarian function. We learn from an early age not to squirm or leave our desk chairs in classrooms. We learn to sit up straight, raise our hands to be called upon, or walk single file to lunch. By the time we reach high school our bodies are often reserved for gym class, the Pledge of Allegiance, or for moving from one class to another. In a sense, we educate from the neck up, leaving the rest of the body to act largely as a physical support rather than as actively involved in our quest for knowledge, thinking, and understanding. Perhaps more sobering to consider are the body searches and metal detectors to which youth are subjected in this era, adding further credibility to Michel Foucault's cultural, historical analysis of the disciplined body (1979). Implicated in this analysis is the importance of agency in relation to activity. Providing curricular opportunities that are experience-based, that encourage the use of the body and engage the senses in learning could create a different kind of *kata* for schooling if learners are encouraged to explore connections between learning, self, and the broader social and cultural frameworks of meaning in which they are situated.

Musical technique serves as the backbone upon which embodied knowledge of *taiko* is built: without a mastery of musical techniques such as rhythm, melody and other aesthetic qualities of sound, of memory successfully encoded in muscle, achieving a level of artistry would be impossible. While *taiko* training certainly involves a disciplined regimen of physical training and repetitive drilling practices, the body is not silent, stilled or dulled into submission; it is not militaristic in aesthetic or purpose. Crucial to understanding the embodied experience of discipline is a larger sense of purpose. In the case of San Jose Taiko, technical mastery is situated within clearly stated artistic goals and critical pedagogy related to the cultural project of San Jose Taiko.

What is the technique of history, math, or science, and in what ways are the skills and practices we teach in schools embedded in the larger purposes of learning such skills? If we want flexible thinkers, people who can make connections across different ideas, issues and concerns and act accordingly, then we need to question how our current learning environments are structured, and how we might design learning environments that educate for the whole person, providing for a continuity and scaffolding of experience. The curriculum of San Jose Taiko provides a variety of cultural tools and forms for multiple modes of perceptual activity that are orchestrated into a cohesive structure. The cardio-physical training needed for playing *taiko*, musical drilling, repetitive bodily gestures and sounds, imitation, and imagery are connected to reflective practice through readings, ongoing discussions about the purposes of technique as it relates to the overall artistic vision and quality of *taiko*. Moreover, a grounding in the cultural-historical significance of *taiko* and its place in Asian American culture helps to orient the purpose of the most minute, embodied sensations involved in learning toward these broader purposes of *taiko*. If it were not for this grounding, these physical experiences could result in a quality of dissociation and alienation from these larger purposes of learning.

My study of the embodied knowledge required of and fostered through *taiko* practice also suggests the primacy of technical mastery and its connection to heightened qualitative experiences that are aesthetic in nature. Paradoxically, when knowledge of *taiko* is embodied to the point of competency, these experiences give rise to a quality of experience that can feel de-centered, or out-of-body. While an out-of-body experience may not be a necessary or even appropriate end-state to learning, mastery of the technique of mathematics, history, science, or any subject matter suggests that learning skills and concepts to the point where they are reflexive is a necessary condition for higher levels of qualitative, aesthetic, generative activity.

There are, to be certain, existing models of education that are organized around aesthetic principles. Just as social action is the basis upon which San Jose Taiko organizes their learning environment, educators such as John Dewey and Maria Montessori took similar issues of community, democratic participation, and freedom as the origins upon which they built pedagogies emphasizing the primacy of aesthetic experience. Dewey (1989/1938) argued that cultural modes of activity integrate and mediate the social, educational, and practical into an aesthetic form, and that the materials of any subject matter provide a medium for aesthetic experience when we interact with them. Montessori (1973) believed in providing very young children with what she called "sensorial foundations," activities meant to enhance higher cognitive functions with activities that stimulated the different senses. This foundation is tempered by her belief in providing "prepared environments," the provision of materials thought to stimulate and enhance sensory experiences and therefore stimulate cognition. Such environments were also thought to be central to preparing children for a sense of community.

I began this chapter with a quote that emphasized the importance of relationship, spirit, and feeling between the learner and the learning. It is, perhaps, a suitable ending to question where we might find these qualities of embodied experience in schools, and how we might design learning environments that bring about mindful feeling.

NOTES

[1]San Jose Taiko generally refers to the second year of the Audition Process, as opposed to the first year, as the "apprenticeship" phase. By using the term "apprentice" throughout this chapter, I intentionally situate this type of educational practice within the academic field of apprenticeship studies, particularly in the tradition of Singleton's edited volume on Japanese apprenticeships (1998) and the work of Lave & Wenger (1991).

[2]My own apprenticeship occurred during Phase I of the Audition Process, the first four months of year 1, as per agreement with San Jose Taiko; I wished to step out of my participation in order to observe the complex nature of individual and group learning processes, and San Jose Taiko wished to focus their resources on those who were planning to seriously continue with the group contingent on their acceptance.

[3]Cleaning and maintenance have been noted elsewhere as important aspects of many Japanese apprenticeships, often considered signs of respect. See, for example, John Singleton's edited volume of situated learning in Japanese apprenticeships, *Learning in Likely Places* (1998).

REFERENCES

Basso, K. (1996). *Wisdom sits in places.* Albequerque: University of New Mexico.

Berliner, P. (1994). *Thinking in jazz.* Chicago, IL: University of Chicago Press.

Blum, A. (1986). *The art of quartet playing.* Ithaca, NY: Cornell University Press.

Csikszentmihalyi, M. (1991). *Flow: The psychology of optimal experience.* New York: Harper Perennial.

Dewey, J. (1989/1934). *Art as experience.* Carbondale, IL: Southern Illinois University Press.

Dreyfus, H. (Ed.) (1982). *Husserl: Intentionality and cognitive science.* Cambridge, MA: The MIT Press.

Feld, S. (1990/1982). *Sound and sentiment.* Philadelphia: University of Pennsylvania Press.

Foucault, M. (1979). *Discipline and punish: The birth of the prison.* New York: Random House.

Fromartz, S. (1998, March). Anything but quiet. *Natural History,* 44-49.

Greene, M. (1995). Art and imagination. In *Releasing the Imagination* (pp. 122-133). San Francisco: Jossey-Bass Publishers.

Hayase, S. (1985). Taiko. East Wind, Winter/Spring, 46-47.

Lakoff G., & Johnson, M. (1999). *Philosophy in the flesh: The embodied mind and its challenge to western thought.* New York: Basic Books.

Lave, J., & McDermott, R. (2002). Estranged learning. *Outlines, 1,* 19-48.

Merleau-Ponty, M. (1962). <u>Phenomenology of perception</u> (C. Smith Trans.). London: Routledge and Kagen Paul.

Montessori, M. (1973). *The Montessori method.* New York: Schocken Books.

Nakasone, R. (2002). *Peripheral cultures, peripheral peoples.* Unpublished manuscript.

Plath, D. (1998). Calluses: When culture gets under your skin. In J. Singleton (Ed.), *Learning in likely places: Varieties of apprenticeship in Japan* (pp. 341-351). Cambridge: Cambridge University Press.

Powell, K. (2003). *Learning together: Practice, pleasure and identity in a Taiko drumming world.* Unpublished doctoral dissertation, Stanford University, California.

San Jose Taiko (2001). San Jose *Taiko* philosophy. In *San Jose Taiko class notes and articles.* San Jose, CA: San Jose Taiko.

Singleton, J. (Ed.) (1998). *Learning in likely places: Varieties of apprenticeship in Japan.* Cambridge: Cambridge University Press.

Steinhardt, A. (1998). *Indivisible by four.* New York: Farrar, Straus, and Giroux.

Sudnow, D. (1978). *Ways of the hand: The organization of improvised conduct.* Cambridge, MA: Harper Colophon Books.

Uyechi, L. (1995). University taiko: Roots and evolution. Manuscript presented at Symposium on North American Taiko, Stanford University Invitational.

JUDITH DAVIDSON

EMBODIED KNOWLEDGE:
POSSIBILITIES AND CONSTRAINTS IN ARTS
EDUCATION AND CURRICULUM

Embodied knowledge, the focus of this book, represents a sea change in perspectives on body and mind and their relationship to instruction and curriculum. As this volume demonstrates, philosophers and researchers have begun to sketch out these implications from theoretical and empirical perspectives. However, there is little available yet in the form of thick descriptions of school life that explore the relationship between theories of embodied knowledge and the enacted curricula.[1]

My purpose here is to examine the ways by which instruction supports or restricts the possibilities of embodied knowledge as a vital aspect of curriculum. Using the model of embodied knowledge developed by Scheper-Hughes and Lock (1987), which I have dubbed "the three bodies theory," as a lens for examining embodied knowledge in classroom practice, I will investigate the implications of embodied knowledge for curriculum, instruction, and the organization of schooling. I will apply this lens to qualitative research data collected from the multi-year "Arts in Education" research study that examined the work of six elementary arts specialists working in three art areas—visual arts, dance-drama, and music[2] (Bresler, 1995, 1998, 1999; Bresler, Wasser, & Hertzog, 1997; Bresler, Wasser, Hertzog & Lemons, 1996; Davidson, 1995a; Davidson, 1995b; Hertzog, 1995; Lemons, 1995; and Wasser & Bresler, 1996).

Arts education provides a unique lens through which to view embodied knowledge and school curriculum and instruction. The arts, by their very nature, value embodied knowledge to a greater degree than many of the traditional disciplines found in schools. However, by virtue of the fact that the arts are placed within the disembodied framework of knowledge that dominates schools, the capacity of the arts to support an embodied framework of knowledge must be compromised to some extent. School art programs, thus, offer special opportunities for viewing the possibilities and constraints that emerge around notions of embodied knowledge within educational institutions.

Liora Bresler (ed.), Knowing Bodies, Moving Minds, 197-212.
©2004 Kluwer Academic Publishers. Printed in the Netherlands

SETTING DEFINITIONS: EMBODIED KNOWLEDGE AND THE 'THREE BODIES'

Embodied Knowledge...or Body-Mind

In Dewey's 1925 work, he makes reference to the "Body-Mind" (Dewey, 1988, p. 191). In so doing, Dewey sought a means of identifying the deeply connected paths of knowing, where body and mind intersect and become entangled. In his discussion of the "body-mind," Dewey describes learning as emerging through experience, that is, action within the world in which we live, action related to solving problems and meeting ends, and through that action, building new structures of knowledge and understanding. Dewey asserts that the body-mind is not simply the acknowledgement of the sensory input that goes to the brain, but it is based upon the interaction of subject within a complex and challenging environment.

Recent studies provide affirmation of Dewey's belief that it is the body and its interaction with the environment that serves as the basis of knowing (See for instance, Damascio, 1999). For instance, Lakoff and Johnson demonstrate the ways metaphors, which they view as the basis for conceptual thinking, are grounded in bodily experiences of time and space: "An embodied concept is a neural structure that is actually part of, or makes use of, the sensorimotor system of our brains. Much of conceptual inference is, therefore, sensorimotor reference" (Lakoff & Johnson, 1999, p. 20).

Far from being creatures whose intellectual minds and physical bodies are distinct from their surrounding worlds—both natural and human-engineered—the embodied nature of knowing indicates instead the permeability of the boundaries that we imagine between self and other—animal or thing (Merleau-Ponty, 1967). As a result of the intersubjective nature of our relationship to the environment, we are more natural, in the sense that we are submerged and intimate in nature, than we have acknowledged (Abrams, 1996). We are also more technical than we might have imagined, in the sense we incorporate technologies into our bodies as we extend our senses through the use of these tools (Haraway, 1991; Idhe, 1990).

For the purposes of this work, I will use the term embodied knowledge to highlight knowledge or knowing as Dewey tried to signify with his term the "body-mind," that is, a recognition of the embeddedness of thought in experience as it emerges in our interactions with the natural and technical world. It is this view of embodied knowledge that undergirds my exploration of the notion of the three bodies described below.

The Three Bodies

Through an examination of the *individual*, the *social*, and the *body politic-*, Scheper-Hughes and Lock (1987) introduce a powerful way to frame notions of embodied knowledge from cultural and structural perspectives. Their intention, however, was to critique issues germane to medical anthropology, whereas I seek to apply the framework to educational concerns, and, thus some translation of their nomenclature is in order.

The individual and physical body

At the first and perhaps most self-evident level is the individual body, understood in the phenomenological sense of the lived experience of the body-self (Scheper-Hughes & Lock, 1987, p. 7).

Consideration of the phenomenological perspective of the body-self, raises many issues, including: the ways we actually experience the body (Merleau-Ponty, 1962/1967); the ways the body serves as a means of constructing knowledge (Dewey, 1934/1980; Piaget 1977; Vygotsky, 1978); How our knowledge of is embodied (Shilling, 1999); and, the means by which knowledge is "held" in the body as a somatic artifact (Dewey, 1988; Idhe, 1990) *Young* children come to school in their bodies—bodies that jump, skip, fall, and kick. Through these physical experiences, scaffold by instruction that builds conceptual knowledge through language, their intellectual understanding unfolds. Those physical roots of one's learning are incorporated in the body through complex memories. As children move through classroom life, the self that acts does so from within a body, saturated with experiences of family, community, and school. Children's views of themselves as learners and actors in the classroom world are wholly dependent and embedded within this embodied self.

The social body

At the second level of analysis is the social body, referring to the representational uses of the body as a natural symbol with which to think about nature, society, and culture...(Scheper-Hughes & Lock, 1987, p. 7)

The ways the body mediates the world, serving, as a lens for interpretation is a critical feature of the *social body*. Two important, linked questions with powerful implications for schooling that emerge from the notion of the social body are: 1) How do we use the body as a tool for shaping roles? And, 2) How do roles shape others' knowledge of ourselves (Crossley, 1995; Finders, 1997; Goffman, 1959)?

Through the use of posture, gesture, clothing, stance, etc., the body is shaped into symbolic meanings body addressed to the outside world. These meanings are both individual and corporate. In schools corporate or structural meanings are embedded in the roles of student, teacher, or principal.

The resources that are used in the course of shaping the body for such symbolic purposes are cultural in nature, and, thus, shared across members of a community. In this sense, the individual and the community work reflexively upon one another. For instance, in America most people recognize the picture of the little red schoolhouse or a school bell as symbols of schooling. While these symbols are broadly shared among Americans, it is not unusual to see teachers appropriate these signs as ways of symbolizing their work as educators, wearing these symbols as jewelry or clothing (Davidson, 2000).

The political body

> At the third level of analysis is the body politic, referring to the regulation, surveillance, and control of bodies (individual and collective) in reproduction and sexuality, in work and in leisure, in sickness and other forms of deviance and human difference. (Sheper-Hughes & Lock, 1987, pp. 7–8)

In other words, how are our bodies disciplined by society, in order to shape our knowledge, behavior, and compliance (Cuban, 1993; Foucault, 1975/1979; Giddens, 1984; Grumet, 1988; Haraway; 1991)?

In schools, children's bodies must mind—they must sit in seats, walk in lines, not chew gum, and abstain from throwing erasers. They must raise their hands when they speak, should not interrupt, and will be in big trouble if they engage in physical roughhouse or fighting. Teachers have to mind the bodies to mind these rules, and principals are responsible for minding teachers to mind the bodies. Classroom, school, lunchroom, and playground are designed to make it possible for bodies to be under constant surveillance by those in charge of minding them.

The notion of the three bodies raises three important questions by which to examine the arts curriculum:

- How is the body a vehicle by which young people experience the art form?
- How do young people learn to use art to symbolize themselves and others or their world through their bodies?
- How are young bodies disciplined, and to what ends, through the practice of school art?

Using the Arts in Education project as my basis for discussion, in the following sections, I explore the ways that these three bodies figured within the music, visual art, and dance-drama education and the implications that the presence of these bodies has for thinking about embodied knowledge in school settings.

THE ARTS IN EDUCATION PROJECT

In this section, I use data from the multi-year Arts in Education Project directed by Liora Bresler to examine the ways that the three bodies are present in schools. In so doing, it is my aim to look at the three bodies as both separate and distinct and intertwined and reflexively connected.

The Arts in Education Project was a qualitative research study of three different disciplinary areas of arts in elementary schools—vocal music, visual arts, and dance-drama—focusing on the role of the arts specialists and the values, methods, and materials by which they composed instruction and curriculum. The eight participants of the study were located two mid-Western communities, seven in public school settings and one in a private Christian school. Over a three-year period (1992–1995), a team of qualitative researchers collected data in the classrooms of the eight, as well as conducting interviews with the participants, and documenting a variety of performances and exhibitions related to the work of the arts specialists. Analysis of the materials was ongoing and consisted of multiple levels of study—coding of fieldwork notes by individual researchers, interpretive meetings of the research team, sharing and discussion of extensive memos, the testing of propositions and feedback from participants, and the preparation of papers for journals and conference presentations (Bresler, 1995; Bresler, Wasser, & Hertzog, 1997; Bresler, Wasser, Hertzog & Lemons, 1996; Davidson, 1995a; Davidson, 1995b; Hertzog, 1995; Lemons, 1995; Wasser & Bresler, 1996).

I joined the project in 1993 with the opportunity to craft a unique position on the research team. Rather than conduct fieldwork (for which there were already ample bodies in the field), I concentrated on interpreting the interpretive meetings, which served as my fieldwork experience (1993–1995). I documented the meetings, analyzed our interpretations, and "played back" these findings to the group in the form of memos and papers. Since that time, I have had the privilege to continue to think with Bresler about the fieldwork materials and the issues they raise in regard to curriculum, instruction, and the organization of schooling (Bresler, Wasser, Hertzog, & Lemons, 1996; Wasser & Bresler, 1996). For the purposes of this paper, I will be writing about only the 1993–1995 data, when I was active on the project.

In presenting examples from the Arts in Education project, the voices of the research team echo in my head—those who collected the data and who shared their insights about that experience in the many meetings they attended. I thank them for their assistance and for the echoes that linger within me of that time.

ARTS EDUCATION AS SEEN THROUGH THE LENS OF THE THREE BODIES

To situate ourselves for this discussion, it is critical to understand the context within which the arts specialists in the elementary school worked and where "school art" took place. Most art courses observed as part of this project were about 30 minutes in duration. The art specialist taught in a separate room (sometimes shared with other specialists) or came into the regular classroom. During these periods the daily classroom teacher absented him or herself, as the art period is often their designated planning period.

The overall sense of a school art class was of an event that is occurs in a borrowed space, on borrowed time, with borrowed participants. Over the period of a week, a public school art teacher might encounter hundreds of these borrowed bodies as she or he moves from class to class and/or school to school. Arts specialists could often be identified in school hallways by the ubiquitous carts that they pushed (suitcases on wheels in some cases) piled high or stuffed with materials for the day's work with various grade levels.

Interestingly, despite this sense of marginal life, it was also the purview of the arts specialist to conduct activities that engaged the entire school through exhibitions or performances, such as the semi-annual music concerts, an art exhibition, or through a dance performance to accompany a special celebration or observance.

The Individual Body: How is the body a vehicle by which young people experience the art form

The learning of an art form is always a balancing act between technique and expression. Technique being the knowledge of skills, materials, history, and usage in the context of practice, and expression the context of evaluation, meaning, and significance in which technique is displayed. Expression is a highly narrative act, embedded in stories and cases that comprise meaning. Technique and expression are interwoven through activity that unfolds in time and space. Moreover, in art, the body is at once an instance of time (rhythm, the thread of execution) and space itself (where the expression occurs).

Music, visual arts and dance/drama present strikingly different ways by which knowledge is embodied through the experience of the art form. In all three, however, the use of the body in particular times and spaces—and the movement of the body through various spaces at different speeds and rhythms are basic organizing principles.

Music

In the vocal music classes studied, for instance, students stood or sat still for the most part, their physical range of motion focused on the use of the vocal chords, and their physical attention focused on pitch and rhythm. Occasionally other physical experiences occurred such as the use of rhythm instruments or the addition of movements to accompany song. Practice was limited, as it is in all school art classes because of the short length of classes.

The music classrooms studied as part of the Arts in Education project varied widely in teacher's perspective on technique, content, and expression. In one classroom, a young, white teacher well trained in formal music emphasized knowledge of musical vocabulary, instruments, history, and technique. In a contrasting classroom, a middle-aged African-American instructor with deep knowledge of gospel music, wove non-European rhythms and expressions into coursework that was almost like a sermon in its attention to values, growth, and responsibility. In this classroom, children were urged as a group to go beyond the restrictions of a melody and to use their bodies and voices in emotional manner. In both rooms, while the body participated within a similar narrow range of activity, there were sharp differences in how children responded physically in the two spaces.

Interestingly, the bodies of the teachers also seemed to experience the classroom differently. The young white teacher moved around the children as they sat, hovering to the sides, ready to respond to them. The African-American teacher led from her piano, by standing in front of the keys and drawing the eyes of the children toward her. She used no written music and played the piano dramatically, to build or emphasize a point, initiate or drive an activity. The piano seemed to be a part of her, and so practiced was she that she seldom needed to glance at the keys.

Visual Arts

While music activities occurred ensemble, in visual art classes, however, activities were conducted individually, or in parallel with others. The standard outline of an art class began with a group introduction, followed by individual practice, and concluded with an evaluation session and clean-up. Moving from introduction to practice to conclusion marked the major form of movement available to students in these classes. The activity of the art work itself was often restricted, the short time available making it difficult to use extensive materials or complicated techniques. Students might draw an object, color-in shapes, and cut-out objects or paste one surface to another. Sometimes they created three-dimensional pieces or used materials other than paper, such as fabric, wood, or clay. The use of tools with sharp or potentially dangerous risks was highly restricted (scissors, paper cutters, glue guns, razors, hammers, etc.) as teachers were limited in their ability to oversee such activities. In the visual arts as with music, the relationship between technique and expression varied widely among teachers.

In the visual art class, the experience of the body was circumspect, limited in many ways to "small motor" activities. Children learned to use pen, pencil, paper, and crayons in the depiction of real or imaginary scenes, to explore the relationships between negative and positive space, the variety of shapes, and the notion of shadows or the mixing of colors.

Dance/Drama

Dance/Drama, a mixture of two art fields, presented yet another contrasting case. In the classes observed, there was much attention to pantomime and drama games that built upon the reproduction of daily activities and the study of the body as a shape and tool for movement.

The following example is an improvisational drama scene.

The first person is a mother. MM (the teacher) whispers something to her and she goes up on the stage and pushes a shopping cart. The scene continues, MM calls on the "actors" and one goes up and acts like a stock boy shelving cans, another is a cashier, another is an old person walking hunched over and slowly through the pretend aisles. After MM stops the scene, she asks two or three people to tell what they saw in the scene. These things are named: shopping, shelving, and paying for the groceries.

The body was also decontextualized in dance/drama class and held up to students as a shape and a tool by such activities as the teacher's request to "find your own personal space" as class is starting. More formal activities of this sort included:

-mirror game; trying to anticipate and make the same movements as another, as if you were looking in a mirror
-freeze game: when the teacher calls freeze, everyone makes like a statue
-exploring movement for shaking, jerking, sustained, smooth, staccato
-making a machine: where several children are connected and moving as if they were a machine
-creating body shapes at different levels: high, medium, low

Dance/drama, unlike music and visual art, made use of large motor skills—jumping, skipping, sliding, etc. Interestingly, however, like the other art areas, the range of movement in dance/drama was noticeably constrained by the limitations of time and space. Classroom space was never designed for the activity and gyms and stages were seldom available for the week-to-week class work. In some cases, the dance/drama class took place in the children's regular classroom, and at those times children's activities took place around the crowded desks.

Formal training in dance steps and techniques, such as one would encounter in a ballet class with bar and floor work routines or in classes for jazz or modern dance, were not part of the dance/drama class. In this sense, it was more like a movement appreciation class, which parallels the ways that music and visual art classes address the basics of instruction.

In summary, children's experience of the individual body as it can be known through the three different art forms presented in school—music, visual art, and dance/drama—allowed them a manner of appreciation for the art form and the physical possibilities whether it be singing, drawing and crafting, and moving in abstract space. In all three cases, however, the range and depth of the experience was severely restricted by the space and the times in which it was offered.

The Social Body: How do young people learn to use art to symbolize themselves and others or their world through their bodies?

The question of the social body is directly related to the actual content of arts education classes, that is, the curriculum and the values and cultural understandings that are conveyed within it. The information and symbols embedded in this content are drawn from a range of disciplinary and cultural sources. The body is both subject and object in the exploration of ideas, forms, and actions within the arts.

In arts education, as in all areas of formal schooling, instruction of the curriculum is enacted within the reflexive relationship of teacher and student, that is, to learn as a student, one must perform the student role, and to teach students particular content, one must perform the teacher role. The ritual performance of schooling, therefore, is a critical element of the social body (McLaren, 1986).

Music

The content of music classes was comprised in large part of songs. Interestingly, despite the seemingly wide gulf in generation, race, and culture of the two music teachers described here, the range of song types used was remarkably similar. These songs included standard songs of holiday and ritual celebration, nursery rhymes, patriotic songs, folk songs, songs written just for children (such as those written for the music textbook), songs designed to teach or use hand motions, and songs from musicals.

Through these songs an image of children and a particular culture of children now prevalent in our society emerged. This image of children depicts them as closer to animals, fantasy, and whimsy than adults. It avoids high drama and death, generally presenting the world as a happy and genial place. In a special assembly, in which music classes would be performing nursery rhymes for children and parents, one music specialist dressed up in the part of a nursery rhyme character, further blending the line between reality and fantasy. For children, the possibilities of doing and being as they were presented in music classes, were sifted through the lens of content and values provided by the song curricula.

Visual Arts

In visual art classes, the majority of observations made over the course of the project were of lessons that examine technical aspects of art, as opposed to narratives such as are part of songs. From my review of the data, I found that, to my surprise, students were seldom given the option to draw or depict themselves or others doing something, nor were they requested to use the visual as a form of narrative, that is, the telling of a story.

There was an interesting exception to this rule in one art class. In this situation, children participated in an art contest sponsored by Pizza Hut that required drawings of a particular character. The art teacher selected a handicapped boy in a wheel chair as the focus character and brought in a wheel chair that students could try out to see what it would feel and look like to be seated in a wheel chair. Then they used the wheelchair to help model the character. This is a section of field notes from that day:

K: (the teacher): ... now the bottom, your bottom is what sits you in the chair. . . Tim, work off your sketch.
Tim: I don't want it like that.
K: Why Tim?
Tim: Because it doesn't look like a kid.
K: This is good Tim, why don't you think it looks like a kid?
Tim: Because he has skinny legs.
K: Well, you know what, kids in wheelchairs have skinny legs because they don't get to use their legs."

In this case, the visual art class brings young people closer to various possibilities for the individual experience of the body, some of which may differ considerably from their own. It is important to note, though, that the subject of the artwork was chosen by the teacher, not the students.

Dance/Drama

Dance/drama classes offered young people a range of opportunities for exploring the social body through pantomime and dramatic sketches. A review of the content or parameters of these events revealed, however, that most focused on mundane daily life tasks, such as shopping in the grocery store, being in the library, or being a home.

Emotions were explored in a decontextualized fashion in special exercises, such as the one dubbed "Conducted Complaining," a favorite of young students. Students selected an issue to complain about, developed three ideas for the complaint, and then created a dramatic skit around the complaining. The complaints children selected included a disliked TV show, dirty kitchen sink, doing dishes, a little sister, Kellogg's corn pops, bad friends, the computer, the problem of parents who always work and don't have enough time to play, and getting money back from a cousin. While there was much powerful emotional content, it was explored in a highly stylized and abbreviated manner.

In reviewing this incident, I thought back to my childhood, when my siblings and I would produce elaborate plays (a rendition of the ballet "The Firebird" is one I remember in particular). Our topics were chosen from plays or films we had seen, mixing in some information about drama, music, and dance gleaned from after-school classes and lessons. Our productions required fairly involved staging, costuming, and rehearsing, often engaging us over hours in the attic. We were not geniuses, nor do I think our play that unique when compared to other children. What is striking to me about these memories is how little our school art experiences contributed to the activity (and we all attended school art classes in visual art and music), and how important it was that we had extended, uninterrupted blocks of time within which to explore our ideas. This personal finding contrasts vividly with the opportunities school art offers for examining technique and expression.

The political body: How are young bodies disciplined through the practice of school art?

Concerns about control were constant within the arts classes, and these concerns emerged on multiple levels. First and most prevalent was the concern with control of individual members of the class, but equally important was the concern of control "for the class," that is between arts specialist and mainstream teacher. Finally, there were indications of the control concerns that exist for arts specialists in regard to performance and evaluation, that is, the controls exerted over them by principals and district and professional oversight organizations.

Again, it is important to consider the unique circumstances of the arts classroom, that is, borrowed students (they belong to the classroom teacher), being taught on borrowed time (time that would ordinarily belong to the mainstream curricula) in borrowed space (space that is often shared, or space that is vacated by the classroom teacher). This three-pronged example of borrowing points up the three areas of school life that figure enormously in the composition of possibilities, and that is, social structure (your rank as a faculty member and in relationship to students); time and space (Davidson, 2002). These three are highly connected and the meanings created in one domain interdependent with meanings created in the other domains.

Music

In the music classroom, teachers placed students in specific seating patterns and defined when they would sit or stand. In music class, there was very little opportunity for students to talk with each other, and touching another student was rigorously prohibited. Almost every minute of the class, students were expected to be focused and participating in teacher directed activities. In music classes, more than the other two arts areas, genders were separated and references to gender figured in statements of control.

Contents of music classes were another arena in which political control was exercised in ways that had implications for the body. Patriotic songs were frequent fare. One school stage an elaborate Veteran's Day celebration in which music was central. All of the schools presented special programming for Martin Luther King Day, a national holiday. Through the singing of the songs, dances, and the rituals accompanying the presentation, new forms of political knowledge were formed and embodied by young people.

Visual Arts

In the visual arts, while improvisation was lauded by the phrase often used by teachers' "Be creative," instructions proscribed the possibility. Materials had to be used in exacting ways and precise parameters were defined for each activity.

Interestingly, it was in visual arts classes alone, that students had the most opportunities for talk among peers on topics of their own choosing. This would occur during class as students worked individually at group tables. During these times they would trade remarks about school or home, giggle, make jokes, and taunt each other.

Perhaps as a result of this situation, one art teacher used a yearlong point system to corral student behavior. She made it a practice of beginning every class with a number on the board, and over the course of the 30 minutes she would judge if student behavior warranted the losing of points. Depending upon how many points were left at the end of the year, the class would receive one of several prizes. This teacher also used seating charts and designated table captains in each of the classes she taught.

It was a visual arts teacher that provided the most vivid example of the ways that arts specialists are positioned vis-à-vis control in regard to the hierarchy of the school, district, and discipline. She described how she taught the names of various arts concepts so that students would be able to produce this knowledge on the statewide achievement tests. She was concerned that low grades on arts content would be subsequently used against her in performance reviews.

Dance/Drama

Of all the arts areas, dance/drama classes were the one arena in which large motor skills were used, and, yet, dance/drama classes, like the other art areas, placed strong emphasis on control. Parameters for movement were always carefully set before the activity began, and the duration of engagement always curtailed by the short periods. Indeed, in rereading the observations the use of movement often feels like a tap being turned on and then quickly off again. In dance/drama class, which often began with the admonition "find your own space," students were allowed physical interaction with each other. This, however, was carefully defined through such activity games as "making a machine."

Arts specialists, because they are using what I have termed "borrowed students," are under strong pressure not to lose control of the group. Perhaps this occurs because losing control could be construed as misuse or disregard of the property of others. Lacking a classroom of their own in the sense that the classroom teacher has a classroom, arts specialists have no "back regions" to which they can retreat when in the school (Goffman, 1959). This may create a state of tension peculiar to that position, and one that is marked by the issues and concerns of control that they face.

In reviewing this discussion of control and the arts education program, I do not mean to imply that teachers were fanatics or that students do not gain much by the controlled use of their bodies in the study of the arts. Many of the controlled activities brought them great pleasure—from singing in a choir to "conducted complaining." Viewed as a whole, however, a strong focus on control emerged within each arts area and, indeed, appears to be emblematic of arts education as it present in the data collected by the project. This notion of control is distinctive from that of the notion of control in support of technique.

DISCUSSION

Across popular and academic discourse, the arts are described as bastions of freedom, places in which we can express our true nature, find solace and contentment, and a place where self-expression is valued. The exploration of emotion, as a component of human activity and narratives, is considered a hallmark of artistic content. The development of this power of expression through the arts is considered to be directly connected to the development of technique—a process that is often highly controlling and repetitive, as anyone who has practiced scales on a musical instrument or done plies at the bar can attest. Through visits to theater, ballet, and musical concerts and interactions with practitioners of different art forms, one becomes familiar with these art forms, conversant with the classics of each form, and knowledgeable of the experimentation going on in various fields.

Our study of arts in elementary schools reveals that school art seeks to locate itself someplace between these the poles of expressive freedom and taut technical mastery. Unable to provide immersion in "real" art experiences, it opts for exposure to information about the arts and short experiences with art materials. The result is a pot pourri of art experiences that could be called "appreciation."

For instance, in regard to the notion of expressive freedom, in school art classes students do have the ability to make some choice within the activities, but there is virtually no time for extended exploration of an idea. Narrative, the glue of human emotional expression, is seldom given free rein. Indeed, by design, the curriculum severely restricts the access to emotionally powerful material and/or the expression of strong emotions.

Our study demonstrates that technical knowledge of arts components, such as knowledge of terms and a correct use of tools was prized in school art classes. True knowledge of the technical skills of an art form, however, could not be acquired from the limited exposure and time allotted. Thus, technique is diluted to technical knowledge, a form akin to "appreciation". By emphasizing technical knowledge or information, as opposed to technique, which is by nature attached to the expression of emotion, school art decouples the act from the content.

The need to de-couple action from content or its expression is consistent with the dichotomous view of mind and body that pervades traditional schooling and is at the basis of the textual or anti-body orientation of schooling that has come down to us from the Enlightenment. It was this dichotomous view of mind and body that Dewey sought to confront with his introduction of the "body-mind." Ironically, whereas art classes may have been introduced, in part, to provide students with the opportunity for more embodied ways of knowing, the actual experience of art in schools is highly restraining of the body and avoids delving into the reservoirs of body-mind experience and knowledge.

School art classes also raise interesting questions in regard to the difficult issues of culture, race, ethnicity, and class that we face in our society. It is the arts programs to which recognition of other races and cultures are often relegated in schools, through programs that present the music or art of another group to students. In this way, the arts program, although an ancillary curriculum to the school's core curricular activities (reading, writing, and mathematics), becomes a necessary adjunct for the presentation of mandated multicultural material. We saw this in our study where the arts programs held major responsibility for activities on Martin Luther King Day celebrations.

Students in arts classes, however, had little opportunity to explore the embodied properties of otherness, such as are raised by issues of race, ethnicity, class or other difference. There were some important exceptions, however, to this rule. At one of the elementary schools, children experienced the uniquely African-American pedagogical style of their music teacher. This same teacher led an African-American gospel choir within the school that drew both white and black students as participants, a highly popular extra-curricular activity. The art teacher who had children draw a disabled child seated in a wheel chair was another example. By and large, however, the content of arts classes were scrubbed clean of experiences that would deepen knowledge of otherness.

An ever-present theme in the observations made of arts classes was that of control, that is, ensuring that the bodies of young people were not out of control, but rather that they were carefully controlled within narrow parameters of condoned physical activity. The strong emphasis on control may be attributable in part to the short time frame of arts education classes, to issues regarding the marginal status of arts specialists (as compared to the regular classroom teacher), or concerns with the "emotional" or "suggestive" content of arts education that educators fear could lend itself to control problems.

In arts education, the possibilities of content, role, and symbol existed within the constraints of instructional patterns that required arts teachers to teach borrowed students on borrowed time in borrowed spaces. These circumstances shaped the ways knowledge was embodied and the forms by which embodied knowledge was expressed in the arts curriculum.

LARGER IMPLICATIONS

The plight of arts education and the arts specialist has much in common with that of other educational reformers, that is, how to move new content, structure, or perspectives into the enduring forms of traditional education as typified by teacher-directed instructional approaches (Cuban, 1998). Progressive educators, for instance, have tried for over a century to make such change (Cuban, 1993).

Traditional education can be said to have forged a compromise with arts education, and all that it might imply for the introduction of an embodied perspective, by allowing arts specialists to circumnavigate on the perimeter, i.e. using borrowed students, on borrowed time, in borrowed spaces. Although our study examined arts classes and the work of arts specialists, not their effect on the connected mainstream classroom, from several years of study, it is probably safe to say that there was relatively little evidence that the arts coursework were shaping schools in powerful or dynamic ways, certainly not with the strength of other initiatives or concerns such as mainstreaming special education students, or standards-based education. There was, however, very powerful evidence that the arts were strongly shaped by school and the norming forces of space, time, and social structure.

In examining the integration of progressive education in traditional structures, Cuban pointed to the notion of hybridity as a means of describing the merging of the two perspectives (Cuban, 1993). In the situation of arts education, unlike those Cuban studied where progressive programs or teachers were eventually folded back into the traditional school, there is a continuing division of the two (mainstream and arts education) within the same overarching structure of school. There is evidence of hybridity, but the majority of the effect appears to be within the arts curriculum.

This is ironic in that it is arts specialists, not mainstream classroom teachers, who are regularly called upon to create school-wide events—such as holiday concerts or special commemorations. It is the arts that are most often asked to serve as representative of the school as a whole (such as in an arts exhibit in a mall).

Specialists and specialized program areas exist in schools in a variety of forms and the findings of this study indicate that there might be interesting things to learn about the possibilities of reform from a comparison of the ways these various disciplinary bodies and specialists exist under the traditional school umbrella (see for instance: Davidson, 2000; Davidson, 2002; Davidson & Olson, 2002; Davidson & Walsh, 1994).

Through the three bodies—individual, social, and political—we mediate the world and, in turn, are mediated by it. Our knowledge of the world is embodied in our individual, social, and political understandings of it. The arts have always served humans as profound means by which to engage the body in the composition, control, and expression of the world. Thus it would seem that the school arts curriculum, of all curricular areas, has the potential to enlarge our understanding through the interaction of the body-mind. For most intents and purposes, however, the possibilities of embodied knowledge are not engaged by the school arts curriculum. Indeed, it may take a philosophical movement of greater magnitude than Dewey's constructivism and the progressive school movement to shift the focus of schooling away from a disembodied and toward a more embodied perspective of knowledge and learning.

ACKNOWLEDGEMENTS

My deepest thanks to Liora Bresler who has made this intellectual journey possible. Also many thanks to my co-workers on the Arts in Education project: Nancy Hertzog, Mary Lemons, and Nelson Fertig.

NOTES

[1] Notable exceptions to this generalization are Nespor's (1997) and *Taught bodies* (O'Farrell, et al. 2000).
[2] This is a part of the study described in Bresler, this volume.

REFERENCES

Bresler, L. (1995, April). *The arts in education project.* Paper presented at the annual meeting of the American Educational Research Association, San Francisco, CA.

Bresler, L. (1998, December). The genre of school music and its shaping by meso, micro and macro contexts. *Research Studies in Music Education, 11,* 2-18.

Bresler, L. (1999, Winter). The hybridity and homogenization of school art. *Visual Art Research, 25*(2), 25-37.

Bresler, L., Wasser, J., & Hertzog, N. (1997). Casey at the bat: A hybrid genre of two worlds. *Research in Drama Education, 2*(1), 87–106.

Bresler, L., Wasser, J., Hertzog, N., & Lemons, M. (1996). Beyond the lone ranger researcher: Team work in qualitative research. *European Journal for Research in Music Education, 7*(4), 13–27.

Crossley, N. (1995). Body techniques, agency and intercorporeality: On Goffman's relations in public. *Sociology, 29*(1), 133–149.

Cuban, L. (1998). How schools change reforms: Redefining reform success and failure. *Teachers College Record, 99*(3), 433–477.

Cuban, L. (1993). (2nd ed.). *How teachers taught: Constancy and change in American classrooms, 1890–1990.* New York: Teachers College Press.

Davidson, J. (2000). *Living reading: Exploring the lives of reading teachers.* New York: Peter Lang.

Davidson, J. (2002). *The role of roles in school reform: The case of the educational technologist.* Manuscript submitted for publication.

Davidson, J. (1995a, April). *Art as experience and the anthropology of experience: Theoretical frameworks for understanding the experience of school art.* Paper presented at the annual meeting of the American Educational Research Association, San Francisco, CA.

Davidson, J. (1995b, April). *Refexivity and the collective self.* Paper presented at the annual meeting of the American Education Research Association, San Francisco, CA.

Davidson, J., & Olson, M. (2002, April). *School leadership in networked schools: Deciphering the impact of large technical systems on education.* Paper presented at the annual meeting of the American Educational Research Association, New Orleans, LA.

Davidson, J., & Walsh, D. (1994, March). *The dilemma of inclusion: Multiple discourses in a complex early childhood program.* Paper presentation at Sociolinguistics Symposium 10, Lancaster, England.

Dewey, J. (1980). *Art as experience.* New York: Perigree Books (Original work published in 1934).

Dewey, J. (1988). *John Dewey: The later works, 1925–1953 (Volume I: 1925)* (J. Boydston, P. Baysinger & B. Levine Eds.). Carbondale, IL: Southern Illinois University Press (Original work published in 1925).

Finders, M. (1997). *Just girls: Hidden literacies and life in junior high.* New York: Teachers College Press.

Foucault, M. (1977). *Discipline and punish: The birth of the prison* (A. Sheridan, Trans.). New York: Vintage Books. (Original work published in 1975).

Giddens, A. (1984). *The constitution of society.* Berkeley and Los Angeles: University of California Press.

Goffman, E. (1959). *The presentation of self in everyday life.* New York: Doubleday Books.

Grumet, M. (1988). *Bitter milk: Women and teaching.* Amherst: University of Massachusetts Press.

Harraway, D. (1991). *Simians, cyborgs, and women: The reinvention of nature.* New York: Routledge Press.

Hertzog, N. (1995, April*). Promise and Compromise: Arts in the elementary school curriculum.* Paper presented at the annual meeting of the American Educational Research Association, San Francisco, CA.

Idhe, D. (1990). *Technology and the life world: From garden to earth.* Bloomington: Indiana University Press.

Lakoff, G., & Johnson, M. (1999). *Philosophy in the flesh: The embodied mind and its challenge to western thought.* New York: Basic Books.

Lemons, M. (1995, April). *Organizing the experience of art for young people: Three case studies of music teaching.* Paper presented at the annual meeting of the American Educational Research Association, San Francisco, CA.

McLaren, P. (1986). (2nd ed.). *Schooling as a ritual performance: Towards a political economy of educational symbols and gestures.* London: Routledge.

Merleau-Ponty, M. (1967). *Phenomenology of perception* (C. Smith, Trans.). New York: The Humanities Press (First published in English in 1962).

Nespor, J. (1997). *Tangled up in school: Politics, space, bodies, and signs in the educational process.* Mahwah, NJ: Lawrence Erlbaum.

O'Farrell, C., Meadmore, D., McWilliam, E., & Symes, C. (Eds.) (2000). *Taught bodies.* New York: Peter Lang.

Piaget, J. (1977). *The essential Piaget* (H. Gruber & J. Voneche, Eds.). New York: Basic Books

Scheper-Hughes, N., & Lock, M. (1987). Mindful body: A prolegomenon to future work in medical anthropology. *Medical Anthropology Quarterly, 1*(1), 6–41.

Schilling, C. (1999). Towards an embodied understanding of the structure/agency relationship. *British Journal of Sociology, 50*(4), 543–562.

Vygotsky, L. S. (1978). *Mind in society: The development of higher psychological processes* (M. Cole, V. John-Steiner, S. Scribner & E. Souberman, Trans.). Cambridge, MA: Harvard University Press.

Wasser, J., & Bresler, L. (1996). Conceptualizing collaboration among teams of qualitative researchers. *Educational Researcher, 26*(4), 5–15.

CHARLES R. GAROIAN

EXERCISE: IDENTITY COLLAGE

LEVEL

The construction and performance of an *identity collage* is an exercise that is designed for high school or college students who are studying the visual arts as well as other academic disciplines across the curriculum. The exercise enables students to examine, expose, and critique the ways in which cultural images and ideas inscribe their bodies and construct their identities with reified cultural assumptions.

JUSTIFICATION

This exercise assumes two kinds of cultural performance: those that are socially and historically determined for students; and, those that they determine for themselves. In cultural performances that are socially and historically determined, students consume and perform identities that have been constructed for them by the cultural environments in which they live. In doing so, they learn to emulate and reproduce the stereotypical images, ideas, and myths of those environments. What they *say* (their cultural discourses), and what they *do* (their cultural practices), represent values, beliefs and attitudes that have been scripted and directed for them by their families, friends, neighborhoods, communities, schools, churches, television, the movies, video games, the Internet, and other cultural agencies. The discourses and practices of these agencies function as a rarefied embodied pedagogy that determines what students' desire and choose in their lives, and how they construct and perform their identities.

By comparison, the "embodied pedagogy" of the identity collage performance is emancipatory. In the exercise students interrogate and perform a critique of the oppressive culture codes inscribed on their bodies; they create new images, ideas and myths based on their memories and cultural histories. Moreover, the exercise enables students to expose the contentious zone of their bodies as a context from which to understand identity construction as a mutable, transformative process. By miming the embodied pedagogy of rarefied culture, they re-claim the self and the body as a creative and political site. By constructing and performing an identity collage from different cultural and disciplinary perspectives, students challenge social and historical assumptions, the ideologies of institutionalized learning, and the spectacle of the mass media from the perspective of their own bodies, their memories, and cultural histories. Such a performance facilitates creative and political agency and critical citizenship within the culture.

213

Liora Bresler (ed.), Knowing Bodies, Moving Minds, 213-218.
©*2004 Kluwer Academic Publishers. Printed in the Netherlands*

OBJECTIVES

The identity collage exercise is designed to facilitate the following objectives: 1) an *ethnographic exploration* and disclosure of the body's physical, cultural, and historical attributes; 2) a *linguistic exploration* of cultural inscription; to "read" and "critique" the oppressive codes of culture which stereotype the body in order to create a language of identity based on memory and cultural history; 3) *political agency* as the dominant codes of culture inscribed on the body are challenged; 4) *social agency* as students bring their respective family, neighborhood, and community experiences to bear in their performances and as they engage in a community dialogue with their peers; 5) *technological intervention* by appropriating, collaging, and miming images reproduced by mechanical and electronic devices; 6) and, *ecstatic experience* as the site of the body and its somatic properties are exposed and re-claimed by students to create new aesthetic experiences, new cultural myths, new cultural identities.

STEPS

The principle of collage is experienced in two ways in this exercise: first, as an object-based medium, students cut and paste disparate images and texts to create disjunctive associations on their bodies; second, as a time-based medium, students write and perform a narrative "reading" of the images and texts pasted on their bodies.

1) Ask students to bring magazines to class containing a variety of photographs and texts pertaining to life in contemporary culture. *Life, Time, Vogue, National Geographic, Mechanics Illustrated, Sports Illustrated, Rolling Stone,* and students' other choices of magazines will work.

2) Ask students to search through their magazines for visual images and texts that they identify with; ones that attract their attention. Visual examples may include lipstick, lips, legs, eyes, cigarettes, buildings, automobiles, apes, snakes, rockets, guns, etc. Text images may vary according to the kind of word that is chosen, to its typography, color, size, and shape. A page of text may function as visual texture.

3) Ask students to cut their selected images and texts from the magazines. The most effective tool is a sharp X-ACTO knife. The images should be cut clean around their contours. Unless necessary, there is no need for students to cut each letter of a word or phrase. Such text can be cut as a block of letters. All images and texts should be removed from their familiar magazine contexts and recontextualized as "floating" signifiers in the identity collage. A tube of lipstick, for example, cut from of its advertisement, and an ape cut from its jungle or zoo photographic context, when recontextualized on a student's face, can yield contradictory readings and new and strange interpretations. As students adjoin the magazine images and texts to the features of their faces, they are able to create new readings and interpretations of their identities.

4) Once students have assembled a random collection of ten to fifteen images and texts, ask them to apply small pieces of double-sided tape to their back side. The

double-sided tape will allow for the image to stick onto a surface without being visually obtrusive.

5) Give students a small mirror and ask them to carefully attach their collage items to their faces in lieu of a conventional ground. The images and texts can be taped in their hair, over their eyelids, on their cheeks, foreheads, chins, in and on their noses and ears, going in or coming out of their mouths, on their tongues or teeth. The purpose is not to conceal the face, but to accent, complement, or parody its visual characteristics. Students should be encouraged to experiment with different compositional arrangements until they achieve a complementary relationship between the forms of their faces and those of the collage.

6) After the students have taped a suitable arrangement of the images and texts to their faces, ask them to look into the mirror and to write a three to five-minute story taking their cues from their identity collage. In producing their stories, the students learn to "read" and "interpret" the cultural text "inscribed" on their bodies. The narrative structure of the story can be as disjunctive as the collage itself or it can be written in conventional prose. For example, students may select random sentences, phrases, and words from their magazines to construct a narrative, or they may choose to write from memory and cultural history; experiences from their personal lives that relate to the collage.

7) After the students have completed their writing task, ask them to memorize their stories or to hold them above the mirror like a TelePrompTer and to rehearse reciting or reading them aloud. Like the disjunctive images on their faces, the testimony of their stories informed by those images, represents a performance that critiques their cultural inscription. The students may wish to revise and edit their work at this point. Encourage them to explore different performance possibilities. For example, they may wish to reconfigure their collage images or to experiment with different voice qualities and facial gestures as they read. They may also want to explore different timing variations for their facial gestures and their readings ranging from a slow to fast pace and/or one that is mechanical and syncopated.

8) After the students have finished rehearsing, ask them to perform their identity collage/stories before a video camera. When videotaping, frame only their faces and those parts of the body that are relevant to their performances. As students are being individually videotaped, ask their classmates to observe the live version before the camera so that they can compare it with the later videotaped version.

9) After all the students have performed before the camera, rewind and playback each of their videotapes so that they can view their identity collages within the context of their video performances. As they watch each other's videotapes, ask the students to "read" and "interpret" the conjunctions occurring between the disparate images, texts, and actions in the identity performances. Have them discuss their interpretations with their classmates. In doing so, their identity collages will lead to conversations about aesthetic issues that are significant to their identities such as family, friends, school, jobs, finances, violence, health, sexuality, philosophy, ecology, religion, and other such concerns.

INTERDISCIPLINARY USES OF THE IDENTITY COLLAGE

Although the identity collage exercise can be applied in a number of discipline-specific classes, it is most effective as an interdisciplinary strategy. It can be used in classes across the curriculum to deconstruct the compartmentalized structure of schooling, to explore the interconnectedness of different disciplines, and to create a community-based learning environment. For example, the exercise can be used in

1) *Anthropology:* as an ethnographic strategy for students to query their memories and cultural histories and to construct a collage of personal identity. As students call upon their cultural experiences to select the images and stories for their identity collage performance, they reveal personal preferences and cultural differences. Their subsequent performances result from a reflexive look back at themselves; a form of ethnographic "fieldwork" where they re-member and re-present themselves as a mutable cultural collage.

2) The *Arts:* to examine, expose and express how the collage of cultural inscription determines students' aesthetic experiences. The identity collage performance can be compared with the way in which space and time, and form and content are composed in the visual arts, music, dance, and theater. How does the temporal character of the identity collage performance compare with the atemporality of collage in the visual arts? What does it mean for the image to be on the body? What sound/music/movement possibilities exist in the identity collage?

3) *Athletics:* as visual cues to "play" the body, to engage its movement in a sport, exercise, or gaming activity. For many students, their sports prowess is an important part of their identities. Like a collage, the turns, adjustments, moves, and maneuvers that students learn from professional athletes in filmed or televised sports, when incorporated with their body's natural capabilities, maximize their athletic achievements. The images of the identity collage suggest possibilities for athletic criticism and experimentation that can lead to new forms of sport. They can serve as symbolic notations to deconstruct and re-present existing forms.

4) *Business:* to critique the body's construction, commodification, and exploitation by the images and ideas of corporate advertising. The students' collaging of commodified images on their bodies suggests that the body and the self are commodified. Under what circumstances does identity function as a marketable commodity? How do magazine and television ads, the movies, and other mass media spectacles influence the choices that students make in their lives? How is it possible for them to enjoy the pleasures of commodified culture while being critical consumers?

5) *Engineering:* to deconstruct the collage metaphors in architecture and in mechanical and electronic technologies. As an engineering metaphor, identity collage construction may serve engineering students to understand the relationships between the structures that they design and build and those of the human body. Considering that technology has served historically as an extension of the exoskeletal system (any technological device or appliance used outside the body), and quick becoming part of the endoskeletal system with prosthetic devices and artificial life-support systems, students can examine, expose, and critique the business and politics of the body's technological intervention.

in poetry and prose. As writing students select, construct, and perform their identity collages they engage in a "live" semiotic process where they learn to examine, expose and critique the codes of reified culture inscribed on their bodies. They learn how visual images and the actions of the body, like verbal texts, signify. As they experiment and improvise new associations between images, words, and the actions of their bodies, they learn about infinite possibilities to create new meanings and new identities.

7) *Foreign languages:* to illustrate how language construction functions as a collage and how a complex of languages comprises a collage of world cultures. Like in the English/literature example above, the identity collage enables foreign language students to explore the signifying character of images, words, and body actions. By engaging in a cultural semiotics, they examine, expose, and critique cultural stereotypes in order to understand and appreciate the differences between their own cultures and those of others whose languages they are studying.

8) *History:* to illustrate how the past is chronicled as a collage and to challenge dominant constructions of history by inviting students to consider their memories and cultural histories as significant content. The identity collage enables students to perform a critique of the histories that they have learned in school, at home, and the mass media. Playing with historical images and texts on their bodies, they are able to examine, expose, and critique the influence of history on their identities and the world in which they live.

9) *Mathematics:* to show how the symbolic language and logic of mathematics "measures" and "constructs" identity and one's place in the world. Students learn how the mathematical relationships can affect their political and creative agency in the world as well as their confinement and oppression. Similar to the mutable process of performance art, which enables students to experiment, challenge, and transform the immutable codes of culture, variant factors in mathematics present the possibility for transforming invariant factors into new ways of measuring themselves to the world.

10) *Philosophy:* to expose, critique, and re-present the socially and historically constructed assumptions of visual culture from the perspectives of the students' personal philosophies. In doing so, the identity collage functions as a "performative theory;" a proposition whereby students learn to create their own assumptions in order to position themselves within contemporary culture.

11) *Psychology:* where students can *tell, listen,* and *interpret* the stories of their identity collages to illustrate how the "testimony and witnessing" process of psychoanalysis reveals the collage structure of cognitive images and those of the unconscious mind.

12) Finally, the use of the identity collage in the *Sciences* renders the biological and physical properties of the body explicit. As science students perform identity collages that contain images of the skeletal, nervous, muscular, digestive and other systems of the body, they experience the dynamic construction of their bodies. As they expose the signifiers of the body's physiology, their concerns about health, and their ecological relationship with the environment, can come into play.

CONCLUSION

The identity collage exercise represents a significant means by which to introduce the issue of identity construction in all aspects of academic practice. In doing so, students learn that the content of their lives, their memories, cultural histories, and their desires count in the larger scheme of education. The identity collage performance is a reflexive process whereby students learn to mime and resist their bodies' inscription and oppression by the rarefied codes of academic culture. With the images and texts collaged *on their faces,* the gestures of their bodies, and their stories, they learn to perform new cultural myths and new identities *in the face* of cultural domination.

Charles R. Garoian is a performance artist, Director of the School of Visual Arts, and Professor of art education at Penn State University, and author of Performing Pedagogy: Toward an Art of Politics (1999), State University of New York Press.

Landscapes: The Arts, Aesthetics, and Education

1. D. Atkinson: *Art in Education*. Identity and Practice. 2002
                    ISBN Hb 1-4020-1084-2; Pb 1-4020-1085-0
2. M. Xanthoudaki, L. Tickle and V. Sekules (eds.): *Researching Visual Arts Education in Museums and Galleries*. An International Reader. 2003
                    ISBN Hb 1-4020-1636-0; Pb 1-4020-1637-9

KLUWER ACADEMIC PUBLISHERS   DORDRECHT/BOSTON/LONDON